W9-ACH-845

Akron's "Better Half"

OHIO HISTORY AND CULTURE

Series on Ohio History and Culture

George W. Knepper, *Summit's Glory*

Leonard Sweet, *Strong in the Broken Places*

John H. White and Robert J. White Sr., *The Island Queen*

H. Roger Grant, *Ohio's Railway Age in Postcards*

Frances McGovern, *Written on the Hills: The Making of the Akron Landscape*

Keith McClellan, *The Sunday Game: At the Dawn of Professional Football*

Steve Love and David Giffels, *Wheels of Fortune: The Story of Rubber in Akron*

Alfred Winslow Jones and Daniel Nelson, *Life, Liberty, and Property: A Story of Conflict and a Measurement of Conflicting Rights*

David Brendan Hopes, *A Childhood in the Milky Way: Becoming a Poet in Ohio*

John Keim, *Legends by the Lake: The Cleveland Browns at Municipal Stadium*

Richard B. Schwartz, *The Biggest City in America: A Fifties Boyhood in Ohio*

Thomas A. Rumer, *Unearthing the Land: The Story of Ohio's Scioto Marsh*

Steve Love, Ian Adams, and Barney Taxel, *Stan Hywet Hall & Gardens*

William F. Romain, *Mysteries of the Hopewell: Astronomers, Geometers, and Magicians of the Eastern Woodlands*

Dale Topping, edited by Eric Brothers, *When Giants Roamed the Sky: Karl Arnstein and the Rise of Airships from Zeppelin to Goodyear*

Millard F. Rogers Jr., *Rich in Good Works: Mary M. Emery of Cincinnati*

Frances McGovern, *Fun, Cheap, & Easy: My Life in Ohio Politics, 1949–1964*

Larry L. Nelson, editor, *A History of Jonathan Alder: His Captivity and Life with the Indians*

Bruce M. Meyer, *The Once and Future Union: The Rise and Fall of the United Rubber Workers, 1935–1995*

Steve Love and Ian Adams, *The Holden Arboretum*

Joyce Dyer, *Gum-Dipped: A Daughter Remembers Rubber Town*

Melanie Payne, *Champions, Cheaters, and Childhood Dreams: Memories of the Soap Box Derby*

John Flower, *Downstairs, Upstairs: The Changed Spirit and Face of College Life in America*

Wayne Embry and Mary Schmitt Boyer, *The Inside Game: Race, Power, and Politics in the NBA*

Robin Yocum, *Dead Before Deadline: . . . And Other Tales from the Police Beat*

A. Martin Byers, *The Ohio Hopewell Episode: Paradigm Lost and Paradigm Gained*

Edward C. Arn, edited by Jerome Mushkat, *Arn's War: Memoirs of a World War II Infantryman, 1940–1946*

Brian Bruce, *Thomas Boyd: Lost Author of the "Lost Generation"*

Kathleen Endres, *Akron's "Better Half": Women's Clubs and the Humanization of a City, 1825–1925*

Akron's "Better Half"

Women's Clubs and the Humanization of the City, 1825—1925

Kathleen L. Endres

THE UNIVERSITY OF AKRON PRESS

AKRON, OHIO

Copyright © 2006 by Kathleen L. Endres
All rights reserved
First Edition 2006
Manufactured in the United States of America.
10 09 08 07 06 5 4 3 2 1

All inquiries and permission requests should be addressed to the Publisher,
The University of Akron Press, Akron, Ohio 44325-1703.

Library of Congress Cataloging-in-Publication Data

Endres, Kathleen L.
  Akron's "better half" : women's clubs and the humanization of the city, 1825–1925 /
Kathleen Endres.—1st ed.
     p. cm.
  Includes bibliographical references and index.
  ISBN-13: 978-1-931968-36-2 (cloth : alk. paper)
  ISBN-10: 1-931968-36-5 (cloth : alk. paper)
  ISBN-13: 978-1-931968-41-6 (pbk. : alk. paper)
  ISBN-10: 1-931968-41-1 (pbk. : alk. paper)
  1. Women—Ohio—Akron—Societies and clubs—History. 2. Women—Ohio—
Akron—History. 3. Akron (Ohio)—History. I. Title.
  HQ1906.A5E53 2006
  367'.977136082—dc22

                          2006002468

The paper used in this publication meets the minimum requirements of American National Standard for Information Sciences—Permanence of Paper for Printed Library
Materials, ANSI z39.48–1984.∞

Cover images: *Front cover, top photo,* the American Hard Rubber Workers, courtesy of the
Special Collections Division, Akron-Summit County Public Library. *Front cover, bottom
photo,* the Goodrich Zipper Girls, courtesy of the B. F. Goodrich Collection, the University of Akron Archives. *Back cover,* the Akron YWCA, 1904, courtesy of the YWCA of
Summit County Collection, the University of Akron Archives.

Contents

Illustrations

Chapter 1

Akron and the Club Movement

There is a peculiar niche in the world's organizations which can be filled only by women. Such has been found in the city of Akron. The local 'niche' which is filled so capably by Akron women, may be said to be a triple nature; namely, charity, literature and music.

—*Akron Beacon Journal*[1]

Akron is organized to death. Everything from the municipal building to the kindergarten is organized, each organization running rampant with shears open, clipping here and there.

—Mrs. Charles Brookover, Akron, Ohio[2]

WOMEN'S CLUBS AND ORGANIZATIONS HAVE ALWAYS BEEN VITALLY important to the health and well-being of the city of Akron, Ohio. They brought much-needed services to the city, created health institutions that continue today, and built Akron's cultural and literary foundations.

The story of women and their organizations is not told in typical histories of the city. Those histories of Akron have concentrated on the industrial, business, and government/political foundation of the city, the rubber barons, and the well-known, affluent men. Yet Akron women and their accomplishments cannot be overlooked. Over the decades, women, usually working through their clubs and organizations, have transformed the city.

In antebellum days, when Akron was little more than a village, women formed temperance societies that assisted families in distress, even as activists tried to get rid of the liquor trade. Other organizations brought wage increases to seamstresses, rescued "fallen women," and raised funds for the local fire companies. During the Civil War, Akron women worked in the Soldiers Aid Society, shipping thousands of dollars' worth of supplies to Cleveland's Sanitary Commission for use in hospitals and assisting families of area soldiers left behind.

And Akron women were only getting started.

After the Civil War, women created organizations that delivered desperately needed aid to the poor and, in the process, created a primitive welfare system for what the women called the "worthy poor." Other women's organizations raised funds to build churches, schools, playgrounds, and more. Akron women also joined the temperance crusades of the day and organized their own structured temperance leagues to carry out the next stage of their antiliquor campaign. During the Gilded Age, there were so many clubs that a small group of activists organized a Women's Council to channel the energies of clubwomen across the city. It was one of the earliest women's councils in the nation.

During the first twenty-five years of the twentieth century, Akron women were caught up in the municipal housekeeping movement that swept the nation. Transferring their household responsibilities to the greater community, Akron women established a new generation of organizations and redefined the missions of long-standing groups to deliver essential services and create institutions that continue today. Sometimes this meant reaching across class and ethnic lines. Some clubs of affluent women focused on the needs of the growing number of workingwomen. They built dorms for women who came to the city to work in the new rubber factories, provided day care for the children of working mothers, and went to workplaces to teach English to immigrant women, even as they quietly pressured employers to improve working conditions for their female employees.

Akron's club movement was not reserved for the native-born, affluent, white matrons of the city. Immigrant, African American, and workingwomen, excluded from membership in most of the women's clubs run by the affluent whites, organized their own groups. They defined for themselves what they wanted and needed, strategized on how to achieve those goals, and selected leaders from their midst.

Thousands of Akron women joined clubs and organizations during the first two decades of the twentieth century. The Women's Council leveraged those groups into a force to exert pressure on civic leaders to create a juvenile justice system, on educators to add kindergartens to the schools, and on corporate executives to cut down on pollution.

If the city needed assistance, civic, business, political, and media leaders called on the women and their clubs and organizations to assume the task. If women saw problems, they formed groups to solve them. The women's clubs made mistakes along the way; they were frequently criticized and sometimes condemned. But they were not going to be stopped.

Akron women and their clubs and organizations changed the city. They transformed Akron from simply an industrial/business center to a place to live. They humanized the city. In the process, Akron women, working within their clubs and organizations, gained for themselves enormous power in the city. The Akron women accomplished this by working within a domestic sphere that they stretched and molded to their own ends. Thus, Akron clubwomen displayed all the characteristics of domestic feminism, using "ladylike" characteristics to reform the community.[3]

The United States has always been a "nation of joiners."[4] From its earliest days, America discovered it could accomplish much through collective action, and Americans were eager to organize clubs, societies, organizations, and associations to get things done. Benevolent societies date back to the early days of the colonies. Charleston, South Carolina, had one of the first, St. Andrew's Society of Charles Town, founded in 1729; Philadelphia followed with its own St. Andrew's Association in 1749. Political clubs that often brought about civic improvement followed. Founding father, American diplomat, printer, inventor, and bon vivant Benjamin Franklin organized his friends into a political/civic club called Junto (Leather Apron Club) in Philadelphia. This group of businessmen and artisans discussed morality, politics, philosophy, and local and national affairs; in 1731, the club organized the first library in the colonies. The Sons of Liberty, a secret society, started simultaneously in New York and Boston to protest the Stamp Act, an unpopular tax levied on the colonies. After Parliament repealed the act, the Sons disbanded but revived to protest the Townshend Acts, which levied taxes on lead, paint, paper, glass, and tea imported to the colonies and suspended the New York legislature until it agreed to quarter British soldiers, in 1766. That organization included printers and editors in all the colonies who exchanged news reports and essays and, in the process, helped foment a revolution and keep morale up even in the darkest days of the war.

European travelers were always intrigued by the proclivity of Americans to organize and join clubs and associations. Traveling to America in 1831–32, French aristocrat Alexis de Tocqueville saw voluntary associations as something special in the new democratic nation:

> The Americans make associations to give entertainments, to form seminaries, to build inns, to construct churches, to diffuse books, to send missionaries to the antipodes; in this manner they found hospitals, prisons, and schools. If it is proposed to inculcate some truth or to foster some feeling for the encouragement of a great example, they form a society.

Europeans did not have that joining spirit, de Tocqueville observed; he speculated that the Americans used their voluntary associations to take the place of the more stable, aristocratic institutions of Europe.[5]

Fifty years later, British historian, statesman, and diplomat James Bryce reported that the voluntary associations were still very much a part of American culture. Bryce observed, "Associations are created, extended, and worked in the United States more quickly and effectively than in any other country." Bryce thought American voluntary associations helped explain the nation's dynamic politics, economic growth, and social development. "Such associations have great importance in the development of opinion, for they rouse attention, excite discussion, formulate principles, submit plans, embolden and stimulate their members, produce that impression of a spreading movement which goes so far towards success with a sympathetic and sensitive people."[6]

When de Tocqueville and Bryce reported on American voluntary associations, they were almost always referring to the societies organized by men. This is not to say that these two European visitors ignored the women. In fact, American women fascinated both visitors because they held such an interesting place in society. On one hand, they occupied a narrow, separate sphere, one confined to home and domestic life. On the other hand, they wielded enormous power and prestige within society. De Tocqueville, especially, was puzzled by that dichotomy:

> As for myself, I do not hesitate to avow, that, although the women of the United States are confined within their narrow circle of domestic life, and their situation is in some respects one of extreme dependence, I have nowhere seen women occupying a loftier position; and if I were asked, now that I am drawing to the close of this work, in which I have spoken of so many important things done by the Americans, to what the singu-

lar prosperity and growing strength of that people ought to be attributed, I should reply—to the superiority of their women.[7]

Bryce also saw the schism in American society. Men occupied the public sphere—their lives revolved around business. Women occupied the private sphere, the home—their lives revolved around the family. Bryce explained, "As mothers they mould the character of their children; while the function of forming the habits of society and determining its moral tone rests greatly in their hands. But there is reason to think that the influence of the American system tells directly for good upon men as well as upon the whole community."[8]

What de Tocqueville and Bryce observed was the "Cult of True Womanhood" or the "Cult of Domesticity," as historians call the ideology that arose during the first half of the nineteenth century. Crafted by antebellum women's magazines, gift books, and religious publications of the day, this image of women was quite different from that of the self-sufficient American woman of the Revolutionary period. Historian Barbara Welter, who coined the term "Cult of True Womanhood," explained that the middle-class women of industrializing America occupied a special place within the home, apart from corrupting influences of business and industry. In her domestic sphere, the "lady" possessed certain characteristics—piety, purity, domesticity, and submissiveness.[9]

Women were to care for their homes (domesticity) and their husbands (submissiveness) and train their children well, in God-fearing, religiously grounded households (piety and purity). The Reverend John Angell James, a popular writer of the day, explained that a happy home finds the woman "yielding" to the greater wisdom of her husband—"her power is in her gentleness." The wife was busy with her family. "A mother's place is in the midst of her family; a mother's duties are to take care of *them*," the minister argued.[10]

Both nature and religion dictated that role. Woman was physically weaker than man; she was unsuited for the stress, strain, and exertion of the business world. As the Reverend F. B. Fulton wrote in 1869, "Woman cannot compete with man in a long course of mental labor. The female mind is rather quiet and timid than fiery and driving. It admires rather than covets the great exploits of the other sex."[11]

Popular writer Elizabeth Poole Sandford explained that St. Paul had been right when he advised women to stay within the domestic sphere. "There is composure at home; there is something sedative in the duties which home involves. It affords security not only from the world, but from delusions and errors of every kind," she wrote. Such was a position shared by Catharine Beecher, American champion of domestic education, and her sister, novelist Harriet Beecher Stowe. They argued that the separate spheres would assure a strong marriage and a happy family. "The father undergoes toil and self-denial to provide a home, then the mother becomes a self-sacrificing laborer to train its inmates." This division of labor was God's will, the two wrote. The family was an "earthly illustration of the heavenly kingdom, and in it woman is its chief minister."[12]

Self-sacrifice, subjugation, domesticity, submissiveness, piety, and purity suggested a restricted role for American women, one with few options. However, as Bryce and de Tocqueville discussed, and as a number of historians have subsequently discovered, American women could—and did—stretch and shape the constricted "Cult of True Womanhood" to their wants and needs.[13]

The ideology of the "Cult of True Womanhood" was built upon the concept that women shared certain characteristics and that they possessed a moral superiority over men. That greater moral sensibility made women ideal wives, mothers, and homemakers. It also provided a shared bond among women and a shared responsibility to bring their greater moral sensibility to the community. Women had a *duty* to care for the forsaken, to help the ailing, and to bring their own good housekeeping to the problems of the community. *Blackwood's Magazine* saw women as the force behind the scenes. They were not only to work in the home but also to minister to all those in need. "Such is her destiny; to visit the forsaken, to attend the neglected, amid the forgetfulness of myriads to remember."[14]

Catharine Beecher saw no conflict between the duties of the home and women's involvement in benevolent causes within the community. "In matters pertaining to the education of their children, in the selection and support of a clergyman, in all benevolent enterprises, and in all questions relating to morals and manners, they [women] have a superior influence," Beecher insisted. Indeed, charity was best left in women's hands. Beecher argued that, working together, women could investigate reports of need, call on indigent families, and determine the proper course to remedy any situation.[15]

The best way to accomplish the tasks that *Blackwood's Magazine* and Beecher outlined was for like-minded women to establish clubs and organizations to help the needy in the community. Just as men started voluntary clubs and organizations, so, too, did the women.

In the United States, women first got involved in benevolent work by organizing auxiliaries to the men's groups. Wives, mothers, sisters, and daughters were welcome to join the auxiliaries that did much of the fund-raising and special-event work of the men's groups. Soon the women formed their own clubs and organizations. These gave women more latitude, more power. Women determined the mission, the goals, and the strategies of their organizations. They formed groups to help workingwomen, prostitutes, and indigent families. During the Civil War, women throughout the North worked diligently in soldiers' aid and relief organizations. It was only because of those local societies that the U.S. Sanitary Commission was able to build its medical support network. After the war, American women geared up for fresh challenges. Some continued their antebellum benevolent work, assisting indigent families in cities and towns across the nation. Others geared up for new temperance and suffrage campaigns. Many took a more conservative route and organized to build churches, schools, and hospitals and then turned over administration of these institutions to the men. Still others were more concerned with their own self-improvement and organized literary, musical, and cultural societies.

The women's clubs and organizations nationwide built upon the social expectations imposed on women of the day. These women used the ideology and rhetoric of domesticity to recruit members, to raise funds, to argue their case to the community, and to accomplish their mission.

Akron, Ohio, was very much a part of this cultural milieu. During the nineteenth century and well into the twentieth century, Akron women embraced the concepts associated with domesticity. Women and men inhabited different spheres. Men lived in the public sphere of business and industry. Women kept the home in a state of domestic bliss. As Akron's *Glad Tidings and Ladies Universalist Magazine* outlined in its "Rules for Wives,"

> I.   Always receive your husband with smiles . . . endeavoring to win, and gratefully reciprocate his kindness and attention.
> II.   Study to gratify his inclination in regard to food and cookery; in the management of the family; in your dress, manners and deportment.
> III.   Never attempt to rule, or appear to rule your husband.
> IV.   In everything reasonable, comply with his wishes with cheerfulness. . . .
> V.   Avoid all altercations or arguments leading to ill humor, and more especially before company.

VI.   Never attempt to interfere in his business unless he asks your advice and counsel; and never attempt to control him in the management of it.

VII. Never confide to gossips any of the failings or imperfections of your husband. . . .

VIII. Avail yourself of every opportunity to cultivate your mind, so as, should your husband be intelligent and well informed, you may join in rational conversation with him and his friends.

IX.   Think nothing beneath your attention that may produce even a momentary breach of harmony, or the slightest uneasy sensation.[16]

Following these simple rules was not a hardship for women. Living within the domestic sphere was an honor. Only there could women—Akron women—receive their greatest accolades. As "Porcia" wrote in the *Akron Offering*, a periodical edited by a woman, women needed to know themselves and value themselves. "Let *man* stand in the *public arena*—it is his place, but let him not forget that *woman* fitted him for his station, and let *woman* rememeber [*sic*] that *this* is *her honor* and a nobler crown than she could ever receive by standing there herself!"[17]

God ordained all this. As a writer for Akron's *Glad Tidings and Ladies Universalist Magazine* explained, "To me, woman appears to fill, in America, the very station for which she was designed by Heaven." It was a role that women played regardless of social class. In even the "lowest condition," women were to be treated with respect and tenderness that their roles as wife and mother deserved.[18]

Just as Akron's social/cultural milieu mirrored nationwide trends, so, too, did the development of its women's organizations, which started as soon as the town achieved a level of economic and institutional stability in the 1840s. During that decade, Akron recovered from the Panic of 1837 and its subsequent depression, saw more and more affluent families settle in town, and witnessed the growth of Protestant churches that fostered and encouraged women's clubs and organizations.

Growing out of the reform impulses of the day, the first women's clubs in Akron were auxiliaries to the men's temperance organizations. But that structure belied the groups' evolution. From the start, the women of the auxiliaries burned with a reform fervor and claimed for themselves far more responsibility than the male parent organizations ever anticipated. In addition, reform-minded Akron women soon began striking out on their own, creating organizations to solve the problems that beset the bustling town. Like their sisters back east, Akron women founded a moral reform organization in the 1840s to rescue women and children from depraved men. In the 1850s, Akron women tried their hand at labor reform by organizing a group to help underpaid seamstresses in the city. This organization, particularly, embraced radical strategies to pressure reluctant tailors to revise the pay structure for seamstresses in the city.

The temperance auxiliaries, the moral reform group, and the labor organization had accomplished the goals of every other volunteer association in the nation—to recruit and motivate a sufficient group of members, to determine their missions, to define their goals, and then to strategize to accomplish those goals.[19] By all accounts, clubwomen in Akron were up to the task and mastered the organizational skills needed for successful club work early.

These women's clubs grew out of reform impulses of the antebellum period. They sought to convert the sinner (the drunkard) and protect the powerless (the seamstress). In Akron in the 1850s, a new kind of women's organization emerged: the "ladies' committee." Growing out of a more conservative sense of civic responsibility as opposed to reform impulses, these committees served as a kind of women's auxiliary to formally organized men's volunteer organizations. Unlike the women's reform groups, these committees lacked a formal structure. Nonetheless, they became important fund-raising allies to the men's groups in the city. In addition, these committees served as training grounds for many women who led the largest women's organization that Akron had ever seen, the Soldiers Aid Society during the Civil War.

Akron women, like women in many towns across the North, formed their Soldiers Aid Society early. That group quickly emerged as the most efficient, best-run women's organization in the city. Burning with a patriotic fervor, the women of the Soldiers Aid Society not only supplied Akron men about to go off to war with tender reminders of their homes but also shipped countless boxes of supplies to the hospitals caring for the sick and wounded. The women of the aid society also looked after the indigent families of soldiers left behind.

After the war, the women of the Soldiers Aid Society went home to rest, but not for long. There was just too much to do. Akron women organized new clubs and organizations to improve the city and themselves. The women worked through many forums. Some of the most active were associated with the churches of the city. From St. Bernard's Catholic Church to Zion Lutheran, from First Congregational to St. Paul's Episcopal, from Temple Israel to AME Zion, Akron women organized missionary and aid societies to do everything from raising funds to help build churches and tending to the altar to caring for the indigent and ailing in the congregation and the city.

Drawing on many of those church organizations, Akron women organized their own temperance crusade. Hundreds of Akron women took to the streets and prayed outside the saloons of Market and Howard streets to end the liquor trade once and for all. After the crusading fever ebbed, Akron women organized temperance leagues and organizations to carry on the work. Other groups in the city—the Dorcas Society, the Buckley Relief Corps, and the Woman's Benevolent Association—delivered emergency welfare that so many Akron families needed to weather the depressions of the 1870s and 1880s.

The new century brought better economic times to the city, but as the old adage attests, "women's work is never done." Akron clubwomen rolled up their sleeves and got busy with a "municipal housekeeping" campaign that was sweeping the country during and after the Progressive Era. Again building on the ideology of domesticity, clubwomen argued that they were merely transferring their housekeeping responsibilities to the community. Women needed to "clean up" the city to protect their family and home. As historian Agnes Hooper Gottlieb observed, municipal housekeeping built on nineteenth-century concepts of the role of women: "municipal housekeeping tradition can trace its roots to the prevailing nineteenth-century ideal that the proper sphere for women was a domestic one." Women activists of the club movement of the early twentieth century "used protection of the 'home' and concerns for its integrity as a motivation to speak publicly about social problems."[20]

The Women's Council of Akron claimed the banner of municipal housekeeping and forced improvements on the city. Bowing to the pressure of its Women's Council, Akron created a separate juvenile justice system, built a detention home for wayward youth, cleaned up some of the more serious health and sanitation messes in the city, and improved the educational system, among many other accomplishments.

The Women's Council was only one small part of the story of the women's clubs and organizations of early twentieth-century Akron.

Some women's groups that got their start in the nineteenth century redefined themselves in the new century. The Akron Day Nursery became the Mary Day Nursery, then the Mary Day Nursery and Kindergarten, then the Mary Day Nursery and Ward for Crippled Children, then the Mary Day Nursery and Children's Hospital. In the process, the women organized the city's first day-care facility for working mothers, first kindergarten, and first hospital for children.

The Tuesday Afternoon Club, which started as a small organization dedicated to improving the musical knowledge and talents of its members, grew into the Tuesday Musical Club that began public concerts in the city. In the early twentieth century, the group, on the brink of financial ruin, redefined itself, created a "people's chorus," and expanded its membership beyond Akron's debutantes and dilettantes, building a strong cultural foundation for the city.

The Akron Missionary Union had a large membership that reached across Protestant denominations but only a vague mission during the nineteenth century. In the twentieth century, guided by strong women leaders, the group reorganized, creating the East Akron Community House to help immigrants adjust to Akron life.

Akron's Woman's Christian Temperance Union (WCTU) had more difficulty growing and changing in the twentieth century. Its crusading spirit spent by the end of the nineteenth century, the group remained busy with its temperance education program, its work in the jails and the infirmary, its campaign to keep the Sabbath sacred, its programming for and with workingwomen, and its push for suffrage in the early twentieth century. But the group was finding great competition in the city, both from new organizations and from its own branches that had been established in many city neighborhoods.

The WCTU's greatest competition came from the vibrant, new Young Women's Christian Association (YWCA). With its innovative programming for girls, workingwomen, and immigrants, its high-profile leadership, and its imaginative full-time staff, the YWCA quickly emerged as one of the largest, most important women's organizations in the city.

The new Woman's Exchange never captured such a following. It offered a different model of philanthropy to Akron women: a retail store where down-on-their-luck, talented women could sell their finest handiwork to affluent women.

When Akron women organized and joined clubs, they sought out others who shared their values, their economic status, and their appearance. That meant that Akron women from underrepresented groups were not always welcome in these organizations. The YWCA and the WCTU had a measure of diversity. The YWCA did have branches in factories that workingwomen joined; African American girls affiliated with the segregated Girl Reserve clubs in the city. African American women interested in joining the WCTU could affiliate with the organization's race-specific branch.

There were other alternatives, however. Workingwomen, African Americans, and immigrants could join groups of their own making and under their own direction.

For African Americans, that meant the Daughters of Jerusalem, which combined a benevolent mission and a cultural cause. Workingwomen joined groups at their places of employment for fellowship, fun, camaraderie, and relief. Immigrant women looked to their country-specific organizations housed in the International Institute.

With so many organizations in the city, Akron women could be called from their homes to do "club work" virtually every day of the week. Was it any wonder that editors and ministers began to question what these women were really up to?

Rabbi Isador E. Philo brought that very question to the heart of the women's club movement in Akron, the powerful Women's Council. In his address in 1905, he equated the women's clubs with taverns, because of the temptations they held. "The American club is the snake which beguiles modern Eves to sin against the home. By eating of the tree of knowledge, of good and evil, they realize their naked-ness, their eyes are opened to the honeyed temptations that seek to entice them away from their consecrated duties," he argued. He accused the clubwomen of los-ing sight of their real responsibilities, venturing out, and corrupting themselves, their families, and their homes with all this club work. Not surprisingly, many clubwomen within the community responded in quite an "unladylike" manner. Mrs. Zelia M. Walters, for example, wrote that club work made women better wives and mothers. "I have known many women with interests outside of their homes, and I have yet to meet one who is not a far better wife and mother than the average woman with a narrower conception of woman's place in the world."[21]

The *Beacon Journal* editor thought there might be some truth to the rabbi's charges. Home was the central place in a woman's life, observed the editor, and anything that worked against it needed to be controlled, curtailed. If club work was a momentary recreation, fine; but if it was more, it threatened the fundamen-tal institution of American life—the family—and it had to be checked. The re-sponse to the rabbi's comments suggested that club work had become something more, the editor observed:

> Let us be charitable, and believe, that the club to Akron women is but a secondary consideration—a place where they can secure an hour's recre-ation when tired out with home duties—a place where their mental ac-tivities may find an outlet, and where they may learn many things which were denied their mothers and grandmothers, but which the modern woman finds indispensable.

Let us believe that those who have sprung so quickly to the defense of the club woman did it more in that spirit of sympathy for a much maligned sister than because of any belief they might have had that they were being criticized.

We can't believe that the mothers of Akron are clubwomen of the sort Rabbi Philo criticized in his speech.[22]

The criticism did not stop Akron's clubwomen. Akron women, working through their clubs and organizations, built churches, hospitals, and community centers. They created enduring cultural institutions. The women carried out campaigns to improve the city's health, morality, and appearance. Akron women—working through their clubs and organizations—improved the city, made it a better place to live. In a word, they humanized the city.

This book is designed to look at Akron women and their clubs and organizations during the first one hundred years of Akron's life—1825 to 1925—a time of tremendous growth in the city and a period of enormous creativity, vitality, and energy among women's clubs. This time period allows a look at the conditions in the city needed to start and nurture women's clubs, a closer examination of the types of women drawn to these groups, and an appraisal of the roles these organizations played within the city.

The book is not designed to provide a comprehensive list of women's organizations that existed in the city during this time period. Two things work against that—the collection practices of libraries and archives in northeast Ohio and the editorial practices of newspapers. Few libraries have retained the organizational records of early women's clubs. Editorial practices in newspapers, especially the general daily newspapers, likewise worked against such a comprehensive listing. In antebellum days, the women's clubs did not keep newspapers informed of their activities; and, even after these organizations mastered media relations and updated the newspapers regularly, the dailies did not always cover the more obscure women's organizations in the city.

Instead, this book looks in depth at key women's organizations in the city. The groups examined in this book reflect the rich diversity of causes that the women's clubs in Akron embraced. They include the better-known reform-based associations and the civic-based "ladies' committees" of the antebellum period and the soldiers' aid and reform societies of both Akron and Middlebury. The profiled organizations of the post–Civil War period cover the gamut of causes, from providing emergency help to indigent families to the temperance crusade, from the municipal housekeeping movement to serving disadvantaged populations, from establishing great health institutions to fostering the culture of the city. The profiled groups also cover the gamut of organizational structures, from women's auxiliaries of male organizations to clubs affiliated with the churches of the city, from the independent women's organizations to the giant federation. Moreover, the groups profiled represent the diversity of female populations. Native-born, affluent women ran the greatest number of the women's clubs profiled in this book. However, the book provides a look at some of the clubs of African American, immigrant, and workingwomen.

Every organization was a product of strong women with a clear vision of where the group should be going. This book also attempts to explore the human element behind these organizations. The women profiled in this book were key individuals in the development of one or more organizations. If their names sound familiar, it is because many came from well-known families in the city's history—the Perkinses, the Schumachers, the Raymonds, the Seiberlings—or because the women were married to prominent corporate and professional leaders of Akron. Other names will not be as familiar. These women came to leadership merely by force of their will, their vision, their personality, and their energy.

This book attempts to tell the story of Akron women and their clubs and organizations, their weaknesses and their strengths. It also tells the story of how clubwomen grew and changed within this vital midwestern city and, in turn, how they changed the city.

Chapter 2

Women's Clubs in Antebellum Akron

Gothic Hall was well filled by an intelligent assemblage of Females, on
Friday last; convened to redress grievances to them almost insupportable;
illy compensated labor.
—*Summit Beacon*[1]

The Ladies cannot be too much praised for their generous efforts.
—*Summit Beacon*[2]

*I*N 1825, AKRON WAS LITTLE MORE THAN A DREAM.
    The reality was stark and uninviting. The Akron of 1825 was an "almost un-
broken wilderness" with some log cabins built by a few adventuresome families. Still,
Akron did have everything needed for urban success in the west—a location with
easy access to a plentiful water supply needed to power factories and mills, families willing to be part of the new town's future, and city fathers ready to spread the
word of the village's enormous promise to anyone who would listen. But most important, Akron was on the planned route of the Ohio Canal. By 1827, the canal
linked Akron with Cleveland and the little village began to throb with commerce.
In 1832, the canal reached the Ohio River, and Akron quickened its pace of growth.
After the Pennsylvania and Ohio Canal cut through the town, nothing could hold
Akron back.
    But the Akron of the 1820s and 1830s was not a particularly nice place to settle
and raise a family. Although the canals promised enormous prosperity, they also
brought disease, filth, vice, and violence to the little town.

In the 1820s and 1830s, especially, Akron was not a healthy place to live. "Touch of malaria" was the common diagnosis for the chills and fever that plagued so many canal workers and village residents. That diagnosis became an easy one to make—even though typhoid fever was probably the real cause of many of the infections.[3] Akron was especially dangerous for women. If they survived the "touch of malaria" and the typhoid fever, they faced the danger of childbirth. Like many towns on the frontier, Akron had a high rate of puerperal or childbed fever. With no known cure, many Akron women died of infection after giving birth.

The canals brought out the worst in the town. There was uncontrolled growth along the canals. Warehouses, businesses, and especially taverns sprang up everywhere. Akron attracted the worst type of scalawags, "finely-dressed, ruffle-shirted, plug-hatted, kid-gloved, lavishly-bejewelled" scoundrels, remembered newspaper editor Samuel A. Lane, who settled in the city in 1835.[4]

The Pennsylvania and Ohio Canal followed Main Street, making it a "disreputable dump," wrote early resident Laurine Schwan. Main Street could be dangerous day or night. At night, decent Akron residents avoided the neighborhood altogether because "tramps and riffraff" would waylay unsuspecting pedestrians. Daylight was not much better; crooks and confidence men tried every scheme to separate the unsuspecting traveler—or anyone else—from his or her money.[5]

Notwithstanding the health problems, the vice, the crime, the corruption, and the violence, Akron was growing and prospering. In 1827, barely 200 called Akron home; by 1830, the population doubled to about 400; by 1836, the population soared to 1,343.

In those early days, there were really two Akrons. One was the Akron of the canal workers. The Irish laborers and their families settled in what they called "Dublin," a community under the steep bluff of North Hill. The Irish huddled in slab and log homes. There was no Catholic church in the city and no priest to minister regularly to the spiritual needs of the Irish laborers. Instead, a priest came periodically to the city to celebrate Mass in one of the homes in "Dublin." The Irish would have to wait until the mid-1840s to have a church of their own.

The other Akron—closer to the canals—was more prosperous. Families of merchants, mechanics, lawyers, doctors, manufacturers, and artisans settled on High, Howard, and Market streets. Everything was close by in the Akron of the 1830s: stores, homes, offices—and Protestant churches. By 1836, Akron was the home to Congregational, Baptist, Universalist, Episcopal, and Methodist churches. The Presbyterian church was in nearby Middlebury. This Akron also prized edu-

Canals brought prosperity to Akron but they also brought vice and violence to the town—problems women's clubs sought to remedy. *Photo courtesy of the Summit County Historical Society, the University of Akron Archives.*

cation; early settlers built a school on High Street, to educate children of all ages.[6]

Everything seemed promising until the Panic of 1837, which transformed the bustling village of Akron into a community fighting for its very survival. Like many western towns, Akron was hit hard by President Andrew Jackson's economic policies that transferred national funds from the Bank of the United States to the so-called state pet banks and by a new national policy that required that the purchase of government lands be in gold and silver. Banks failed. People lost their savings. Factories closed their doors; people lost their jobs. The entire economy wobbled.

Things were especially bad in the west. Akron was in real trouble. For approximately five years after the Panic of 1837, Akron was reduced to what newspaper editor and historian Samuel Lane called a "truck and dicker" economy—barter. Woolen cloth became almost "legal tender," Lane explained. A carriage maker would sell a wagon for cloth. The cloth then would be traded for lumber, firewood, or other goods. Employees were paid in cloth, farm produce, or store orders. Lane himself had to sell his Akron house and lot for forty brass clocks and then traded those for the lumber and other materials needed to build another house.[7]

Few businesses survived in this economy. According to one history, only three of Akron's fourteen businesses in 1837 weathered the crisis. For more than five years, the *Summit Beacon* carried story after story of well-known, prosperous businessmen filing for bankruptcy and selling their property at sheriff's auctions.[8]

The Panic of 1837 could not keep Akron down for long, however. By the early 1840s, Akron was recovering. In 1843, *New York Tribune* editor Horace Greeley reported that the town had "five woolen factories, an extensive blast furnace, a machine shop, a card manufactory, nine dry goods stores and about as many other stores, two weekly newspapers, four large flouring mills, a court house, four churches [all Protestant] and two more being erected." Many of the merchants who had resorted to bankruptcy and sheriff's sales just a few years before were rebuilding their businesses, their wealth, and their reputations within the community. The town itself was looking better. One longtime resident recalled that by the mid-1840s Akron was a "quaint village with dirt roads lined with trees."9

It was during the early 1840s that Akron women first organized their own clubs and organizations. A number of conditions coalesced at that time to make Akron an ideal environment for these organizations.

Economically, the town had recovered from the Panic of 1837 and the subsequent depression. New businesses started; others grew. Canal traffic picked up, and Akron flourished with the new trade. Women's clubs in Akron needed that economic stability to organize.

The economic prosperity of the early 1840s also drew the population base the early women's clubs needed. In the early 1840s, Akron's population increased. More businessmen, lawyers, physicians, artisans, and laborers moved into town; especially important, from the perspective of women's clubs, was a growing corps of affluent families. Women within these families had domestics, time to devote to activities outside the home, and a certain sense of civic responsibility. Antebellum women's clubs were not just the work of the elite. The less affluent women of the town shared the religious zeal and the desire to sweep evil from the city.

The development of women's clubs also depended on the presence of institutions in the town. Akron in the 1840s was home to a range of Protestant denominations—Congregational, Universalist, Methodist, Episcopal, Church of Christ (and Presbyterian in nearby Middlebury). Catholics also finally had a church of their own. The Protestant denominations were especially vital to the beginnings of women's organizations in Akron. The churches served as networking locations, convenient places where women could talk about organizing or joining women's clubs. Moreover, the ministers of these churches, especially those from the Congregational, Methodist, and Universalist denominations, encouraged members to get involved in the reform movements of the day. Finally, the churches, the ministers, and the publications—local and national women's magazines and general news-

By 1855, when this photo was taken at Halls Corner, Akron had recovered from the Panic of 1837. By this time, also, women's organizations were thriving in the city. *Photo courtesy of the Summit County Historical Society, the University of Akron Archives.*

papers of the day—articulated a view of women that espoused the concept of a separation of spheres. Men were to handle the business and women were not to meddle. Women were told "never attempt to interfere in his business," wrote one correspondent to the Universalist women's magazine in Akron. Women held a higher moral ground, more appropriate to family and home. As one writer to the *Akron Buzzard* observed, "Her house is the residence of religious sentiments, of filial piety, of conjugal love, of maternal affection, of order, peace, sweet sleep and good health." A writer to the *American Democrat*, another Akron newspaper, emphasized the qualities of the good wife. "The best qualities to look after in a wife are industry, humility, neatness, gentleness, benevolence and piety—where you find these there is no danger. You will obtain a treasure and not regret your choice to the last period."[10] Because of their higher moral sensibilities and their sense of industry, benevolence, piety, and gentleness, Akron women were encouraged to save the souls of sinners and care for the downtrodden in the community. That message was especially emphasized at the revivals that spread throughout the nation in the 1830s and from the pulpits in Akron subsequently.[11]

When the Akron women first organized their Martha Washington Society and the Daughters of Temperance in the 1840s and formed groups to help seamstresses in the city in the 1850s, they were part of a nationwide reform movement of women committed to eliminating sin and helping the downtrodden. These organizations emerged from the religious fervor of the day and would draw their membership from the reform-minded affluent and artisan families of the city.

In the 1850s, however, another type of women's organization emerged in Akron—one quite different from the reform groups. More closely modeled on the male organizations of the day, these new groups—called ladies' committees—were dedicated to civic improvement, rather than reform. They concentrated on raising funds for the small volunteer fire department or other civic improvements planned by the men of the town. They drew their membership from the elite, affluent, civic-minded families of the city.

These would be the two competing models of women's organizations in antebellum Akron. Both would accomplish much, but each was different in its attitudes, tactics, and membership.

TEMPERANCE AND MORAL REFORM SOCIETIES

It is difficult to say with certainty which women's organization was established first in Akron. Few organizational records survive, and newspapers did not always cover women's clubs.[12] The earliest reference appeared in January 1842, when women were acknowledged for their work with the Washington Total Abstinence Society. The Washingtonians had been established in Baltimore in 1840 by a group of reformed alcoholics. In the early days, the group drew its membership from a population that heretofore had never been involved with temperance reform—lower-middle-class and working-class men. Their wives got involved through the woman's auxiliary, the Martha Washington Society. The Washingtonians added much to temperance reform. They built their activities around the "experience meeting," where reformed drinkers talked about their battle with the bottle.[13]

The Washingtonian movement spread quickly through the North. It arrived in Akron by December 1841, but the town's chapter seems to have been quite different from Baltimore's. Although lower-middle-class and working-class men may have made up the bulk of its membership—no membership list exists, so it is impossible to determine the membership with certainty—the *leadership* of the Akron Washingtonians was drawn from the upper crust of Akron politics. Akron Mayor

Gen. Lucius V. Bierce; attorney G. Bliss, who would go on to be mayor of the town; Judge C. G. Ladd; tax collector A. R. Townsend; manufacturer Reuben McMillan; and lawyer Henry W. King all served as officers or executive board members of the early Akron Washingtonians.

A few things had not changed. The Akron Washingtonians were committed to the same aims as the other chapters. Members had to sign the "pledge" neither to sell nor drink alcoholic beverages. "The sole and only object of this society shall be the promotion of entire abstinence from all intoxicating drink as a beverage—the rescue of the unfortunate inebriate—and the reformation of the moderate drinker," the constitution of the Summit County Washingtonian chapter read. Akron Washingtonians continued to rely on the "experience meeting" with reformed alcoholics telling of their difficulties with alcohol. The organization had a tremendous following in the city. In 1843, the Akron society reported it had 868 members, one of the largest organizations in Summit County.[14]

The organization also relied heavily on its women's auxiliary. Membership lists no longer survive of this organization, and the newspaper did not report the names of its officers. If Akron followed patterns in other cities, the Martha Washington Society was made up of wives, mothers, sisters, and daughters of the members of the male Washingtonian group. Thus, this membership would include wives and female relatives of the elite in the community (the leaders of the male organization) and of the artisans (the rank and file of the group).[15]

The women of the Akron Martha Washington Society had the responsibility for the social entertainment of the Washingtonians—the picnics, socials, and all other fund-raising events. The enormous success of these special events was testament to the capabilities of the Martha Washington Society.[16]

Akron's Martha Washington Society also established one of the first welfare programs for the less fortunate in the town. The group began its welfare work with the families of inebriates. The auxiliaries in other communities across the North did similar work; but, in Akron, the Martha Washingtonians took their welfare work one step further. As the women worked with the families of inebriates, they came into contact with the underclass within the town, families without relatives, friends, or a church community to help. Although the male organization acknowledged only their work among the families of the inebriates, Akron's Martha Washingtonians had expanded their work to destitute families generally. In this work, Akron's Martha Washingtonians relied primarily on their own means as well as on their fund-raising to provide food and clothing for these families. Only occasionally did the women call for help from the general public. In November 1844, however, Akron's Martha Washingtonians needed clothing and bedding for the growing number of poor in the town. These goods would be used for "gratuitous distribution among the poor and needy," the women wrote.[17]

The town's male Washingtonians did not always comprehend how the women's auxiliary had stretched its organizational mission. Akron temperance leader H. W. King saw what had taken place and congratulated the women's auxiliary, in March 1843, for "their accustomed zeal and fidelity" to "leave nothing undone when suffering, and distress are to be relieved, they may be made the source of incalculable benefit to the destitute and afflicted." But the resolution passed by the Washingtonians the next month mentioned only the women's work with the families of the drinkers. The women's auxiliary was applauded for all its hard work "in the cause of humanity, so strikingly manifested in their numerous acts of disinterested kindness, and charity, in seeking out the victims of intemperance, relieving their wants, and contributing to their comfort."[18]

This benevolent work opened a door for Akron women. The Martha Washingtonians of Akron did not challenge the social customs or expectations of the day. Working within the construct of women's separate sphere, they used the rhetoric of domesticity to gain needed support for the indigent within the town. Although the male Washingtonians never fully appreciated how much their women's auxiliary had expanded its mission beyond assisting the families of inebriates, the Martha Washingtonians established important precedents for temperance women who followed. It would be an important lesson that another group of temperance advocates, the Daughters of Temperance, would build on—and, in the process, strengthen the welfare services within the town.

By 1846, much of the vitality within the Akron Washingtonians had been spent. Nonetheless, the "liquor problem" within the town remained. In 1845, after almost four years of agitation by the Washingtonians, Akron was still the home of two distilleries and "16 doggeries" from "fashionable resorts . . . to the meanest hole on the canal," one temperance newspaper in the town reported. Akron's population had also come to accept the "rum sellers" who went to church even while their taverns were "the theatre of profanity, blasphemy and drunkenness," wrote a temperance advocate.[19]

The temperance movement in Akron was re-energized in 1846 with the introduction of the Sons of Temperance in the town. Established in 1842 in New York, the Sons of Temperance was a fraternal lodge with secret initiation rites and insignias. The organization initially faced resistance in Akron. The town—and the entire Western Reserve of Ohio—harbored resistance to secret societies. Yet the temperance spirit won out over the suspicion. Eventually, two divisions of the Sons of Temperance were established in Akron (Cascade and Akron) and another one was set up in nearby Middlebury (Summit). Because it was a secret society, neither the leaders' nor the members' names were published in the newspapers of the town, but if Akron followed trends in other towns, many Washingtonians affiliated with the Sons of Temperance.

The Washingtonians and the Sons of Temperance had common goals. Both wanted to eliminate the evils of liquor from the city, but the Sons of Temperance had a mutual assistance aspect. Members of the Sons contributed about six cents a week to a mutual benefits fund from which members could draw in times of sickness and disability. At the death of a member or his spouse, the organization provided funeral benefits, and a "contingent fund" provided support for the widows and orphans of members. The relatively high membership costs—initiation fees ranged from two dollars to five dollars; regular dues were four dollars per year in addition to the mutual fund contributions and the periodic assessments—suggest that members of Akron's Sons of Temperance were at least middle class.[20]

Soon after the Sons of Temperance was founded in Akron, its women's auxiliary—Daughters of Temperance—debuted. Like the men's group, this was a secret society. The Daughters of Temperance had their own uniforms and secret insignias. Like the men's group, the women's auxiliary had a mutual benefits plan that insured wives against the sickness and death of male breadwinners.[21] Nationally, the Daughters of Temperance had a constricted role. Unlike the Martha Washingtonians, who spoke at temperance rallies as well as at organized fund-raising events, the Daughters were not welcome to speak at the Sons' conventions or don their uniforms in public. That constriction of roles did not take place in Akron, according to the city newspapers. Both the Sons and the Daughters were welcome—indeed expected—to participate in the various temperance demonstrations. In full dress uniform, both the Sons and Daughters of Temperance paraded at temperance rallies as well as at funerals.

Like the Martha Washingtonians, the Daughters were expected to arrange fund-raising events benefiting the temperance cause. Most of these were conventional affairs—suppers, fairs, and the like. But at least one tested the bounds of community acceptance. In October 1849, the Daughters hosted a temperance festival that drew large numbers, and one of the great attractions was the dancing—held in another location, lest certain people be offended. As the *Summit Beacon* reported, "*It is said* there was some dancing, in an adjoining apartment, but we cannot swear it as we did not see it." The Daughters were extremely successful in raising money. The Sons of Temperance Hall—underwritten at least in part by the fund-raising of the women—was dedicated in November 1849.[22]

It is unclear what the Daughters of Temperance did as a welfare group. In the rare instances that the temperance women reached out to the general community for assistance, they followed many of the precedents set by the Martha Washingtonians. They used appeals that drew upon the idea of the separate spheres of men and women; men were busy with business, so women had to tend to needy families of the town. Like the Martha Washingtonians, the Daughters did not limit their welfare work solely to the families of inebriates; and they even sometimes signed the appeals "Martha Washington." In October 1849, for example, the women reached out to the "Benevolent of Akron." "Mothers are asking us for old clothes, to make garments for their shivering children. Will not gentlemen who are laying aside old garments enable us to respond to this call, by sending them to our depository at Mr. Gale's, on or before the day of our next meeting. We earnestly request those who deem it a pleasure to alleviate human suffering, to make donations of food, clothing or fuel—anything that can be converted into bed 'comfortables,' or clothing for children."[23]

The Martha Washington Society and the Daughters of Temperance marked the beginnings of women's organizations in Akron. Both grew out of the reform impulses of the day. The women of these organizations embraced the notion of the separate spheres for the sexes and the higher moral sense of women and used those ideas to achieve their goals and gain for themselves new power and responsibilities within the community. By transferring the notion of woman as caregiver to the community, both the Martha Washingtonians and the Daughters of Temperance claimed the right to carry out important welfare services to the community.[24] In the process, Akron's Martha Washingtonians and the Daughters of Temperance were learning important skills. They were transferring their role as hostess within the home to event planner within the community and fund-raiser for the male organization with which they were affiliated.

These women had learned important organizational, fund-raising, and networking lessons. They would soon apply those lessons when they moved beyond auxiliaries, formed their own organizations—and controlled the funds they raised. One of the first women's groups to try this, in 1846, was the Akron Female Moral

Reform Society, a group committed to saving women and children from the ravages of morally depraved men. Little is known about this women's organization in Akron. Not surprisingly, newspapers carried few details of what these women were doing—and few women's organizations of the antebellum period had learned publicity lessons that they mastered during the Civil War. The group only highlighted its work on the pages of the reform newspaper of the town, the *Cascade Roarer.* The Akron Female Moral Reform Society used personal intervention to save women and children from depraved men. According to one news report, women rescued an invalid orphan from the repeated attacks of her guardian. The man was identified at the meeting, although his name was not revealed to the press in deference to the child.[25]

The Female Moral Reform Society was not peculiar to Akron. Many of these moral reform organizations operated in small towns across the North. Like the Akron group, the other societies assailed the sexual double standard and exposed licentious men. However, the Akron society never achieved widespread acceptance among the organizational women or the general public in the town. There were several reasons for this. First, distinct, separate women's organizations were an innovation in Akron in this period. In other towns where the moral reform society achieved wider success, there had been a long history of independent women's benevolent activities. Second, this particular organization was more closely identified with the women members of the Presbyterian Church.[26] During this time, the closest Presbyterian church was located in Middlebury.

SUMMIT COUNTY FEMALE LABOR ASSOCIATION

In both their temperance work and their moral reform work, the benevolent women of Akron had come into contact with the least affluent women of the city. The Martha Washingtonians and the Daughters of Temperance gave indigent women the emergency food, fuel, and clothing needed to sustain them. The Moral Reform group rescued women and children from abusive situations. The concerned, affluent women helped the needy families only in times of emergency; they did nothing to address the underlying economic problems these women and their families faced in Akron. In 1854, a new organization was formed that redefined women's organizations and welfare in the city. The Summit County Female Labor Association was a true partnership between the affluent and the working-class women. The group went beyond emergency help and attempted to bring about lasting economic changes.

In 1850s Akron, there were few options for women who needed to work. The better-educated women taught in public or private schools in the town. Less-educated women worked either as domestics or in the sewing trade. The Summit County Female Labor Association, organized in March 1854 in a flurry of publicity, pledged to "aid and assist each other in carrying out the principle of a just remuneration for labor, and to widen the field of female labor." The group focused primarily on improving the conditions of women in the sewing trades. This organization represented a radical departure from earlier groups in tactics, organization, leadership, and membership.

In the early days of this association, certain men from reform circles in the town, like former mayor Lucius V. Bierce, editor Samuel A. Lane, and the Reverend Baily, lent their names and their support. But this was a woman's organization. A man was elected president but women held all the other positions. They served as vice presidents and secretaries. They drafted the resolutions. They defined the public appeals, traveled throughout the town to gain public support for their organization, reached out to workingwomen to earn their support, and pressured merchants to go along or face a boycott. Here was a different, more forceful model of women's organizational activism in Akron.

It is unclear what precipitated the organization of the Female Labor Association. For years, seamstresses in Akron had been poorly paid and no one seemed particularly concerned. But in 1854, the time was right to remedy the situation and get decent wages for the women. The Female Labor Association decided on a strategy that had not been tried before by women in Akron. Instead of offering emergency aid, the organization forced tailors to increase the rates paid to seamstresses in the town. With input from the "German Tailors," the group developed a new price index for piecework. The price list was broken down by shop work and custom work. The increases recommended were substantial but not unreasonable, wrote the women.

The Akron seamstresses were to be paid as follows:

For shop work

Common cheap vest	37 cents
Cheap silk and satin vest	50 to 75 cents
Best satin vest	75 cents
Coarse plain bottom pants	37 cents
Common spring bottom pants	50 cents

Fine cassimere [*sic*] and broad-cloth pants	50 to 75 cents
Fine over coat	$2
Fine sack coat	$1.50
Dress coat	$2
Linen Coat	37 to 75 cents
Satin coat	$1
Fine tweed coat	$1
Coarse tweed and satinette coat	62 to 75 cents
Fine single breast frock coat	$1.50
Coarse single breast frock coat	$1.25
Overalls	15 to 18 cents
Drawers	18 cents
Common white shirts	25 cents
Striped shirts	18 cents

Custom work

Single breast, frock coat	$2
Double breast frock coat	$2.50
Dress coat	$3
Linen frock	$1
Linen vest	75 cents
Linen pants	75 cents
Fine vest	$1
Fine cloth pant	$1[27]

To achieve that piecework rate, the Female Labor Association had to convince the seamstresses, the merchants, and the general public to go along.

In addressing the public, the group framed its appeals so that women of *all classes* could identify with the plight of the seamstress. These were not faceless laborers; they were mothers, sisters, and daughters forced into sewing work by financial reverses. They had lost their fathers or husbands. They had no contingency funds. They had to go to work to survive. "To whom can she look for aid?" the women of the labor association asked. "Not surely to her own unaided efforts, for at the low prices she would receive for work, however well done, would barely afford the means of keeping soul and body together to say nothing of clothing and educating her children, and placing them in a respectable position in society—objects dear to every true mother's heart."[28]

But in order for these new wages to go into effect, the organization needed the support of both the seamstresses and the merchants.

The seamstresses had to demand the living wage, even if merchants offered them less. The women of the labor association pleaded with the seamstresses to go along.

> Ladies, we appeal to you. Have you not labored long and hard enough to obtain a bare subsistance [*sic*]? Then arouse yourselves to a sense of your duty, and have confidence enough to tell a man what you can afford to labor for: and work for nothing less. Place no confidence in any statement that they can get their work done cheaper east or west, north or south. Admit that they could do so; would not any man of honor give out his work in his own community, when he is depending upon that community for his support? We think he would. It is our duty to assist each other, and we are determined to do so, as far as lies in our power."[29]

There was much that was within the labor association's power. The members of the Female Labor Association were not just going to rely on prayers and appeals. These women were going to experiment with boycotts and public recriminations. Merchants who failed to go along with the new prices were identified. In April 1854, for example, the women announced that all the clothing establishments in Akron had agreed to the new prices, except for "Messrs. Koch & Levi, and S. B. Hopfman." These merchants would accede to the new prices, the women were sure: "We have too good an opinion of these gentlemen to believe that they will stand back and resist demands so manifestly just."[30] Those two retailers soon agreed to pay the higher rates.

The labor association women did not rest on their early successes. They followed up with clothing merchants and seamstresses regularly. When they discovered that some merchants had reverted to lower wages, the women of the Female Labor Association called for an accounting. In June, the women found that "Messrs. S. A. Lane [an early supporter of the organization] and I. P. Sanford had violated the rules." And the women could prove it, they wrote in the *Summit Beacon.* "We have pieces of the garments, names and places of residents of those doing the work, and can produce them, if necessary."[31]

The women also encouraged Akron consumers to boycott any establishment that failed to honor the higher wages. "Gentlemen, be on your guard, if you are willing to 'live and let live,' and do not patronize those who will not pay a living price. There are some that *will* pay for their work—such men we wish to see sustained," the "LADIES" wrote.[32]

The threat of a boycott made the Female Labor Association a formidable power. It represented a significant departure in tactics for women's organizations in Akron during the antebellum period. Here was a group who had learned to use the press to publicize their work and to disavow merchants who failed to follow the higher prices. Here was a group who reached across class lines to establish a powerful partnership. Seamstresses and affluent women worked together to bring about lasting improvements in the prices paid workingwomen. When a clothing merchant failed to pay the higher wages, seamstresses informed the Female Labor Association, which used intimidation, publicity, and threats of economic boycotts to get the agreed-upon higher prices for seamstresses. It was empowering for the women of the labor association but also for the seamstresses. But there were limits to this association. The group never followed through on the second part of its objective, widening the field for female labor, and never looked into the wages paid the domestics, some of whom were toiling in the households of the members of the Female Labor Association. Compared to other women's organizations of the day, however, here was a group that tested the boundaries of the "separate sphere." These women directly intruded into man's business sphere to protect the women working there. With the input of "German Tailors," women came up with a new price structure for the seamstresses, a price structure that gave women an opportunity to support their families.

By the 1850s, press customs were beginning to change. In the 1840s, the names of the leaders and organizers of women's benevolent groups were never revealed in the newspapers. By the 1850s, that taboo had broken down. The names of the leaders of the Female Labor Association were publicized, as were the leaders of another type of women's organization in the city.

The Female Labor Association built upon the reform tradition of the Martha Washington Society, the Daughters of Temperance, and the Moral Reform group. In the 1850s, a new women's organizational model emerged, the ladies' committee. Unlike the women's organizations of the reform tradition, these committees emerged from more conservative, civic-responsibility impulses. These committees served as women's auxiliaries to the male-run organizations, like the Young Men's Association and the Fire Department. However, the ladies' committees did not appear to have a formal structure. The committees came together to do specific jobs and then dissolved. The women of these committees came from the highest reaches of Akron society; they were members of elite, affluent families in the city. A number of these women went on to be leaders of the largest woman's organization that Akron had ever seen—the Soldiers Aid Society during the Civil War.

LADIES' COMMITTEES

The best known of the ladies' committees were associated with the Young Men's Association and the Fire Department. The Young Men's Association, not to be confused with the Young Men's Christian Association, was a civic organization made up of young, affluent business and government leaders of Akron. The ladies' committee of this organization was made up primarily of the wives of the officers and members of the YMA. These committees acted like the women's auxiliaries of the male temperance groups, except their roles were far more constricted. Unlike the temperance groups, the ladies' committees did not have a welfare component. The women of the ladies' committee had only special-event responsibilities; they organized dinners and socials for the group. The women also did not apparently have input into how the money was to be spent. Thus, Mary Ingersol Tod Evans, widow of an Akron physician and sister of Julia Ford and Grace Perkins, both notable civic leaders in their own right, helped prepare the Washington Birthday Celebration Dinner for the Young Men's Association.[33]

A larger number of women were busy with the ladies' committee of the Firemen's Festivals. Each year, prominent business and government leaders in the town held a large festival to raise funds for the small fire department in the town. (A stock company that needed an annual infusion of funds to buy new equipment and replace worn hose underwrote the fire department at the time.) The ladies' committee had the responsibility of organizing the arrangements and cooking the dinner. This was no small task. In 1849, the celebration drew two thousand. "The Ladies cannot be too much praised for their generous efforts on the occasion," said the *Summit Beacon*.[34] The composition of the ladies' committee varied from year to year. In 1852, Mary Ingersol Tod Evans helped out at the Firemen's Festival, as did Elizabeth Smith Abbey, wife of a jewelry store owner; Roxana Jones Howe, wife of a civil engineer, and Agnes Grant Mathews, wife of the manager of a fire insurance company. Each woman worked in the Soldiers Aid Society ten years later.[35]

Mary Ingersol Tod Evans had the right family connections for a leadership position in the women's committees in the antebellum city. She was the daughter of a judge, widow of a physician, and sister of Julia Ford and Grace Perkins, two community leaders in their own right. *Photo courtesy of the Summit County Historical Society, the University of Akron Archives.*

Women's organizations grew up with antebellum Akron.

By the Civil War, Akron already had a small core of experienced organizational women. These women knew how to frame their appeals, plan and execute successful fund-raising events, and set up and carry out emergency welfare services within the community. A few were even experienced in networking across class lines. Akron women were going to need each of those skills as they embarked on a new type of organization, a kind that Akron had never seen before.

Chapter 3

Women's Clubs of Akron during the Civil War

This truly is a blessed work.

—Mrs. E. T. Chapman to Miss M. C. Brayton, February 5, 1864[1]

I can assure you we feel lost without our weekly meetings. . . . It was a pleasure to be present at those little gatherings, and 'twas no little thing that kept us away; to me especially 'twas a great trial to be absent. We shall often [refer to] . . . our Aid Society with pleasure.

—Mrs. E. T. Chapman to Miss M. C. Brayton, August 17, 1865[2]

ON APRIL 17, 1861, FIVE DAYS AFTER CONFEDERATE FORCES FIRED ON Ft. Sumter and two days after President Abraham Lincoln made his call for 75,000 troops, Akron citizens rallied in support of the war. The crowd condemned secession and rebellion. Men rushed to enlist—more than enough to fill the city's quota for troops. Almost as quickly, the women in the city "enlisted"; but instead of volunteering for a mere three months, the typical length of enlistments for men, women were "in for the war."[3]

The Civil War was a pivotal period for Akron women and their organizations. The women could stay home and carry on their traditional responsibilities, caring for their husbands and children and sending packages to friends and relatives off fighting the war. Or they could follow the antebellum club pattern, working in small groups or in auxiliaries to male organizations, providing supplies to Akron men and boys in the Union army. Or they could redefine women's organizations and what they could accomplish and start an aid society the likes of which Akron had never seen. Akron women chose the last option.

The women of Akron formed their Soldiers Aid Society in May 1861. It quickly became the largest, most active women's organization in the city. Under the wing of this organization, women learned how to organize, stage special events, and do fund-raising on a scale never before imagined. This organization allowed women to expand their friendship networks beyond neighborhood and church, but not beyond class. It remained an association of middle- to upper-class women committed to helping the men away at war. The aid society women accomplished much; the group provided much-needed supplies to the sick and wounded soldiers of the Civil War.

Other groups besides the matrons of the city availed themselves of the same opportunities. The "girls" of the city formed their own groups—the High School Girls Soldiers Aid Society and the Girls Soldiers Aid Society. In a sense auxiliaries to the Akron Soldiers Aid Society, these juvenile societies trained the next generation of women to take their places in community and benevolent organizations.

The women of Middlebury could not achieve the same type of unity of purpose or organization. Instead, the women of Middlebury formed two groups— the Soldiers Aid Society in June 1861 and the Soldiers Relief Association in 1862— that competed for membership and donations. It is unclear what led to the split, but it was irreparable and bitter. As Janette Adams, secretary of the Middlebury Soldiers Relief Association, wrote to the president of the sanitary commission in Cleveland, "We do not wish to be connected with the Aid Society of our town but wish our donations to be credited to Soldiers Relief Association." The feud had taken a toll. According to the Middlebury Soldiers Aid Society, donations fell off considerably in 1862.[4]

The two Middlebury organizations and the Akron societies shared similar goals. All were committed to assisting those who were off fighting the war—"doing what we could for the sick and suffering," wrote the president of the Akron society, Pamphila Stanton Wolcott.[5]

At the start, the Soldiers Aid Society members of Akron and Middlebury harbored parochial attitudes about aid and relief. The women preferred that their supplies go directly to the hospitals caring for Akron and Middlebury men. As early as June 1861, Pamphila Stanton Wolcott explained, "it was preferred by the Ladies to work for them [Akron soldiers] first, more especially as they have gone

Soon after this photo was taken, Akron women organized their Soldiers Aid Society, where women worked to send necessities to the men away at war but also learned networking and organizational skills. *Photo courtesy of the Summit County Historical Society, the University of Akron Archives.*

and are expecting to go into active service, and may very soon have need of these articles."[6]

That parochialism caused problems between the Akron and Middlebury groups and the Cleveland Sanitary Commission, the hub for aid societies across northern Ohio. The commission wanted all shipments to be sent to Cleveland so it could decide where the food, clothing, and medicine would be sent. Instead, as the Akron and Middlebury women gained confidence in themselves, the local groups started making distribution decisions, sending supplies to specific hospitals where Ohio soldiers convalesced or suggesting to the Cleveland Sanitary Commission where their supplies should be sent. The women of the Akron and Middlebury aid societies also ventured out to examine conditions at hospitals for themselves.[7] Ironically, the parochialism of the Akron and Middlebury women led to a degree of independence and confidence in their own abilities.

At the beginning of the war, few Akron women had the club or association experience to organize or lead a large, complex society. But the Akron and Middlebury women, inspired by a deep patriotic spirit, learned quickly.

The woman credited with organizing the Akron Soldiers Aid Society was Pamphila Stanton Wolcott. On the surface, she seemed an unlikely candidate for organizing and leading the society. She was young, just thirty-four in 1861, and had three young children at home. She was not originally from Akron; she and her husband had moved to the city in 1844. However, she brought assets to the job that few could have imagined. Pamphila was, perhaps, politically the best-connected woman in the city. She was married to Christopher Parsons Wolcott, a brilliant young attorney who became a senior partner in the law firm of Wolcott and Upson. Soon his name was bandied around in political circles. Ohio Governor Salmon P. Chase appointed Wolcott state attorney general. In that position, he traveled the state, leaving his wife to manage the household and raise the children alone. In 1861, Christopher Wolcott was appointed judge advocate general. He did not keep that job long; he was soon in Washington, D.C., serving as assistant secretary of war under Edwin Stanton, Pamphila's brother. Thus, by birth and by marriage, Pamphila had strong local and national political connections—if she chose to use them.[8]

In addition, Pamphila Wolcott had developed extraordinary management and organizational skills by the time of the Civil War. Because her husband was a workaholic—the newspaper reported that his typical day ran from 6 A.M. until 2 the next morning—Pamphila had primary responsibility for running a bustling household. Moreover, her youth was also an asset. Most of the leaders of the Akron and Middlebury aid societies were matrons with grown children, while a large number of the women volunteering in the aid societies were younger, closer to Pamphila's age. Thus, her political connections, her apparent management and organizational skills, and her youth made her the ideal first president of the Akron Soldiers Aid Society.

In May 1861, Pamphila Wolcott made the first overtures to the Cleveland Sanitary Commission. In the early days of the society, Pamphila looked to the commission for guidance and suggestions, for, she admitted, Akron women had "willing hearts" but were not entirely sure what to do. She was not disappointed. The experienced commission leader Rebecca Rouse mentored the young woman, sent her circulars and papers, and provided "explicit" instructions on what to do. Pamphila learned quickly and soon was sending out circulars of her own, developing an auxiliary in a school, moving the society's headquarters to a "more convenient" location, and reorganizing the leadership of the society.[9]

Although she seemed to have grown in confidence and ability, Pamphila Wolcott withdrew from the leadership of the Akron society at the end of her six-month term. Friends urged her to reconsider, but she declined. It was a great loss to the society, said Adeline Myers Coburn, who took her place as president. Adeline should have understood the reasons. Pamphila's husband was in Washington, D.C., and his health was failing. Christopher Parsons Wolcott died in April 1863 at the age of forty-two. He had literally worked himself to death, the *Summit County Beacon* observed.[10]

The Akron Soldiers Aid Society went on, competently led by Adeline Myers Coburn. Born in New York, Adeline came to Akron with her physician husband, Stephen, in 1848. The two had only one child, a married daughter, who was also active in Akron's Soldiers Aid Society. The Coburn family was affluent, not just because Stephen was a competent doctor but also because the family had invested in real estate and done well. Thus, at the time of her election to president of the city's Soldiers Aid Society, Adeline was affluent, had few child-rearing responsibilities, and had time to commit to the Soldiers Aid Society—and several other organizations as well. She also became president of the Akron chapter of the Ladies National Covenant, a nonimportation group, a member of the Akron committee for the Sanitary Fair in Cleveland, and a leader of an Akron organization that collected clothing for freedmen. The Soldiers Aid Society marked only her introduction to civic betterment. After the war, she shifted her organizational and leadership skills to the temperance crusade.[11]

Unlike Pamphila Stanton Wolcott, who had strong ties to the Cleveland Sanitary Commission, Adeline Myers Coburn was more independent—and more committed to *directly* helping Summit County men away at war. She repeatedly directed the Akron society to send boxes to companies from Summit County or to hospitals where Akron men recuperated. In 1862, for example, Akron women went to Louisville to visit men in the camp and the hospital and took them clothing, reading material, and jellies. That meant that the central sanitary commission had to wait for contributions, "and as our Soc. is not a *fast* one[,] it may be some weeks before we are able to send another to you," Adeline wrote the Cleveland Sanitary

Commission. When she again diverted contributions, she explained her reasons: "I assure you our sympathies are a good deal aroused when we hear that our neighbors are wanting comforts which we can furnish."[12]

Adeline Coburn had difficulty delegating authority; she handled all correspondence with Cleveland herself and closely supervised the aid society work in Akron. It was little wonder that she looked forward to the end of her presidency. She was tired—so tired, in fact, that her daughter was helping with some of her mother's responsibilities. As Adeline wrote to the Cleveland commission, "A few weeks will bring a change in the administration of our soc. and I hope some of the offices will be more efficiently filled, especially that of president." Adeline completed her term in 1862 and, like Pamphila Wolcott, withdrew from the society, allowing a new group of officers to take over.[13]

The new leaders under Isabella Green, a native of New Hampshire and wife of the deputy provost marshal of Summit County, seemed ill equipped to handle the challenges. They could not keep the Akron women focused and motivated. Shipments to Cleveland fell. The situation became so serious that the head of the Cleveland commission wrote Isabella, reminding her of her responsibilities. That helped matters, she observed. "Your letter urging us to do something for you this week has helped me much in getting our ladies aroused again," she wrote. But the commission needed to do more to keep the struggling Akron society on track. "If you will occasionally send us a letter stating your *great* need of certain articles, it would be of much service to us," Isabella wrote.[14]

Nothing improved. By late 1862, the Akron Soldiers Aid Society was floundering. If the society was to endure and be effective, the organization needed different leaders—strong, experienced ones. The group turned away from Isabella Green and her officers and elected some old friends. Adeline Coburn returned but this time as vice president. Friend and neighbor Elizabeth Smith Abbey took over as president, and another neighbor, Sarah T. Peck, served as both secretary and treasurer.

Elizabeth Abbey became the driving force behind Akron's Soldiers Aid Society for much of the remainder of the war. Elizabeth was older, fifty-one at the time she was elected president. She had strong ties in the community. She and her husband, the owner of a successful watch and jewelry store, had moved to Akron in 1835, and she quickly settled into her matronly duties. She joined the Congregational Church, the denomination of many of the political, social, and economic elite in the city. She got involved in civic activities, serving as a member of the Ladies' Committee of the Fireman's Festival in 1852.

Elizabeth Abbey was also a good manager. She delegated responsibilities to other officers, something that the three previous presidents had not been able to do. Secretary Sarah Peck took over all correspondence with the Cleveland Sanitary Commission. Elizabeth was too busy organizing lavish fund-raising events and rebuilding the Akron Soldiers Aid Society's treasury. The group also strengthened its ties with the local newspaper, informing it of every planned event, every new appeal, and, seemingly, every donation made to the organization. That brought unexpected benefits. Not only did the newspaper publicize the events before the fact and cover them as stories after the fact, but the publication also editorially supported the group. Akron women, the *Summit County Beacon* reported, had to be involved in the Soldiers Aid Society "to furnish their proportion of the Sanitary stores now so greatly needed by the wounded soldiers in the hospitals of Mississippi, Tennessee and Kentucky."[15]

The society also reached out to other groups, forging new alliances. Farmers were encouraged to contribute fresh produce, and children were encouraged to do their own fund-raisers.[16]

Soon the Akron Soldiers Aid Society turned around. Never had the group been so dynamic, energetic, or successful. As Sarah Peck wrote, "Our Society has never been more flourishing than at present." Elizabeth Abbey committed the society to support the aims of Cleveland's Sanitary Commission. Direct shipments to Akron troops and individual hospitals ended. Supplies for the soldiers were routed through Cleveland alone, although the aid society did open its coffers to the soldiers' indigent families left behind in the city. As Sarah Peck wrote the Cleveland commission, "We mean to send all our goods to your Rooms to be distributed as you think best, well knowing that your facilities far know where they are most needed are much better than ours." But that did not mean the Akron society would blindly follow the Cleveland directives. When the commission wanted a report from the Akron group, the officers refused. "Some think it an unnecessary expense," Sarah reported.[17]

Pamphila Stanton Wolcott, Adeline Myers Coburn, and Elizabeth Abbey showed the growing independence and capability of the leaders of the Akron—and Middlebury—soldiers' aid societies. They also illustrated the elite nature of the women who were leading these organizations. Based on the information about these women obtained from the census, city directories, church records, marriage and death records, and city histories, the officers of the aid and relief societies were not typical Akron or Middlebury women. The twenty-six officers of the Akron and

Middlebury societies came from the elite families within these towns. Most of these (twenty of the twenty-six) were married or widowed. Their husbands were owners of successful businesses or thriving professionals, primarily attorneys or physicians (twelve). These were women who could afford to delegate their household responsibilities to servants. Officers seemed to be older—an average age of 47.6 years for the six leaders whose age could be determined. Ten were native born and five were Protestants.

Those involved in the Akron and Middlebury aid societies represented a wider cross section of the community but were hardly reflective of the entire population of either town. The women of the aid societies were not from the laboring class; these women were from at least the middle class.

In all, newspaper reports named 166 women contributing to or associated with the Akron Soldiers Aid Society.[18] Most of these women (146, or 87.9 percent) were married; only seventeen (10.2 percent) were single, and the marital status of another three is impossible to ascertain. (There may have been substantially more single women in the aid societies, but their involvement was masked by general organizational references, such as Girls Soldiers Aid Society or High School Soldiers Aid Society, instead of the names of specific donors.) The average age of twenty-eight women associated with the aid societies was 37.5 years, ten years younger than the average age of the leaders. Of the forty-three women whose religious affiliation was determined, all were Protestant. More than half of these women (twenty-two) were members of the Congregational Church; seven women were Universalists; six were Episcopalians; four were Methodists; three were members of the Church of Christ; and one was a Lutheran.

The women affiliated with the aid societies were middle- to upper-class women. Almost half of those positively identified (thirty-four, or 47.2 percent) were married to business owners. Some, like Janette Murphy Adams, the wife of the president of Akron Sewer Pipe, were quite wealthy; others, like Cornelia Wadsworth Beebe, wife of the owner of the *Summit County Beacon*, probably had more modest means. A significant number of members (fifteen, or 20.8 percent) were married to professionals, including attorneys, physicians, and ministers. Elizabeth Howard, for example, was married to physician Elias W. Howard; Frances A. Oviatt was married to an attorney who moved into politics during the Civil War.

A smaller number of women (fourteen, or 19.4 percent) were married to skilled tradesmen. These women introduced diverse elements into the picture of the aid societies. For example, Catherine Burkhardt, wife of machinist George Burkhardt, had been born in Germany. In contrast, Anna Potter Grant was married to a miller and was native born. None of the women positively identified through the census, city directories, church registers, or marriage and death records were married to laborers.

Soldiers Aid Society women tended to live in certain neighborhoods. The majority of those women identified lived in the First Ward. The largest concentration of them lived in a two-block radius of the corner of East Market and High streets, within easy walking distance of each other. This was an affluent neighborhood where many families of business owners, professionals, and skilled craftsmen resided. Far fewer women were located in the other wards. In Ward Two, the largest concentration of aid society women resided within a two-block radius of Middlebury and High streets, although far fewer resided there than in the Ward One's neighborhood of activism. Those who resided in Ward Three lived along Walnut and Maple streets. These neighborhood concentrations meant that many of the women probably knew each other before becoming involved with the Soldiers Aid Society. They were neighbors; a number went to the same church; their husbands worked together. Indeed, that familiarity helps explain membership recruitment patterns within these organizations. Women encouraged their friends, relatives, and neighbors to join them at the society's rooms located within walking distance of the Ward One concentration.

No Catholic or Jewish women could be identified. Few of these women were foreign born or the children of immigrants, even though Akron had a large thriving immigrant population.[19]

These class, religious, and ethnic patterns explained much about the aid societies and their strategies and practices during the Civil War. First, the women of the aid societies built on middle-class views of the domestic roles of women to solicit members and donations. As caregivers, the women had special responsibilities to the soldiers—husbands, fathers, sons—away fighting the war; Akron women needed to get involved in the aid societies that provided the much-needed supplies to the hospitals that tended to the wounded and sick husbands, fathers, and sons away. That same theme appeared in appeals for donations and special events. The women were "indefatigable in their labors and efforts to aid in the good work of providing sick and wounded soldiers with hospital comforts and delicacies," and so both women and men had a responsibility to attend the dime parties, the dinners, the concerts, and the speeches sponsored by the aid societies.[20]

Because so few of these women had experience in organizing and running associations with substantial fund-raising goals, they searched for models on which to build. In the aid societies, the women embraced a hierarchical model commonly associated with businesses and male organizations. Each society elected officers and directors. Most leaders came from the elite families in the community, wives of business owners or professionals. These actions patterned behaviors within male community organizations of the time.[21]

This hierarchical model also spilled over to relations between the Cleveland Sanitary Commission and the local aid societies. The Akron and Middlebury aid societies were to supply the Cleveland commission hub with supplies. Input from local societies was neither solicited nor welcomed. The Cleveland commission then determined where the need was most pressing and sent the supplies accordingly. At first, the presidents of the Akron and Middlebury aid societies—most of them wives or widows of professionals—chafed under those expectations and sent supplies directly to hospitals where Summit County soldiers convalesced, although they continued to supply the Cleveland commission.[22]

Slowly the commission's authority and the hierarchical structure prevailed. In Akron, once Elizabeth Abbey—the wife of a business owner—was elected president, the aid society stopped diverting supplies to individual hospitals. Elizabeth saw the superiority of the commission's expertise, intelligence, and access to reduced transportation rates. Middlebury societies followed a similar pattern. When the leadership of those aid societies was turned over to the wives of business owners, those groups also bent to the commission's will. As Amanda Merrill, secretary of the Middlebury society, wrote to the commission, "We like your systematic plan."[23]

However, when it came to planning grand fund-raising events or dinners or socials, Akron and Middlebury women used their own experiences as hostesses within their families as the model to follow. The women, again, transferred their expertise in the home to a community-based forum.

The aid societies in both Akron and Middlebury relied on "dime parties" to keep the coffers of their organizations full. The local newspapers publicized these "dime parties," so named because admission to the festivities required ten cents. All proceeds went to the aid society. Most commonly, these parties were held in the homes of well-known Akron and Middlebury residents. Interestingly, the newspaper always reported that the home was owned by the husband and never alluded to the wife's affiliation with the aid society. Apparently, the aid society women who wrote the circulars sent to the newspapers—a kind of early press release—identified the household through the man's name, illustrating how these aid societies used the social conventions of the time for their own ends. Thus, the Middlebury

Soldiers Aid Society announced that one of its dime parties would be held at James Viall's home. James Viall at the time owned a business that ran a line boat between Pittsburgh and Cleveland. His wife, Mary, was a director of the Middlebury Soldiers Aid Society, although that affiliation was not mentioned in the story. Instead, readers got the impression that these male civic leaders were independently involved with—and supportive of—aid society events.[24] The dime parties of the Akron Soldiers Aid Society were also held in private homes, primarily those of business owners in the city. Aid society parties were held in the homes of James Christy, owner of a leather store; Henry Abbey, owner of a watch and jewelry store, and James H. Peterson, a well-known surgeon/dentist. The wives of each of these individuals were active in the Soldiers Aid Society, although that affiliation again was not disclosed in the story.[25]

Some of these dime parties were designed to build on friendship networks that existed within churches. The dime party for the Methodist-Episcopal Church was held at the home of Dr. I. E. Carter, a dentist whose wife was a member of the Akron Soldiers Aid Society. Members of the Congregational Church were invited to the dime party hosted by Dr. James H. Peterson.[26]

Other special events were grand extravaganzas designed to be "the" place to be on a given evening. The dime party held at Empire Hall promised to be "one of the richest affairs of the season," the *Beacon* reported. Wives and children would go for the fun, but fathers went for patriotic reasons. Typically, these large events were timed to coincide with a holiday and usually netted hundreds of dollars. The dime party and oyster supper given at Akron's Phoenix Hall before Valentine's Day was a grand success; the society made $195 on the dinner. The July 4 dinner at Grace Park was even more successful, earning the organization $290.[27] Most of these grand fund-raisers were held at convenient locations in Ward One, adjacent to or in the "neighborhood of activism."

Each successful dinner, dime party, and social not only replenished the society's coffers but also enhanced the reputation of the Soldiers Aid Society in the community—and the morale of the members. As the *Beacon* reported after a particularly profitable dinner, "This will greatly encourage the members of the Society, who will enter with renewed zeal into the good work in which they are engaged."[28]

Having a good reputation within a community was vital to the success of these groups. Without it, the Soldiers Aid Society would not have continuing access to the newspaper. Without it, appeals fell on deaf ears.

If there was one skill that the women of Akron Soldiers Aid Society mastered during the Civil War, it was media relations. Never before had a woman's organization in Akron had such access to the newspaper. Media relations between the *Summit County Beacon* and the Akron Soldiers Aid Society were especially strong—and were, no doubt, assisted by society members Cornelia Beebe and Adaline Elkins, the wives of the owners of the newspaper. But it was the aid society's "communication committee" that explained the group's continuing press coverage. That committee, a team of women responsible for the group's media relations, sent out circulars and letters updating the newspapers on every event, every contributor, and every shipment sent to Cleveland, in an early form of press releases. The published reports, in turn, enhanced the reputation of the Akron Soldiers Aid Society by demonstrating that the group was a well-run, frugal, efficient, effective organization that was helping soldiers away at war. This coverage was complemented by another public relations campaign under the committee's oversight. Akron members got involved in a letter-writing project, which turned out to be a public relations coup for the Akron aid society. Members wrote letters to soldiers, which were tucked into the shirts and dressing gowns shipped to the hospitals. Soldiers were encouraged to write back. These letters, in turn, were used as internal checks of where shipments from Akron were being sent, as devices to raise the morale of Soldiers Aid Society members, and as yet another way to demonstrate the effectiveness of the Akron group in the press. Copies of the soldiers' letters were sent to the newspaper to be published. The communication committee also wrote the handbills and circulars that were distributed in the neighborhoods.[29] Of all the innovations introduced by the Akron Soldiers Aid Society, certainly the communication committee was among the most significant.

The Middlebury societies never had this type of access to the press and suffered as a result. As an officer of the Middlebury Soldiers Aid Society complained to the Cleveland commission, "It would be of *very* small consequence were it not for the doubts expressed by some of the good people of this place in regard to the expenditure of our funds, saying they have read the paper carefully and have never seen any notice whatever."[30] This lack of access—and the resulting suspicion that it triggered—explained why the Middlebury Soldiers Relief Association split off from the town's Soldiers Aid Society. But the Middlebury relief organization had no better access to the *Beacon* columns than did the town's aid society.

The Akron Soldiers Aid Society appreciated the diverse circumstances their members faced at home. Accordingly, the group cultivated practices that worked to each member's strengths and individual situations within the household. If demands of the family required women to be at home, society work could be done there. If women had more time or desired the support and companionship of others, they could work in the Soldiers Aid Society rooms. In Akron, aid society rooms were located in Ward One. These rooms bustled with activity and seemed to be open "constantly," the *Beacon* reported.[31]

When women had finished sewing or canning at home, they dropped their donations off at the society rooms. The women who worked at home usually stayed to exchange pleasantries with those who worked in the aid society rooms. Women working in the society rooms had many responsibilities—from sorting through donations to making sure that clothing was usable, from checking on the safety of donated food to packing giant boxes to be shipped to the Cleveland Sanitary Commission. Some women were dispatched to outdoor markets to distribute handbills that encouraged farmers to donate fruits and vegetables. More stayed back in the society rooms quilting, making down pillows, or anything else that the Cleveland commission said it needed.

The aid societies were also organizational enterprises. Akron's Soldiers Aid Society conducted its weekly business/working meetings Friday afternoons. The women of the two Middlebury societies were more haphazard in their scheduling. They held meetings once or twice a week, depending on the needs outlined by the Cleveland commission. These were special times for aid society workers. They were learning about their successes, encouraging each other to work harder, and enjoying each other's company. They talked about their families and their plans after the war. These meetings were not to be missed—"It was a pleasure to be present at those little gatherings," one member explained.[32]

At the end of the war, the Cleveland Sanitary Commission tried to get the individual aid societies across northern Ohio to give some sort of final report. The Akron and Middlebury societies had problems with the request. The women had not kept complete records and even the sketchy ones were lost after the war. One Akron banker tried to put a price tag on the donations, estimating five thousand dollars as their worth. But he admitted that the figure was little more than a guess.[33]

During the Civil War, women in the aid societies of Akron and Middlebury accomplished much. They helped outfit the Summit County troops before they marched off to war, not with the tools of battle but with the comforts of home—clothing, edible delicacies, and some morally upright reading material. The aid societies sent supplies—food and clothing—to the hospitals where soldiers recovered. Teams of aid society women from Akron and Middlebury went off to the hospitals to investigate conditions there, reported back, and arranged for more needed supplies to be sent. The aid societies of Akron and Middlebury also sent hundreds of boxes crammed with food, clothing, drink, reading material, and much more to the Cleveland Sanitary Commission which, in turn, shipped them where the need was greatest.

But there were more intangible benefits that the aid societies provided their members and their communities. In a time of tremendous stress and uncertainty, the aid societies gave the women a sense of purpose. Aid society women used their traditional skills—sewing, cooking, and canning—to help the men away at war. And the women were praised and applauded for all their hard work. The aid societies, their rooms, and their meetings also gave these women a sense of place. Here they could spend time with like-minded women.

There were lessons learned in the aid society rooms as well. The women learned organizational skills. They learned how to recruit members and reach out to different groups in the community to establish alliances. They learned how to set goals, strategize, and come up with plans to reach those goals. They learned how to stage fund-raising extravaganzas. They learned how to use the press for the best possible news coverage. In short, they were learning the skills needed to launch a women's club movement in the city.

But not all women learned those skills. The aid society women were, primarily, from the middle- to upper-class families of Akron and Middlebury. The class basis of the aid societies explained much about the organization of these groups. The aid societies in Akron and Middlebury shunned a democratic leadership, opting to follow the patterns of male organizations. Leaders were drawn from the leading families of the city.

After the war, the women of the aid societies returned to their homes to do the jobs that had gone undone; but they had not forgotten anything. They remembered what they had accomplished, friends that they had made, lessons they had learned. After some rest, these women came together again and turned their "attention to other objects of benevolence."[34]

And the city was better because of it.

Chapter 4

Women's Clubs of Akron in Reconstruction and the Gilded Age

At our first meeting we came together almost strangers, now we greet each other as dear friends.

—Woman's Missionary Society, Trinity Lutheran Church[1]

God bless the faithful women in all our churches, who are doing so much to advance our dear Redeemer's Kingdom.

—*Grace Church Reformed Herald*[2]

However much we may differ from methods adopted and policies laid down to accomplish the end sought by this [Woman's Christian Temperance] union, no one can help admitting the sincerity of purpose exhibited by those most deeply interested or recognizing the good that is being done by earnest efforts in more ways than one. The various forms of work engaged in by the Akron organization . . . give ample proof of this.

—*Akron Beacon and Republican*[3]

AFTER THE CIVIL WAR, AKRON AND MIDDLEBURY WOMEN, WHO HAD been active with aid and relief societies, were tired; they returned to their homes and the routine of family life. After a brief respite, however, many looked for fresh challenges and renewed kinship with like-minded women. During the post–Civil

War period, also, a new generation of women—some newcomers to the city, others longtime residents just awakening to women's organizations, many brought up by mothers long active in women's groups in Akron and Middlebury—yearned for that sense of kinship and challenge.

They did not have to wait for long. From soon after the end of the Civil War through 1900, Akron throbbed with activism again.

Many Akron women organized through their churches and synagogues. Protestants, Catholics, and Jewish congregations all had some sort of woman's association. These groups were organized with either an inward mission—to financially support and provide services to the religious establishment—or an outward vision—to provide services to the needy and infirm of the congregation or the city.

That organizational structure helped bring about the next turning point in Akron women's history—the temperance crusade of early 1874. Here Akron women, many of them already members of ladies' aid societies and missionary organizations at their churches, sounded the alarm for a holy war against "demon rum," recruited others to the battle, developed strategies that pressed the bounds of propriety, and then created an organizational structure to continue the fight against the liquor trade, work for woman's suffrage, help workingwomen, and protect families within the city. In this crusade, the Akron women built on the lessons learned in the Civil War. The temperance women became masters of special-events staging and publicity to gain maximum exposure for their work. They built on the religious diversity that the Civil War women had found to be so important; but, unlike the societies of the Civil War era, the temperance women were able to draw on the strength of newly established women's church organizations. The Woman's Temperance League, renamed and reorganized as a branch of the Woman's Christian Temperance Union (WCTU), soon became the preeminent woman's organization in Gilded Age Akron. Few other organizations could match the WCTU's membership, generational appeal, far-flung mission, social and political activism—or power.

The temperance crusade also created strong ties that bound women together as they organized other societies to bring services to the city. Temperance involvement became a common thread—along with an affluent socioeconomic class—that bound the leaders of the Dorcas Society and, to a lesser degree, the Woman's Benevolent Association. The Dorcas Society, like the temperance crusade, harnessed the energy of Protestant women's organizations for the delivery of systematic benevolence to a city that reeled in the depression that followed the Panic of 1873.

Following the temperance crusade, the tenor of the women's organizations of Akron changed. These women's organizations displayed a new confidence as they defined their own course and determined their own direction. Even auxiliaries to men's organizations showed an independence that was not always welcomed by the male group.

Some post–temperance crusade organizations learned lessons of diversity. A few—especially those affiliated with churches and the ladies' auxiliary to the veterans' group—established ties across class and ethnic lines, but that was a rarity in Akron. Most women's organizations were trapped in the class, ethnicity, and race of their founders.

The women's organizations of Akron were also trapped in the traditional view of women and their role in society, even as their organizations were taking steps that tested the limits of that sphere. Most women's organizations of Gilded Age Akron continued to use the rhetoric of domesticity in their appeals to the community, to explain why women were best suited to care for the sick and ailing, to provide relief for the needy, to carry out mission work in foreign countries, to establish much-needed training for girls in the city. It was a balancing act that *thousands* of Akron's organizational women, young and old, had to deal with—extending their reach within the community while espousing the traditional values of home and family.

The temperance crusade brought an unwelcome change to Akron and its women's organizations as well. Up until the temperance crusade of 1874, women's organizations in the city had been above reproach. The reputations of the affluent women leaders provided a certain measure of protection against criticism. That changed with the temperance crusade. As the women prayed in the streets outside the saloons, not even the reputation of the most affluent, God-fearing women in the city who had lent their names to the crusade could protect the temperance women from criticism. During the Gilded Age, women's organizations might be respected, but were no longer revered. Increasingly, women's organizations would be criticized for their leadership, their strategies, and their goals. That criticism would only increase with time.

POST–CIVIL WAR AKRON

The growth, activism, and diversity within the women's organizations reflected what was happening in the city generally. Between the end of the Civil War and 1900,

Akron went from a town "of the second class" with a population of just 5,000 to a bustling metropolis of 42,720.[4] Akron became a city with a diversified industrial base, a thriving retail center, a progressive education system, new churches, and enormous energy.

The men and women who rushed to Akron during the Gilded Age found employment in the industries that were relocating to—or expanding within—the city.

There were giant cereal mills, owned by Ferdinand Schumacher and others. With brand names like "Rolled Avena" and "Farina," Schumacher's company had become the foremost miller in the world by 1885; the company's headquarters as well as many of its mills were located in Akron. In 1886, the cereal empire literally went up in smoke, when a fire—one of the worst in the city's history—swept through the mills on Mill, Summit, Broadway, and Quarry streets. Hundreds were thrown out of work and Schumacher seemed ruined. But Akron was not out of milling. The Akron Milling Company—with the financial support of the Commins, Robinson, Inman, and Allen families—challenged the crippled Schumacher Milling and hired many of that company's displaced workers. By the 1890s, Schumacher rebuilt his fortunes by allying with others to create the American Cereal Company, which evolved into Quaker Oats.

Milling was not the only story. Akron was also a center for clay production. Well before the Civil War, Middlebury—annexed by Akron in 1872—was a "clay products village" that gained a reputation for producing water and sewer pipes. New companies expanded the product line. After the Civil War, Akron clay factories were producing everything from crocks and jugs to sewer pipes. They were also making fortunes for their founders. The Merrill, Robinson, King, Adams, Ebright, Viall, Hill, and Harrison families made their money with stoneware and sewer pipes.

But it was with the rubber industry that Akron created its lasting identity. In 1870, a young chemist, Dr. Benjamin Franklin Goodrich, came to the city to scout sites for a new manufacturing venture. He liked what he saw in Akron—a great location, a large, available labor pool, and a group of eager investors. In December 1870, Goodrich, Tew and Company went into business. Early on, the company concentrated on producing the finest rubber fire hose in the nation, "White Anchor." For a decade, the company struggled. Finally, in 1880, B. F. Goodrich incorporated, with investors Col. Simon Perkins, George W. Crouse, Alanson Work, and R. P. Marvin Jr. By the 1890s, Akron was well on its way to becoming the rubber capital of the world. In 1892, the precursor of Miller Rubber—underwritten by Jacob

Pfeiffer, John Grether, and John Lamparter—started; in 1894, Sherbondy Rubber (renamed Diamond Rubber by its founder, the "match king" O. C. Barber) began; in 1898 Frank and Charles Seiberling began Goodyear, specializing in carriage and pneumatic bicycle tires.[5]

Akron's industrial base thrived because it was connected to the rest of the nation through the railroad system. Between 1865 and 1900, Akron became a key depot in midwestern rail traffic. The Cleveland and Canton Railroad; Valley Railroad; Pittsburg, Youngstown and Chicago Railroad (soon to be the Pittsburgh and Western); Baltimore and Ohio; Akron and Chicago Junction; and the Akron and Barberton Belt Line all wove through the city, bringing cargo and passengers—and enormous wealth to investors. Akron had its own railroad magnates—David L. King, John F. Seiberling, David Hill, Lewis Miller, Col. A. L. Conger, O. C. Barber, and others.

In the post–Civil War decades, Akron also became a retail and service center for the county. With clothiers like Koch and Levi, china and glassware merchants like G. C. Berry and Son, booksellers and stationers like H. G. Canfield and W. G. Robinson, druggists like F. W. Inman and Son and Sisler and Hoye, jewelers like H. E. Abbey and J. B. Storer and Son, and furniture dealers like A. Baldwin and D. G. Sanford, Akron thrived.[6]

The family names of these industrialists, railroad developers, and merchants resurfaced in the women's organizations of the Gilded Age and the Progressive Era. The wives, daughters, mothers, and other female relatives of these business magnates played prominent roles in the leadership of Akron's women's organizations of the late nineteenth and early twentieth centuries.

Another group of women leaders came from the new schools being built in Akron. There was enormous energy and innovation within the Akron public school system under superintendents Samuel Findley and Elias Fraunfelter. By 1900, Akron had a high school, eleven elementary schools, and five thousand students. Parochial schools provided alternatives. St. Vincent's, St. Bernard's, and St. Mary's educated Catholic children; Zion Lutheran offered education to the children of German-speaking Lutherans. In 1872, Akron got a college of its own. Buchtel College (now the University of Akron) was started as a Universalist Church institution. The college (and the church) recruited faculty and administration from across the nation. Liberal in attitude, the college was coeducational from its founding. Women were hired as faculty and, less frequently, as administrators. Women faculty, like Carita McEbright, Jennie Gifford, and Mary Jewett; the wives of male

Jennie Gifford, a faculty member at Buchtel College, was only one of the many women students and faculty who were committed to organizing and leading civic organizations during the Gilded Age. *Photo courtesy of the University of Akron Archives.*

Wife of the first president of Buchtel College, Sophie Knight McCollester remained active in the community until her husband gave up his position in 1878. *Photo courtesy of the University of Akron Archives.*

Grace Belle Gorton Olin, an 1887 graduate of Buchtel College, was a member of the Tuesday Musical Club and a charter member of the College Club; both groups are still in existence in the city today. *Photo courtesy of the University of Akron Archives.*

faculty and administrators, like Katharine Claypole, Sophia McCollester, and Grace and Marie Olin; and the alumnae of this institution introduced new women's organizations into the city and took the leadership in many of the already existing ones during the Gilded Age and in the new century.

Akron was also a city of churches. In 1869, when Akron's population did not yet reach ten thousand, the city was the home of eleven Christian denominations. By 1894, there were forty churches or missions in fifteen different denominations. Almost every church, temple, or synagogue had one or more women's societies. Some carried generic names like the Ladies' Aid Society, the Mission Society, and the Altar Society. Others were peculiar to the church or temple, like Schwesterbund and the Franz Joseph Society.[7] Every minister, priest, and rabbi came to see that the women in their congregations were important assets, if their energies could be properly channeled.

CHURCHWOMEN'S ORGANIZATIONS IN AKRON

Akron churches had come relatively late to organizing women's societies. The Zion Lutheran Church had one of the first,[8] in 1866; Jewish women organized Schwesterbund, in 1868, to identify and give financial aid to those in need in the Jewish community. Women's organizations in the Methodist-Episcopal, Universalist, Disciples, Baptist, and Congregational churches soon followed.

Even before the various denominations had formally structured organizations, women church members were active in their congregations. During the Civil War, Catholic women of St. Bernard's organized fairs to raise funds to build the new church. Akron newspapers also reported that the women of the Methodist-Episcopal Church and Congregational Church gave fairs to raise funds to build or expand their churches or to finance needed improvements.[9]

These women's groups, whether formally organized or working within less formalized structures, embraced one of two missions. Some women's groups had an "inward mission," concentrating on needed improvements within the church. These groups hosted dime parties and fairs to raise funds to build a new church or addition or purchase an organ or some other needed supplies. These groups—often part of conservative denominations—sometimes took over the light maintenance at the church, maintaining the linen, or caring for the altar. Other groups assumed an "outward mission," concentrating on assisting the needy within their congregation or the broader community. Often called mission or aid societies, these groups did fund-raising and went into the community to locate and help families in need.

Most groups met weekly to work, pray, or study. Whether the group embraced an inward or outward mission, these organizations strengthened ties that already existed between the women and their churches—and they established connections among the women themselves. As one secretary to a mission society observed, "Few ties aside of the family are stronger than those which grow out of efforts to advance the Kingdom of our Divine Savier [sic], especially when these involve hard work, self denial, love, prayer, or perhaps enough opposition to keep every energy on the alert, eager, without the indulgence of a single unkind thought, or action."[10]

The success of a women's group in any Protestant church depended on the support of the minister, the stamina of his wife, and the enthusiasm of the congregation's women members. Church histories almost always credit the minister for suggesting that women start their organizations. At the Congregational Church, a new minister, the Reverend Dr. T. E. Monroe, saw the importance of a mission society, but it was his wife, Hannah, who formally organized prominent church-women into a functioning missionary society. Not surprisingly, given Hannah's interest in civic betterment as well as the involvement of many of these members in city organizations already, the Congregational Church's missionary group embraced an outward focus and provided aid to needy families within the congregation and outside of it.[11]

The Reverend Julius Herold brought many changes to the First German Reformed Church. Not only were families allowed to sit together—heretofore, men and women were required to sit separately—but women's organizations were formed. The Ladies' Aid Society was the oldest organization in the church. Its slogan—"When the Consistory has done its best, the Ladies' Aid will do the Rest"—pointed to that group's inward mission. The group did the fund-raising needed to pay for everything from painting the church to buying Sunday school books.[12]

The Reverend C. C. Smith of the First Congregation of Disciples (now High Street Christian Church) was credited with starting the first woman's organization in the church, the Home Society. The group had a twofold purpose. The women were to assist the sick and recruit new members for the church. The Home Society, like the other women's organizations at the Disciples Church, had at its base an outward focus.[13]

A new church, Trinity Lutheran, had women's organizations almost from its start. Both the Dime Society and the Ladies' Aid Society started under the Reverend J. F. Fahs's—and his wife's—direction. The women's organizations blossomed under the Reverend M. J. Firey and his wife Cynthia, when the church's Home and Foreign Missionary Society started. Each of these organizations had an "outward" mission.[14]

It is difficult to say precisely what kind of women joined the churchwomen's groups during the Gilded Age. Few Akron churches kept membership lists of *any* early organizations. Two exceptions were the Woman's Missionary Society of the Trinity Lutheran Church for 1887–88, which kept records of its charter members,[15] and the Dorcas Committee at the Grace Reformed Church in 1896.[16] If these two organizations were reflective of churchwomen's organizations across the city, then these groups encompassed a depth of economic diversity not generally found in clubs of the nineteenth century.

Trinity Lutheran Church was established in 1868 as the first English-language Lutheran church. (Zion Lutheran held its services in German.) Almost from the beginning, Trinity Lutheran had women's organizations. The missionary society was not the first woman's organization established, but it grew quickly into an important group within the church. Trinity Lutheran Church Missionary Society drew its membership from a cross section of the congregation. Of the forty-two charter members of the missionary society, thirty-seven were positively identified using the 1880 census and/or the city directory for 1887–88.[17] The largest number of these women (eleven) were married to business owners, executives, or sales personnel. Trinity Lutheran was the religious home of John F. Seiberling of Akron Straw Board, John Hower of Hower and Company, and O. L. McMillen of Akron Cabinet Company; their wives, Catherine, Susan, and Magdalena, joined the church's missionary society. But then, so, too, did Mrs. Frank Glass and Kate Morgan, whose husbands worked in the factories of the city. Both Frank Glass and Charlie Morgan worked at Buckeye Works. Six wives of semiskilled or unskilled laborers were members of Trinity Lutheran's missionary association. Five wives of professionals joined the group. First on the list of charter members was Cynthia Firey, wife of the minister. Cynthia Foltz, fifty-one, wife of physician William Foltz, and Rosena Black, wife of "Black the Druggist," also joined the group. Three women were married to skilled craftsmen. Two of the charter members were employed—one as a teacher, the other as a seamstress.

An even greater amount of economic diversity could be found in the Dorcas Committee of Grace Reformed Church in 1897. Established in 1842 as part of St. Paul's Protestant Church, a union of Lutheran and Reformed denominations, the reformed church split off in 1853. A further split took place over the issue of language. Those who preferred to worship in the English language established the Grace Reformed Church. The Dorcas Committee was not the first organized women's organization formed at Grace Church. In 1876, the Ladies' Aid Society was organized; the Sewing Circle followed in 1892.[18]

The Dorcas Committee had fifty-four women members in 1896. Forty-five of these women were positively identified using the city directory of 1896.[19] Like Trinity Lutheran's missionary society, the membership of the Grace Church Dorcas Committee was drawn from a cross section of the congregation. In the Dorcas Committee, however, the wives of skilled craftsmen and semiskilled and unskilled laborers predominated. Half of those positively identified (twenty-five of the forty-five) were married to skilled craftsmen or semiskilled/unskilled laborers. The largest number of these husbands (fourteen) worked in Akron's factories: Ann Fulmer's husband, Camp, at the Rubber Works; May Cox's husband, Daniel, at Goodrich; Agnes Foust's husband, Benjamin, at the Buckeye Works. Eleven women were married to skilled craftsmen. Minnie Waltz's husband, Luvander, and Ada Mantz's husband, Nelson, were carpenters; Elizabeth Rishel's husband, Benjamin, was a painter; and Ella Beckwith's husband, Fred, was a printer. Seven women were married to men employed in business. Ella Frank's husband, William, was the president of Frank, Laubach and Nutt; and Sarah Sprigle's husband, Emmanuel, was a general contractor and builder in the city. Others held clerical or sales positions. Kate Heller's husband, Thomas, was a clerk with Dague Brothers; and Eliza Coleman's husband, W. F., was a traveling salesman. Only two women were married to professionals. Two women of the Dorcas Committee worked outside the home: Anna Schaffer worked at the Rubber Works, and Laura Cooper was a dressmaker. Both were single.

Most of the women associated with the Dorcas Committee were married. Eight women were widows. Like Grace Reformed's Dorcas Committee, the greatest number of Trinity Lutheran Missionary Society members were married: twenty-nine of the thirty-seven positively identified in the census and/or city directories. Three women were single: Ida Wunderlich, the teacher; Grace Seiberling, daughter of Akron entrepreneur John Seiberling; and Anna Wachter, daughter of a carpenter. Five women were widows, including Josephine Corson, a seamstress.

All of the women affiliated with these churchwomen's groups were white, but not all were native born.

When the women of the Missionary Society of Trinity Lutheran Church elected their officers, they looked to the wives of professionals and business executives for leadership, following a model used by men's organizations. The first president was Cynthia Firey, the minister's wife. Other presidents were wives of executives, such as Sarah Rinker, wife of the owner of Murdoch and Rinker, and Hattie Miles, the wife of an executive at J. F. Seiberling and Company. In contrast, the women of the Dorcas Committee turned to wives of skilled craftsmen and semiskilled/unskilled laborers for leadership. The president was Margaret Wise, wife of Samuel Wise who worked at Hankey Lumber. Other officers included Anna Fulmer, wife of Camp Fulmer who worked at the Rubber Works, and Celestia Wood, wife of a paperhanger.

The common thread that held all these women together was a deep religious faith. These two groups introduced a socioeconomic diversity that few civic organizations in the city were able to attain. The shared religious faith was enough to bring these women together and to allow them to work for a common goal. When it came to selecting their leadership, however, these two groups embraced different models. Trinity Lutheran women turned to the affluent, best-educated in their group; the Dorcas Committee of Grace Church preferred officers most like the majority of their membership—women who were married to skilled craftsmen or unskilled/semiskilled workers.

Although these women came from a variety of backgrounds, they worked comfortably with one another, at least according to the minutes of Trinity Lutheran's missionary society.[20] There may have been some disagreements, but nothing could take away from the "spirit of acquaintanceship and sociability" that the women enjoyed in their missionary society. The group met weekly to learn about mission work in other parts of the world and to hear reports from the visiting committee, who looked in on the sick and ailing. Those meetings never interfered with the member's home duties. "Think whether I individually have done all I consistently could do, without neglecting home duties, for the upbuilding, prosperity and encouragement of this organization," the secretary wrote.

By 1889, a generation gap had opened in Trinity Lutheran's association; the younger members wanted to form their own organization. The parent group, which included many mothers of the teens and young adults who wanted to branch off on their own, did not oppose the separation. As the secretary of the mission society wrote, "May the two societies, like mother and daughter, work earnestly, and devotedly in our respective places, for the advancement of God's kingdom and may our feeble efforts be blessed by the giver of all perfect gifts." Following that split, the women of the original group waged an aggressive membership drive. After that, attendance was better than ever, except in the fall and spring when matrons were otherwise occupied with their seasonal cleaning.[21]

Of course, Trinity Lutheran's missionary society was not the only women's group in the city. Other denominations had missionary groups and ladies' aid societies. The organizations with an outward mission visited the poor and infirm who were members of the congregation; other groups were ecumenical, caring for any family that women knew to be in need.

By 1874, most of the Protestant churches in the city had at least one woman's organization. Most of those groups had an outward focus, sending women—particularly the affluent leaders of these groups—into the community. They visited homes in extreme want. They visited families who had been put in jeopardy because of the drinking of one or more parents. They listened to the sermons of ministers who condemned liquor and inebriation as sins. By early 1874, a number of these church-women were ready to become the backbone of Akron's greatest temperance crusade.

Akron did not start the temperance crusade in Ohio. The women of Hillsboro and Washington Court claimed that honor. The temperance crusade rumbled through the state like an unrestrained force. It reached Akron in February 1874.

Akron women knew about the crusade almost from its beginning. The newspapers in the city reported on the unorthodox crusade to end drinking once and for all. Women—with their higher moral sense and duty to rid the community of sin[22]—prayed outside saloons or went inside them, to convince the bar owners to stop selling liquor and to urge fathers to return to their families and give up drinking. Ministers of congregations that traditionally supported temperance also spoke about the crusades from the pulpit.[23] It was only a manner of time before the Akron Protestant women,[24] so active in their churches and their church organizations, would embrace the temperance crusade and fashion their own war against saloons and liquor in the city.

In Akron, the opening volley was fired on March 4, 1874, when more than one hundred prominent women called for a temperance rally at the First Methodist-Episcopal Church. A few, like Elizabeth Johnston and Adeline Coburn, were well known for their work with Civil War aid and relief societies. More were known because of the reputations of their husbands, prominent businessmen in the community. German immigrant Hermine Schumacher was the wife of the cereal king Ferdinand Schumacher, who was a committed prohibitionist. Hannah Herrick was the wife of Burke E. Herrick, who made a name for himself because of his crockery business and his involvement in the Young Men's Christian Association (YMCA) and the Bible Society. Others were the wives of ministers who were committed to the temperance cause. Susan Smith, the wife of the pastor of the Congregational Church, and her daughters Hattie and Nellie all signed the call.

These women—some young single women, others wives of up-and-coming professionals and businessmen, more affluent matrons who had been too young or too busy to get involved in the Civil War relief groups, and a few veterans of many civic associations—wanted Akron women to join them in a holy war against demon rum. These women did not expect much from the Catholic women in the city who had already been warned to keep away from the crusade,[25] but they did expect Protestant women in the city to join them.

And the women responded as few predicted. Sentiment for the crusade had been building for days, the *Beacon* reported. "The grand tidal wave of Temperance

Reform . . . has at last reached the limits of our quiet city, and the fair wives and daughters of Akron . . . are fully alive to the importance and responsibility of the work it imposes upon them."[26]

When the women crowded into First Methodist-Episcopal Church the next day, Akron was not disappointed. With the encouragement of the four ministers who spoke, one hundred women voted to support the crusade. Subsequent meetings found the temperance movement gaining strength in Akron; soon there were three hundred eighty-five volunteers, then over five hundred and then more than seven hundred. Akron women were ready to start their own temperance crusade. The women decided to follow the example of other crusaders. They would "visit" the city's saloons and urge the owners to give up selling liquor. It took some time to decide on just the right strategy, organize the visiting bands—twenty women to a group—and decide which neighborhoods and saloons to visit.[27]

On March 11, the women were ready. If the women thought they would gain immediate converts, they were sorely mistaken. Focusing on the saloons on Market and Howard streets, four bands of twenty women went "visiting." How the women were received was the subject of debate. A reporter from the *Akron City Times* thought most bar owners treated the women "courteously." The *Beacon* reporter did not think the saloon owners behaved themselves. Jacob Good of 209 East Market Street refused to allow the women in. A neighboring saloon keeper, Nick Wagner of 218 East Market Street, locked the women out, and "Mr. Dussell [of 112 South Howard Street] stopped the ladies at his door and was quite hostile but tried to keep the rowdies who followed the ladies there from mis-behaving in their presence." J. Seiber, a wholesale and retail leader in wines, liquors, cigars, and tobaccos at 138 South Howard Street, was "bitter and denunciatory." But nothing could compare to Andrew Langerdorf's "most shameful demeanor" toward the women; he made matters worse by giving free drinks to "drunken loafers" who followed and harassed the crusaders.[28]

Both newspapers agreed that the women were causing quite a stir. As they prayed and sang outside the saloons, crusaders were greeted by "the jeers and groans and shouts of the half-drunken rabble, [who] made a scene only a little less hellish than the wretches engaged in it," the *Times* reporter observed. If the saloon owners had any hope of controlling these crusaders, the reporter argued, they had to behave themselves and make sure that their customers treated the women with respect, especially since there was already a strong sentiment against the crusaders.

If the saloon keepers expect to gain any sympathy from the respectable portion of the community, they had better treat the women respectfully. There has been a strong sentiment against the movement in the minds of many of our most respectable citizens. But there can be no way taken to so effectually dispel this feeling, as for the saloon keepers to heap abuse upon the ladies, such scenes . . . will educate public sentiment faster than the songs and prayers of the women can possibly do it.[29]

The saloon owners got the message. The next week, the women crusaders were met with the utmost respect. Although a large crowd followed the women, those men were "quite orderly." This time, women targeted any business that sold liquor— saloons, groceries, drugstores, and restaurants. Some saloon owners, like Frederick J. Wettach, Jacob Good, Nicholas Wagner, and J. D. Palmer, welcomed the women. Grocers W. and J. Bittman and James Costigan did likewise. Henry J. Huber, a keeper of a restaurant/saloon, also allowed the women in. More, however, refused to admit women. Saloon owners Balster Cook, Richard Feederlee, William Franz, and Andrew Langendorf refused to let the women come in and pray. Druggist E. Steinbacher, wholesale and retail liquor dealer J. Sieber, grocer Christopher Schmidt, and others also denied the women entry into their places of business. Although the crusaders might have found their afternoon visits discouraging, their hopes were raised in the temperance meetings in the evening. Every night women crowded into the appointed church—First Methodist-Episcopal, Congregational, Baptist—to get the news of saloon owners who had given up the fight.[30]

Notwithstanding the encouraging reports at night, Akron women were having little luck with the saloon keepers. So the women changed their strategy. They focused on ending the sale of liquor in the city's drugstores. There were fewer of them, and the proprietors were more susceptible to the pressure of the women. By the end of March, the *Beacon* reported that all but two drugstores had quit selling liquor. The women also started to shift their focus to the men who imbibed. These were fathers, the women said, who failed to take care of their families because they spent all their money on drink. As one letter writer to the *Akron City Times* explained, "Women are now trying to save lives—men are slaves to drink—it is a war on the nerves and flesh, which sooner or later yields to King Alcohol."[31]

That shift in strategy was needed because community sentiment was turning against the crusaders. Unsigned letters to the editors of city newspapers complained that crusading women were doing more harm than good. These crusaders were ma-

During the temperance crusade of 1874, Akron women "visited" saloons on Market and Howard streets in the hopes of convincing bar owners to give up their businesses. They achieved only limited success. This is one of the few existing photos of the temperance crusade in Akron. *Photo courtesy of the Summit County Historical Society, the University of Akron Archives.*

nipulated by others, one letter writer to the *Akron City Times* said. In an editorial, the *City Times* reported that there were mutterings in the community that "women, in engaging in the crusade work, over-stepped the natural limitations of their sphere, and derogated from the inherent purity and dignity of their character." Even the *Summit County Beacon*, which had been a consistent supporter of the crusades, reported that "croakers" in the community denounced the temperance crusaders as "unwomanly, unchristian and degrading."[32]

Those same "croakers" also complained when the temperance women began to push for a new city prohibition ordinance. Women had no place in politics, the critics argued. But the women crusaders would not listen. They practiced the purest form of grassroots politics to get support for the measure in 1874. They distributed handbills in their churches and the streets. Almost two hundred women paraded to the Akron City Council meeting and listened while one of their leaders, Isabella Berry, wife of a dry goods retailer, spoke for the women of the city on the need for the prohibition measure. The *Beacon* dismissed her talk as a "charming little address." But that evening, pressured by the women crusaders and an over-flowing crowd of temperance supporters, the city council approved the measure. "The uproar at the passage of the ordinance was most deafening," the *Akron City Times* reported.[33]

The women had accomplished their goals—or had they?

If the editors thought a city council measure would end the pressure from the women, they were sorely mistaken. Temperance women had just discovered their voice. They found that a united front could accomplish much. Even the newspapers in the city saw it. These women had shown that they were "competent to render hard, persevering, self-sacrificing toil" in a good cause. Nothing could stop them—"Storm, and abuse, and insult, and scorn, have not deterred or disheartened them." The women had shown that "God-fearing women, adherents of divers creeds and members of different communions" could work together for the greater good.[34]

What the women needed were leaders, an organizational structure, and a clear vision of what to do after the crusade, for visiting saloons was only the first battle in women's war on liquor in Akron. When the crusades first started, Akron women had little experience in public speaking and so relied on ministers. Then they turned to experienced women speakers from outside the city. Mary Livermore—writer/editor, women's rights advocate, and temperance supporter—came in March to bolster the spirits of Akron crusaders. Increasingly, however, the Akron temperance advocates grew more confident in their abilities and developed women leaders of their own.

The best known of Akron's early women temperance leaders was Angeline Manley,[35] the wife of a prominent Akron photographer and business owner. One of the first women to sign the call for the temperance rally in Akron, Angeline was not only a leader of the women in the streets but an organizational strategist for the city, the county, the state, and the nation.

Angeline Manley did not come from a background that would cultivate that kind of leadership ability. She was the daughter of Adam Clark Stewart, a carpenter and justice of the peace in Jefferson County, and Sarah Beebout Stewart. There were eight Stewart children. Nothing is known of her early life, her schooling, or how she met and became the second wife of George W. Manley. Once she moved to Akron, Angeline affiliated with the First Methodist-Episcopal Church and got involved with its women's organizations. The Methodist-Episcopal Church was one of the congregations most strongly behind the temperance crusade of

1874. Thus, Angeline's involvement in the temperance movement was expected, but her leadership in the crusade and the subsequent organizations could not have been predicted.

During the crusade itself, Angeline Manley gained a good deal of organizational experience and credibility (at least within temperance quarters) when she commanded a band of some six hundred crusaders in the streets. But her lasting contributions to Akron, the temperance movement, and women's organizations in general were based on her overall vision. Without some permanent organization, she reasoned, the temperance crusade would stall. It was Angeline who suggested and then led the first temperance league in Akron—the Summit County Temperance League. It was Angeline who called for a statewide convention of temperance workers in Cincinnati. She recalled years later that she was overwhelmed by the response. "Soon the replies poured in 'We will meet you.' By the basketful they brought to me the responding letters and telegram, and the convention was an assured fact."[36] It was that group—the first state convention of its size held in the United States, according to the *Summit County Beacon*—that hoped to thwart a proposed liquor license amendment to the state constitution. The women drafted a temperance memorial against the amendment and then sent Angeline and a committee of women to the constitutional convention. When Angeline and her committee delivered the memorial, they made history. The *Beacon* reported that it was the first time any woman had attended a state or national constitutional convention.[37] The legislators were not impressed; they promptly tabled the temperance memorial and approved the amendment. If Angeline was disappointed with that action, she must have been more encouraged that women voted to create a state organization. Angeline headed the committee to draft its constitution. Because of an illness in the family, she could not carry through on her commitment. Harriet C. McCabe replaced her, and became the first president of the state temperance group.

Angeline Manley also had a role in the formation of the national union, the *Beacon* reported. At the Chautauqua Assembly, she is said to have insisted that a meeting be held to organize a national temperance women's group. The meeting was held in November 1874 in Cleveland. The result was the Woman's Christian Temperance Union, a group that would change the face of temperance and women's organizations forever.

Angeline Manley never figured in the leadership of the national or the state temperance groups. She concentrated on the local level. During the remainder of

Angeline Manley, wife of a prominent Akron photographer, was a key leader and organizational strategist for the temperance organizations in the city, the county, the state, and the nation. *Photo courtesy of John Manley, Massillon, Ohio.*

her time in Akron—she and her husband moved to Canton in 1890—Angeline focused on building a strong foundation for temperance in the city. One way to accomplish that was by strengthening the league's ties to the Protestant churches in the city—and across generational lines. Under Angeline, the league established a "young ladies'" temperance group that had teen/young women representatives from the Congregational, Baptist, Universalist, First Methodist-Episcopal, Episcopal, Disciples, and Grace Reformed churches.[38] A number of these young women were second-generation temperance activists. Lizzie Berry, one of the women representing the Congregational Church, was the daughter of Isabella Berry, who would soon become the driving force in the city's temperance union. Susie King, just eighteen when she represented the Episcopal Church to the "young ladies" group, was the daughter of Betty King, one of the original signers of the temperance rally call.

One of Angeline Manley's lasting contributions to the WCTU was her willingness to withdraw from active leadership and work behind the scenes. She concentrated on the industrial efforts of the WCTU, working with employed women in the city. As the *Beacon Journal* reported years later, Angeline "has been known as one of the most enthusiastic and faithful members of the local W.C.T.U. and has given much of her time to the work, especially the industrial side of the accomplishment of the organization." Her withdrawal from WCTU leadership gave her extra time for her literary pursuits. In 1883, (writing under the name of Angie Steward Manly) she published a novel, *Hit and Miss: A Story of Real Life.* There is no evidence that she was involved in the WCTU after she moved to Canton.[39]

When Angeline Manley stepped aside, a new group of women came forward to lead the WCTU in Akron and Summit County. The new leadership of the WCTU fit a certain mold. Almost all were affluent, married to successful businessmen or professionals (primarily attorneys and physicians). Most of the officers of both the Akron and the Summit County chapters were familiar names around Akron—Hannah Monroe, active in the women's organizations at the Congregational Church where her husband ministered; Adeline Coburn, a civic leader who had been involved in everything from the Civil War Soldiers Aid Society in Akron to the Ladies' Rural Cemetery Association; Isabella Berry, wife of a dry goods merchant who had charmed the Akron City Council with her stirring address for prohibition in 1874. A few officers did not fit the benevolent matron mold. Katherine Kurt, for many years treasurer of the WCTU, cast a feminist shadow; she was single and the first female homeopathic physician to work in Akron.[40]

Once the WCTU expanded into the less affluent neighborhoods—by 1929, there were thirteen unions in Akron—fewer affluent women were elected to office. For example, the president of the new Frances Willard Chapter in the south end was Mary Sherbondy, wife of a boilermaker. However, throughout the Gilded Age, most of the WCTU leaders were affluent matrons, married to successful businessmen and professionals. Their daughters often dominated the leadership of the city's Young Woman's Christian Temperance Union.

The temperance crusade and the WCTU had a lasting influence on many of the women's organizations in the city during the Gilded Age.[41] The WCTU leaders reached forward into many of the important benevolent groups in the city, including the Dorcas Society and the Woman's Benevolent Association. They reached into their religious roots and helped define the direction of many of the women's church organizations, including St. Paul's Episcopal Ladies' Aid Society, King's Daughters, and First Methodist-Episcopal Missionary Society.

This web of influence was strengthened when the Akron WCTU opened its Friendly Union. Proposed in 1875, the union was originally envisioned as a place to start a "temperance and industrial union," but it evolved into a central meeting place for women's organizations in the city.

The Friendly Union became a kind of women's organizational incubator. Women's groups were no longer isolated. Here was a central place where women and their organizations could organize, define the missions, plot strategy, and work. Akron's women's groups came into contact with each other and learned from each other, making collaboration possible.

The WCTU benefited as well. Women's groups paid a fee for meeting there and helped finance the Friendly Union. The WCTU also shared in the spirit that made the union such a dynamic location. The Friendly Union gave the WCTU a home where it could offer special services to workingwomen, a safe place where young people could learn about the evils of liquor and the sordid life it brought, a command central where the group could plot its next battle against liquor.[42] From that central location, the women of the WCTU circulated petitions in favor of the "local option" by which neighborhoods could vote themselves "dry" (without saloons). It was there that WCTU members held their weekly prayer meetings and their mothers' meetings. It was there that WCTU members planned the push for a prohibition statute. Invoking their higher moral calling, the women had a "God-given mission" to make voters embrace the temperance cause. Statewide the temperance women could not muster the support, and the prohibition amendment failed.[43]

It was at the Friendly Union that the temperance women decided, in 1885, that they must have the vote if they were to carry forward their sacred battle against drink. Talk of woman suffrage had often circulated around in Akron. But in 1885, the Akron WCTU made winning the vote its first priority. Henrietta Wall, thirty-five, wife of a dry goods merchant in the city, particularly championed the move.

As secretary of the national WCTU's Suffrage Department, Wall had a lot at stake. National President Frances Willard endorsed the suffrage move in Ohio, and Wall pushed WCTU's more conservative members to the side of suffrage by framing it as a way for women to achieve God's will and win the temperance fight once and for all. Akron's WCTU was unsuccessful that year. In 1892, the WCTU joined forces with the new Akron suffrage organization. Finally, in 1894, the Ohio legislature passed a bill to let women vote in school board elections, but Akron women would have to wait until the Nineteenth Amendment was ratified before voting in presidential, congressional, or gubernatorial races.[44]

In spite of defeats on suffrage, Akron WCTU members remained optimistic. One of the reasons for the optimism was the "city temperance missionary" hired by the WCTU in 1884. The daughter of a cabinetmaker in the city, Florence Savage, twenty-seven at the time she was hired by the WCTU, coordinated many of the union's activities and then went out into the city to bring the word of temperance to all. As the WCTU reported, "Our Friendly Visitor [Florence Savage] has taken many long, weary trips up and down the streets of Akron, carrying temperance literature, visiting homes, and holding temperance prayer meetings." According to Florence's accounts, she distributed thousands of pieces of temperance literature throughout the city.[45]

Florence Savage also brought a fresh perspective to the WCTU. At her behest, the WCTU began offering services to a population group that heretofore been ignored by the benevolent women in the city. In 1884, the WCTU reached out to the domestics in the city. The WCTU working girls club met every two weeks, and the young women spent their evenings together "read[ing] aloud, sew[ing], hear[ing] lectures, hav[ing] music, or recitations or talk[ing] on some topic of general interest." But, perhaps more important, the WCTU afforded a place where domestics could get together, away from their employers; "it is nicer to invite our friends to meet us here [in the parlor of the WCTU], to spend an hour, than to take them into the kitchen, or walk the streets with them," one member reported. Some affluent women even joined the group periodically. According to one woman, those evenings showed how much women had in common; "we find there is not so much difference between a Christian woman who works for the church, or Sunday school or some other public benevolence, and the one who works for the family of the first, so she can have time for other duties."[46]

Under Florence Savage's watch, also, the WCTU started a placement service for domestics. The Woman's Exchange was a central place where young women who wanted domestic work could register and matrons who needed assistance could make inquiries. The working girls club had made the WCTU more sensitive to the perspective of the domestics. The union urged Akron matrons to be more businesslike in their dealings with domestics: "Let the employer be a little more businesslike so that the one employed may clearly understand her duties and, keeping the golden rule in view, arrange for a respite during the week to which she may look forward."[47]

Before Florence Savage left the WCTU, she took the union into new parts of the city. She helped organize the south Akron WCTU, started another working girls club in another part of the city, and then took over the temperance work at the jail and prison, a job that few members of the Akron WCTU wanted.[48]

Florence Savage illustrated just how important a full-time employee of a woman's organization could be. She brought fresh perspectives to Akron's WCTU; she initiated new programs, took over the jobs that the women volunteers did not want, brought the WCTU into new neighborhoods, and introduced more women—different types of women—to the organization. It would be these groups, together with the affluent women who remained WCTU members, who would determine the direction of the organization in the new century, would wrangle for control, and then watch as the WCTU lost its relevance to the women in the city in the new century. But during the Gilded Age and much of the Progressive Era, the WCTU remained a force with great energy and importance in Akron, even as other women's clubs were organizing to bring much-needed relief to the poor and ailing in Akron.

WOMEN'S BENEVOLENT GROUPS IN AKRON

In 1874, Akron reeled in a deep depression. Everyone in Akron suffered, from the heretofore "comfortable" families of businessmen, some of whom were driven into bankruptcy, to the families of the already financially stretched laboring class. Nationally, 18,000 businesses failed, and unemployment reached 14 percent. Wages were slashed, hours cut. Financial and physical hardship was widespread. In Akron, times were especially hard. It is against this picture of great distress that the Dorcas Society, an amalgamation of women active in the Congregational, Methodist, Baptist, Episcopal, Universalist, Reformed, and Lutheran churches, was organized.

The Dorcas Society started in 1874 to provide "systematic benevolence" to the "worthy poor," individuals who through no fault of their own faced great need.

Summit County's "poor house" (by then called the infirmary farm) and infirmary could neither investigate all claims of need nor provide consistent support to all those claiming to be in want. Taking its name from the biblical woman who was full of good deeds, the Dorcas Society was designed to step into the breach, investigate claims of need, and provide immediate aid to those found "worthy."[49]

Published calls in the city's newspapers asked for women of all religious denominations—or no affiliation—to meet in the YMCA rooms to help with the new society's relief efforts.[50] The temperance crusades earlier in 1874 had proven that ecumenical calls to women could work effectively. However, the Dorcas Society's call for women with no church affiliation was unusual. Akron, then as now, was a city of churches. Church attendance was encouraged—expected—of all self-respecting, God-fearing women in the city.[51] Thus, the Dorcas invitation to nonchurch members represented a departure.

It is unknown how many women without church membership joined Akron's Dorcas Society. The records of the organization have not been preserved. The city newspapers, however, regularly reported on the group's activities and its leadership.

Notwithstanding the initial call, the Dorcas Society built its leadership structure on the denominations that supported it. Dorcas had an elected president and seven vice presidents, one each from the Congregational, Methodist-Episcopal, Baptist, Episcopalian, Universalist, Disciples, and Lutheran churches.[52] Other Protestant denominations were not included, nor were the Catholic churches or the Jewish population in the city. Thus, Dorcas drew from the same Protestant base that drove the temperance crusade just a few months before. In addition to the president and vice presidents, women served as secretary and treasurer. The early leaders—or those who could be positively identified[53]—were drawn primarily from the upper-middle to upper classes. These were, primarily, wives of businessmen or professionals. Some were women in their twilight years; Mrs. Adeline Coburn, who had been so active in Akron's Soldiers Aid Society and was the wife of a physician/surgeon, served as a "work director" for the new Dorcas Society. Others were just beginning their benevolent careers: Mrs. Lucy Tibbals, wife of an attorney, was only twenty-nine. Lucy was also one of the organizers of the Dorcas Society in Akron.[54] Like all the leaders positively identified, she was a native-born, white woman.

Almost all these women shared another characteristic: some involvement in the temperance crusade. Some, like Mary Bates, the wife of a banker, was forty-five when she was first selected for the visiting committee for the First Ward, had signed the petition that first called the crusaders together; others, like Hannah Monroe, wife of the pastor of the Congregational Church, not only signed the temperance petition but also went on to be an officer of the Woman's Christian Temperance League.

Subsequent leaders of the Dorcas Society did not always have such close ties with the temperance movement. For example, L. Louise Brewster, the wife of a coal dealer who was only twenty-four when she was elected treasurer of Dorcas in 1880, confined her involvement to women's associations that provided relief to needy families. In contrast, Mrs. Louisa H. Uhler, thirty-seven and a member of the 1880 visiting committee for the Third Ward, had strong ties to the temperance movement, even serving as the president of the local WCTU. The 1880 Dorcas leaders were drawn from the same socioeconomic class as the original group, and all but one positively identified were native born. That one exception was Hermine Schumacher, wife of the cereal entrepreneur Ferdinand Schumacher.

Throughout its ten-year existence, the Dorcas Society operated in the same manner. Most of its work was done by committees. The "visiting committee"— two women per ward—was responsible for investigating claims of want, visiting the homes of the needy, determining if those individuals were "worthy," and de-ciding the amount of aid to be given.

In their work, these wives of business owners and successful professionals came face to face with instances of want that few imagined. Families were found in desperate conditions, living in makeshift hovels even in the coldest winters. Some families were deemed "unworthy" if the head of the household was "shift-less or drunken." The women of the visiting committees and the director of the county infirmary found that most were "worthy," facing poverty because the father and mother could not find work in the city. The Dorcas Society provided emergency aid—food, clothing, and fuel—to help the families through their emergencies.[55]

"Worthy poor" were expected to work for any assistance given, so Akron's Dorcas Society created a "work" (later called employment) committee, staffed by volunteer members. During the depression of the mid-to-late-1870s, the com-mittee did not try to find jobs for out-of-work men, as there were few jobs for anyone in the city; instead Dorcas volunteers concentrated their efforts on the mothers in needy families. These mothers were given material—muslin, calico, flannel—to make clothing for themselves, their families, and others. In that way, the needy mothers were "earning" their assistance. This activity was not peculiar to the Dorcas Society or Akron. Throughout the late nineteenth century, relief groups headed by women expected some sort of reciprocal arrangement from the families receiving assistance. As the city recovered from the depression, the women of the Dorcas work/employment committee tried to find jobs for out-of-work men, so the men could "help themselves."[56]

The Dorcas Society looked to its Ways and Means Committee, also run by women, to solicit donations of needed goods and services, budget the resources of the organization, and do fund-raising. At a time when the city reeled from a depression, the Ways and Means Committee often had problems with fund-raising and soliciting the needed food, clothing, and fuel. As the *Akron City Times* reported, "The Dorcas Society is worthy of hearty support from all charitable persons, and we hope next year to record a more general public interest in it than the figures for this year indicate."[57] Fund-raising improved when the general economic climate of the city brightened.

The Dorcas Society grew into its role within the city. During its relatively brief life, the women of the Dorcas Society created an industrial school, housed in the WCTU rooms, and pushed to create a "Free Dispensary," where the indigent could get medical treatment free of charge. Once that dispensary became a reality in 1883, the women of the Dorcas visiting committee were given the additional responsibility of reporting cases of illness among the poor.[58]

For ten years, the Dorcas Society served the city well. But in 1884, when yet another panic hit the nation and a depression followed, it was clear that Akron's Dorcas Society could not keep up with the demands of caring for the poor in the city. In March 1884, the Dorcas Society was circulating a subscription campaign to raise money to carry it through the remainder of the winter. In December 1884, the Dorcas Society was again out of funds, and the *Summit County Beacon* speculated, "It is uncertain whether that society [Dorcas] which has done so much good in the past, will do any benevolent work at all this Winter."[59]

But who would carry the work forward?

A new women's organization in the city stepped up to the challenge in December 1884, the *Summit County Beacon* reported. The Women's Relief Corps of the Buckley Post, a woman's auxiliary of a Civil War veterans group, began carrying out general relief efforts in the city.

Just organized in February 1884, the Women's Relief Corps was set up to care for sick, needy, and ailing Akron veterans and their families. The Buckley Post felt that Summit County authorities had failed to provide sufficient assistance to the sick and destitute veterans and their families. For some time, there had been discussion within the post on how best to deal with this problem. Drawing on nineteenth-century concepts that women had the primary responsibility of caretaker in the family, a small group of Buckley Post women, primarily wives of business owners and professionals, came up with the idea of the relief corps. "The zeal and energy with which the ladies take hold of this matter bespeaks for its complete success," the *Summit County Beacon* concluded.[60] That zeal and energy explained many things about this new group—here was an organization that crossed class lines, redefined its mission, and challenged the male authority within the Buckley Post. By December 1884, the women of the Buckley Post had already expanded their mission. The *Summit County Beacon* reported, "Ladies' Relief Corps of Buckley Post is doing a good work throughout the city, and is helping people outside of the soldiers' families." The newspaper even speculated that the relief corps might "become the benevolent society of the city."[61] The Buckley Post women were probably not ready to assume the kind of systematic welfare work that the Dorcas Society had done. Nonetheless, the new group did its part in the relief work of the 1880s and 1890s.

The Women's Relief Corps was new in many ways. There was little cross-membership between the Dorcas Society and the Women's Relief Corps of the Buckley Post, even though a number of Dorcas women were married to Civil War veterans. The Women's Relief Corps did not cultivate ties with the churches in the city. This is not to say that the women had no church affiliation, only that the group did not establish formal ties with any denomination.

Women's Relief Corps members also did not have any special ties with temperance or the WCTU. In fact, many of the leaders and members of the relief corps kept their organizational activities to a minimum, concentrating their work on the corps and the women's organizations in their own religious denomination. Sarah Battels, wife of one of the city's photographers, was typical. She was the first president of the local relief corps and later served as president of the state organization, but she held no leadership positions in other groups. Amelia Codding was a widow who was elected chaplain of the group in 1884 and had no other known organizational activities beyond the corps.[62]

Other officers seemed to carry on a whirlwind of activities. Laura Fraunfelter, wife of the superintendent of Akron schools, not only was vice president of the corps but was also soon involved with the Woman's Benevolent Association and the Women's Council. Huldah Jacobs, wife of a successful physician, balanced her commitments to the Akron Board of Charities with her involvement with the corps's Finance Committee.

Laura Fraunfelter, wife of the superintendent of Akron schools, served as vice president of the relief corps of the Buckley Post, but also was active in the Woman's Benevolent Association and the Women's Council. *Photo courtesy of the University of Akron Archives.*

The amount of involvement in outside women's clubs seemed to be related to the socioeconomic class of the individual. The more affluent the woman, the more likely that she would be involved with other women's organizations.[63] The less affluent women were not as heavily involved. This variety of civic involvement reflected the diversity in the membership of the relief corps. Just as the Civil War drew soldiers from every class, so, too, did the membership of the Buckley Post and its Women's Relief Corps.

Fifty-eight of the ninety-two Women's Relief Corps members in 1884 were traced through the census of 1880 and/or the city directory of 1884.[64] The largest number of these women (thirteen) were either widows or wives of businessmen—owners, officers, or salesmen. The wives of the businessmen probably lived comfortable lives. That was not necessarily the case for the widows. Some, like Amelia Codding, lived with relatives. Amelia lived with her son, a teamster, and his wife. Others, like Ann Holmes, widow of James, who had been a much older pattern maker, lived independently. Holmes opened her home to six boarders in 1880.

Wives of skilled craftsmen (carpenters, millers, potters) were the next-largest group (eight). Another group of seven women were married to men whose occupations were vaguely identified through their place of employment ("works at knife works," "works at Buckeye Works"), suggesting semiskilled or unskilled occupations within these factories.

The remainder of those positively identified were married either to professionals or men in other occupations, typically individuals working for the city or county, such as a firefighter or the superintendent of streets. Two members of the relief corps were employed outside the home. In 1884, Alice Malone, the widow of iron molder James Malone, ran a boardinghouse, according to the city directory. The other, Fannie Hine, was a dressmaker, according to the 1880 census.

The leadership structure of the Women's Relief Corps differed from that of the Dorcas Society. There was a president, two vice presidents, a secretary, a treasurer, a chaplain, a conductor, and a guard. The latter three offices were a reflection of the corps's affiliation with the veteran's group. The relief corps also differed considerably in the women who were elected to leadership position. The Dorcas leadership was drawn from the highest reaches of Akron society—wives of prominent business leaders and professionals. That was not the case in the Women's Relief Corps. Although a number of its officers were the wives of business owners, the relief corps leadership was more egalitarian. In 1884, there were eight officers of the corps, seven of them positively identified through census records or city directories. Three of those seven were wives of professionals or business owners—Sarah Battels, wife of a photographer and business owner; Laura Fraunfelter, wife of the superintendent of schools; and Celia Baldwin, wife of the general superintendent of the Akron Iron Company. Two—Amelia Codding and Mary Morrison—were widows. One—Emeline McMillan—was the wife of a skilled craftsman, a carpenter. The final officer, the treasurer, was an unmarried daughter of a veteran—Fannie Hine, a dressmaker.

Like the Dorcas Society, the Women's Relief Corps worked primarily through committees, although the structure was quite different. Because the corps was initially organized to provide relief to Civil War veterans and their families, the organization did not use the ward-by-ward visiting committee structure that had worked so effectively for Dorcas. Instead, three women ran a "relief committee," which handled reports of veterans (or their families) in need. The finance committee, along with the treasurer, handled the business affairs of the organization. The Home and Employment Committee helped veterans or their family members find jobs in the city. The Executive Committee, a group of more than fifteen women, determined the mission, evolving direction, and activities of the relief corps. It was this committee along with the officers who redefined the mission of the organization, much to the chagrin of the male leadership of the Buckley Post.[65]

As noted, by December 1884, the Women's Relief Corps had already expanded its welfare activities beyond the veteran base. If the leaders of the Buckley Post were unhappy about the expanded focus of the relief corps, the dispute was kept within the organization. In 1887, however, the controversy went public, when Sarah Battels, by then president of the state organization, brought an expanded vision of the Women's Relief Corps to the state structure. Battels was brought before a secret GAR court of inquiry in Akron and charged with a variety of things but, according

Sarah Battels, first president of the local relief corps of the Buckley Post, went on to serve as president of the state organization, but she ran into trouble there when she attempted to expand the group's mission. Sarah Battels was eventually brought up before a secret GAR court of inquiry in Akron to answer to the charges that she was attempting to make the relief corps independent of the GAR, instead of an auxiliary of it. *Photo courtesy of the Summit County Historical Society, the University of Akron Archives.*

to the *Akron City Times*, the main charge "is that Mrs. Battels has endeavored to make the [relief corps] organization independent of the G.A.R. instead of auxiliary to it." The male leadership of the Buckley Post, Judge N. D. Tibbals and Gen. A. C. Voris, conducted the prosecution. Other male members of the post along with unnamed "ladies" represented Battels. The *City Times* expected Battels to be exonerated of all charges.[66]

That court of inquiry was in keeping with the tension that was beginning to surface toward organizational women in Akron generally during this time period. The tension first became evident during the temperance crusade of early 1874; it resurfaced during the secret court of inquiry in 1887; but it boiled over and made headlines in 1886 when the men of the Board of Charities accused women of usurping their authority, introducing new programs, and squandering resources.

The Board of Charities was organized to carry on the "systematic" relief efforts of the Dorcas Society. Unlike the Dorcas Society, the Board of Charities was a benevolent group of both men and women. The officers of the board were all men, primarily Akron business leaders. The shift from the female-led Dorcas Society to a male-led Board of Charities started at the Tibbals home in the fall of 1884.

One of the founders of the Dorcas Society, Lucy Tibbals, and her husband, Judge Newell Tibbals, engineered the transition when the Dorcas Society appeared to be on the verge of dissolving. The transition started innocently enough. Thomas C. Raynolds, editor of the *Summit County Beacon*, was visiting the Tibbalses one evening, when the three started talking about what would happen to the poor in the city if—or when—the Dorcas Society dissolved. Without consulting the Dorcas Society, the three decided to ask the Akron City Council to call a meeting of all those interested in charitable work.

In early January 1885 at the invitation of the city council, a small group of men—ministers, business owners, and professionals—met to talk about how best to proceed. The women of the Dorcas Society and other prominent Akron women leaders were not invited. Then, an even smaller group of men was directed to draft a report. That report, which proposed the creation of a Board of Charities, was presented at a public meeting late in January, where "a good part of their audience were ladies who have heretofore worked in charitable societies and organizations," the *Summit County Beacon* reported.

Under the new structure, the Board of Charities would be a benevolent group of men and women. Its aims were simple: "1. To see that all deserving cases of destitution are properly relieved. 2. To prevent indiscriminate and duplicate giving. 3. To make employment the basis of relief. 4. To secure the community from imposture. 5. To reduce vagrancy and pauperism, and ascertain their true causes."

That mission did not differ markedly from the Dorcas Society's. The Board of Charities also used the Dorcas Society's method of investigating cases of want. The board had a visiting committee that was split into wards. Two men and two women in each ward were appointed to investigate cases of want. The Board of Charities would then coordinate relief activities—"Poor Boards, church societies, charitable organizations, and private persons of benevolence . . . to prevent wasteful and mischievous alms giving." Like the Dorcas Society, the Board of Charities embraced the concept of the "worthy poor." The poor were encouraged to work. The new organization would raise "the poor from a condition of dependence by fostering their self-respect, and by promoting habits of forethought and self help, and better and more sanitary modes of living."[67]

The women and men assigned to the visiting committee were among the most affluent in the city. The men were captains of industry with long records of civic activity, but little time to actually visit those in need. Ohio C. Barber, the match king; Burke C. Herrick, who made a fortune in the crockery business; retailer Michael O'Neil; railroad mogul Charles Ingersoll; and Akron postmaster James Morrison were just some of the men named to the first visiting committee of the Board of Charities.

The women appointed to the committee came from the same socioeconomic class. Emily Sanford, wife of a prominent lawyer; Mary Church, spouse of a dry goods merchant; Hannah Monroe, married to the pastor of the Congregational Church; Elizabeth Stone, wife of a successful lumber dealer; and Lucretia Hitchcock, married to a physician/surgeon, were among the women who served on the board's first visiting committee.

Those women were not strangers to the Akron community. Like the Dorcas women, most had ties to the temperance crusade or the WCTU. Hannah Monroe had signed the petition that started the crusade in 1874, served as an officer of the local WCTU, and helped manage the Friendly Union. She had also been involved with the Dorcas Society, even serving on that group's visiting committee. Elizabeth Stone's involvement with the temperance movement was just as strong. She signed the petition beginning the crusade, served on the WCTU membership committee, and helped organize the Friendly Union in 1875. Mary Church had signed the temperance petition. Emily Sanford's ties to temperance could not be documented.

Nonetheless, Emily had a long history of civic activism. She had been one of the original members of the Dorcas Society, serving on the visiting committee in 1875 and as vice president of the group in 1880.[68]

The women of the Board of Charities had credibility in the community because of their high socioeconomic class and their long records of civic involvement. The women of the mothers' committee faced losing much of that credibility when the male leaders of the Board of Charities questioned their motives, their judgment, their honesty, and their behavior. Lesser women might have folded under the pressure. These women got angry; they seceded from the Board of Charities and started their own benevolent organization in a very public controversy that dominated the headlines of the city's newspapers.

The anger might have stemmed from the fact that the women of the Board of Charities had done so much of the fieldwork needed to establish a systematic relief effort in the city. These women visited overcrowded tenements, run-down homes, and shanties in alleys. They found destitute widows and their families, elderly immigrants, and men desperate for work. The women had to differentiate between the "worthy poor" and the "professional beggars" and then turn legitimate cases over to the board.[69] It was easy to determine those legitimate cases.

One family of eight lived in a tenement house in South Akron and was recovering from a "long siege of typhoid fever." All slept in one room, "breathing the poisoned air." The family had to rely on the generosity of neighbors and "what the overseers of the poor furnished them, which it is generally known is not of the kind of food that a sick person needs." (The infirmary normally provided salt pork to those requesting food.) Because of the prolonged illness, the family fell behind in the rent. Nonetheless, there was hope. "The mother, amidst all this squalor and wretchedness, talked hopefully of the future." Three of the children were going back to school; the other three were too young, "hanging about their mother, each with a piece of dry bread in his hand which they appeared to be enjoying as much as your little darlings . . . enjoy the dainties bestowed by a fond mother."

Visitors had to go up a "narrow, dark, steep flight of steps" to reach another apartment where a family of five lived. The father found work only "now and then," and the mother took in washing. That was a "killing job" because she had to carry the water from the canal up "two flights of narrow dilapidated stairs." The mother said she would prefer to do sewing, and the woman visitor arranged to supply work.

Men, especially, were having trouble finding work in Akron during the mid-1880s, the women reported. One young married man had been "driven almost to desperation on account of his inability to get anything to do." He had been out of work all winter, and he and his young, sick wife faced eviction.

The aged were especially at risk. One sickly German couple on Locust Street had lost all hope when their only son died. "Unless speedy relief is given them[,] they will be compelled to go to the Infirmary." An aged Irish couple lived in an alley. "The wife is not quite as feeble as her husband and goes out to work whenever she is able, but what little she can earn scarcely keeps them in food, saying nothing about their rent, fuel, etc." On South Main, another aged couple survived "in the most abject poverty." The man had rheumatism and was confined to the house; his "quite feeble" wife made doormats that she sold door to door. "They do not wish to beg, but do ask for something to do to keep them from starving."[70]

Women turned "worthy" cases of need over to the trustees of the Board of Charities for assistance. The visiting committee women were also responsible for soliciting funds from the affluent in their wards. The money and pledges were also turned over to the Board of Charities.

Shortly after the Board of Charities was organized, the women associated with the group were suggesting new ways of handling cases of want. The most progressive ideas came out of the Mothers' Work Committee, and male trustees of the board found those actions objectionable. First, the women invited the *general public* to get involved with their work; second, they opened a "work room" where needy women—and lady volunteers—sewed clothing to be distributed to the poor in the city; and third, the committee began offering services to the indigent who heretofore had never received assistance.

The entire history of the Mothers' Work Committee was controversial. Some trustees said the committee had gone through the proper channels and received the approval of the leaders of the board; others branded it a renegade group that never received official support. What is not debatable is that the Mothers' Work Committee did invite Akron women, who heretofore had not been involved with the Board of Charities, to get involved with relief efforts. That call elicited a large number of women volunteers.

The committee operated out of the work room. This work room had two functions: it was a place where volunteer women and indigent women sewed clothing to be distributed to the poor in the city, and it was also a place where needy women could get special services. These services grew out of the committee's work investigating cases of want, going to the homes and apartments of families, and talking to indigent women.

According to the trustees of the Board of Charities, the women of the Mothers' Work Committee had lavishly furnished their work room with oil paintings, expensive carpeting, and costly furniture purchased by funds donated to help the poor. Nonsense, the women responded. Volunteers, patrons of the cooking school, and friends had donated most of the furnishings. The trustees' charges were groundless, and "the people of Akron will see how contemptible was the insinuation which those disaffected members of the Board of Charities peddled around the streets of Akron all Summer and Fall," the women replied.

The volunteers did not deny that they provided services that the trustees considered trivial. Yes, the women admitted, the work room did have a bathroom where "poor mothers of families could, after a day of toil, enjoy a grateful bath." That was a welcome respite for women who lived in tenement houses and shacks with no running water. Besides, the volunteers responded, associations in neighboring cities offered similar services—and "cleanliness is next to godliness."

Yes, the women admitted, they had taken indigent women for a picnic out of town. But that was no reason to slur the name of women who had worked so hard for the Board of Charities. The picnic was much needed. For some poor women, it was the first day of recreation in years. "There were women who came to the committee upon that . . . notable day, and with tears in their eyes thanked them for the pleasure that had been given to them," the women explained in the *Summit County Beacon.*

Trustee charges that the women had taken funds earmarked for the board were also ridiculous, the women responded. The women had held fairs, collected donations within the wards, and turned the funds over to the board. Indeed, it was the women who had replenished the coffers of the Board of Charities.

Charges and countercharges followed. Male board trustees whispered that the Mothers' Work Committee had never been part of the Board of Charities, that the women had been *"swindling the public"* and had no right to any funding. So widespread were the charges that the children of the head of the Mothers' Work Committee came home from school with the story that their mother had "misappropriated (perhaps 'stolen' . . .)" hundreds of dollars earmarked for the board.[71]

With tempers overheated, controversy raging in the city, and headlines screaming in the local papers, there was little room for compromise. The women of the Mothers' Committee seceded from the Board of Charities and formed their own organization in 1886. The Woman's Benevolent Association (WBA), formed in the Mothers' Work Committee work room in the Christy Block, promised "to prevent indiscriminate and duplicate giving; to secure the community against imposture; to see that all 'deserving cases' of destitution are properly relieved; to make employment as far as possible, the basis of relief; to employ any and all means to secure relief to the unfortunate especially to encourage their efforts to be self sustaining, and acquire by donations or otherwise all necessary property and funds."[72]

The mission did not differ markedly from the Board of Charities. Men were allowed to affiliate, but this would be a woman's organization, run by women. "Any lady of good moral character resident of the city of Akron may be elected a member of the Association." Dues were reasonable, not less than twenty-five cents per year. The controversial work room—"where the needy mothers might come, be welcomed, and provide for her ragged and raimentless children at home; a place whose association would give new life and ambition to the hard working, discouraged mothers of our city; a place where pure benevolence would be freely bestowed"—became the heart of the new association.[73]

Mary Long, wife of an executive at the Akron Iron Company, who had suffered so much abuse at the hands of the male officers of the Board of Charities as head of the Mothers' Work Committee, was elected president. Anna Booth, an officer of the old work committee and the wife of a carpenter, was elected secretary of the new organization. Emily Conger, the wife of the president of more than one corporation, agreed to handle the job of treasurer. The women established a visiting committee, with members looking into cases of want in each of the wards.

Forty-eight women became charter members of the new organization. A number relinquished their membership in the Board of Charities; others merely joined the new organization, while retaining their ties with the board. The largest number of these women were affluent matrons, wives of business executives who had long been involved in civic associations. May Goodrich, wife of B. F. Goodrich, and Sarah Barber, wife of O. C. Barber, joined the new association. Widows—some of whom had great wealth, like Etta Work, widow of Alanson, who had been vice president of B. F. Goodrich—were the second-largest group. A few were wives of professionals: Alice Chapman, who had been a charter member of the old Dorcas Society, was the wife of a dentist, and Julia Upson was the wife of an attorney who became a judge. Only two women were wives of skilled craftsmen. Thus, the charter members of the WBA, like the leadership of the Dorcas Society before it and the women leaders of the Board of Charities, were drawn from a select population of affluent matrons with some history of civic activity.[74]

The heart of the WBA was its work room. Here needy mothers could get supplies for their children. But the women had to be worthy. Help would not be given to individuals "who *persist*[ed] in a criminal course of life, or in the use of intoxicating liquors, nor to the willfully idle." The WBA, like the Dorcas Society and the Board of Charities, wanted to cultivate good work habits and a sense of self-reliance. Needy women were given sewing work to be done in the work room or at their homes; as the WBA women explained, "we prefer not to give charity without recompense if ever so small."[75]

When the Woman's Benevolent Association started, the group needed some financial resources. In light of all the money the women had raised for the Board of Charities, they naturally thought that the board should share some resources. Incredulous, the Board of Charities refused. The women had no more right to the money they collected "than the 'Odd Fellows or the Methodist Church,'" the trustees of the Board of Charities asserted. The feud again raged in the newspapers. Finally an unidentified writer called for the Board of Charities and WBA to end the squabbling—"Cork up your ink bottles; bottle up your wrath"—get to a table, and work out a compromise. That seemed to be good advice, so committees from each organization worked out a deal: the Board of Charities would pass a resolution, saying that the women of its old Work Committee had not exceeded their authority, the two groups would cooperate in the visiting of the indigent in each ward, the WBA would provide welfare services, and the board would share some of the money collected by the old Work Committee. The compromise was quickly accepted by the WBA. The trustees of the Board of Charities rejected the measure. Even the *Akron Daily Beacon* could not believe that action:

> The Akron Board of Charities may have committed suicide last night when
> it neglected the treaty of peace agreed upon by the joint committee, which
> the Women's [*sic*] Benevolent Association ratified at once and without a
> dissenting vote. The test of this will be found in the opinions and actions
> of the public, who are the real arbiters of the fate of both societies.

A day later, however, cooler heads prevailed, and the trustees of the Board of Charities approved the cooperation pact.[76]

The women of the WBA were free to carry on relief work as they saw fit. With the city in the depth of a depression and the feud with the Board of Charities finally resolved, the needy—especially the indigent mothers—looked to the

WBA for help. Needy women came to the work room to sew; WBA members went to their assigned wards to investigate instances of want; donations flowed in; food, fuel, clothing, boots, and shoes went to those in need. Hundreds of families looked to the WBA for survival in just the first six months of the group's existence.

The work room in the Christy Block soon became too small for the welfare work of the women. The WBA moved to a new home on South High Street, which was large enough to offer the services that the women of the WBA thought were needed. The bathroom was "well patronized." Needy mothers and their children paid twenty-five cents a bath. Every Sunday, the WBA offered Bible readings and a Mission Sabbath School. There were so many things for the women of the WBA to do, they had to hire someone to help. Miss Lou Lusk became the group's missionary, visiting all cases of sickness and distress, reporting back to the WBA and the proper authorities so that those in want could receive the "necessities and delicacies required."[77]

As the depression of the 1880s eased, the WBA looked to expand its mission. The WBA built on what it knew. The women of the WBA believed in the ideal of domesticity. The home was woman's kingdom, "the domain of her greatest and most lasting influence."[78] But in their visits to the homes of the needy, the WBA

The Woman's Benevolent Association Home, located on South High Street, was the central location for that organization's work. It was from this home that the group investigated cases of need and then provided assistance. *Courtesy of the Summit County Historical Society Collection, the University of Akron Archives.*

women discovered that the lessons of womanhood—housekeeping, sewing, and the like—were not being taught. Here would be the WBA's new focus, educating the next generation of women, the daughters of the needy. The WBA opened an industrial school, where young girls learned to sew. In January 1889, the first month of operation, the school had sixty-eight pupils and eight teachers. Later in the year, the WBA opened a "kitchen garden" to teach the fine arts of cooking and housekeeping. In so doing, the women of the WBA ensured that the girls in their charge would be well trained for traditional roles as wife, mother, and caretaker of the household; but it also meant that these young women would be well trained for domestic jobs, jobs that in Akron were low paying. In the process, the women of the WBA had access to a ready supply of well-trained domestics.[79]

In 1889, the WBA and the Board of Charities merged. The new group, open to both women and men, was renamed the Union Charity Association of Akron. Of the two groups, the women emerged as the dominant force. Most of the founders were women, as were most of the officers and trustees of the new group. WBA also brought the most tangible asset to the union—a "home" on South High Street, which became the headquarters for the new association. WBA programs continued. Miss Lou Lusk remained but was given a new title. The new association had the same goals as the WBA and the Board of Charities. The Union Charity Association continued until 1905, when its building and programs were given to a new woman's organization in the city, the Young Women's Christian Association.[80]

The Dorcas Society, the Women's Relief Society, and the Woman's Benevolent Association provided services that the city needed during times of great distress. They provided the food, clothing, and fuel needed for hundreds of indigent families in the city. These benevolent groups were assisted by many church missionary and aid societies that were committed to helping the needy in the congregation and the community.

The benevolent/philanthropic civic organizations and the church associations represented only a portion of the women's groups in Akron during the Gilded Age. Other women formed literary, musical, health, child-focused, and educational organizations. Many men's groups had "ladies'" auxiliaries as well. It would have been difficult to keep track of all the women's clubs in the city.

The proliferation of these women's groups was not lost on four women who had witnessed all the groups crowding into the WCTU's Friendly Union or gathering in the churches of the city or meeting at the homes of individual members. The four wondered why all these women's groups could not come together and form a council of cooperation and collaboration in which thousands of Akron women could be represented through their clubs in a kind of women's parliament. Because women did not yet have the vote, this council might be a way for the thousands of Akron organizational women to gain a voice on issues they cared strongly about. In February 1893, the call went out for cooperative action; by the end of the year, Akron had its Women's Council, one of the earliest formed in the nation.

THE WOMEN'S COUNCIL

The four women who spearheaded the Women's Council, Katherine Claypole, Henrietta Chase, Isabella Berry, and Abby Soule Schumacher, had collaborated before. In 1892, the four had worked together when the Woman's Suffrage Association and the WCTU held a joint meeting on suffrage.

Isabella Berry, wife of a dry goods merchant, and Henrietta Chase, widow of a prominent physician, were the powers behind the powerful WCTU in Akron, Isabella being its longtime president and Henrietta its longtime vice president. Both were members of an affluent socioeconomic class, and also of the Congregational Church.

Katherine Claypole and Abby Schumacher came from a different religious heritage. Both were Universalists. Both were also part of the Buchtel College women's community that was growing so strong within the city. Katherine was the wife of a Buchtel College faculty member; Abby, the young wife of milling executive Franz Adolph Schumacher, son of cereal king and prohibitionist Ferdinand Schumacher and his wife, Hermine, the temperance and benevolent women's organization leader, was a graduate of the college (class of 1885). The two shared an organizational tie as well: both were founders and officers of the Akron Woman Suffrage Association.

From its start, the suffrage association in Akron had strong ties to the Buchtel College women's community. Formed in 1889, the suffrage association was committed to winning the vote by a national amendment. Three of the four officers of the new group—Dora Merrill, Mary Jewett, and Abby Schumacher—had a Buchtel College connection. Dora and Mary were faculty members. (Both women left the institution in the early 1890s and moved to New York City, Dora Merrill to take a teaching position at a fashionable young ladies' finishing school, Mary Jewett to attend New York University's medical school and become a physician.) By

Abby Soule Schumacher, an 1885 graduate of Buchtel College, was one of the founders of the Akron Woman Suffrage Association and the Women's Council. *Photo courtesy of the University of Akron Archives.*

1890, Katherine Claypole was leading the group and boasting that more than one thousand people in Akron and the vicinity believed that women should have the right to vote. How many of those one thousand joined the suffrage association is unknown.[81]

The suffrage advocates used two arguments in their campaign in Akron. For the constituency that had so much at stake in the ideal of domesticity and the separate sphere for women, the suffrage advocates argued that women would bring "the promotion of morality and good order" to politics. For the college-educated women the group was attracting, the advocates added the "simple justice" argument, harkening back to the historical "no taxation without representation" refrain. The suffragists were also employing the grassroots strategies that the WCTU

Mary Jewett, an 1876 graduate of Buchtel College, taught English literature, logic, and rhetoric at her alma mater. She was also one of the founders of the Akron Woman Suffrage Association. Jewett left Akron to attend medical school at New York University and practiced medicine in Winterhaven, Florida. *Photo courtesy of the University of Akron Archives.*

in Akron had used so effectively. The suffragists used "missionary work" throughout Summit County—and the group was quite effective at it, for any number of reasons, as the *Cleveland Press* reported:

> The members of the society are doing considerable missionary work among the ladies of Summit county, and new members all enthusiastic in the work, are being recruited into the ranks. It is a significant fact that they are all handsome women, and should they take it into their heads to send a committee to Columbus it is extremely likely that the bill would become a law.[82]

In 1892, the WCTU and the suffrage group collaborated in a number of different ways. The two groups held at least one joint meeting on suffrage, a position

Women graduates of Buchtel College (now the University of Akron) represented an important force in the city's women's clubs. They were an important part of the suffrage group and among the founding members of the Women's Council (now the Akron and Summit County General Federation of Women's Clubs). *Photo courtesy of the University of Akron Archives.*

that the Akron WCTU had endorsed since 1885. In turn, the suffragists supported WCTU-led measures, including signing the petition supporting a police matron to attend to female inmates.[83]

The creation of the Women's Council in Akron was very much in keeping with that spirit of collaboration. In February 1893, the four—Isabella Berry, Henrietta Chase, Katherine Claypole, and Abby Schumacher—called for the women's organizations in the city to join them in forming a council, in which each association would have an equal voice, no matter what the group's numbers.[84]

At the organizational meeting, thirty societies were represented.[85] More than a third of the groups represented Protestant churchwomen's organizations. As might be expected given the organizational affiliations of the four who called for the council, the WCTU and the suffrage association were represented, as were ethnic, benevolent, and literary clubs. What was not expected was the representation of the Daughters of Jerusalem, an organization of African American women in the city. The group became an early member of the council, and its representatives spoke out about the special problems facing African American women in the city. "The advancement of the Afro-American women formed a considerable part of the address. The help in this line, she [Ella Simpson] believed, was largely through the efforts of the society she represented," the *Beacon* reported after an early council meeting. The Daughters of Jerusalem, however, did not continue its affiliation. By 1896, the group was no longer a part of the Women's Council.[86]

The mission of the Women's Council in Akron was to "bring all women's organizations into closer relationship thereby increasing the knowledge of each as to the work of others and affording a means of carrying on any enterprise of general interest." To that end, council meetings began with a representative of each member organization relating news. Sometimes, the representatives provided a historical perspective; other times, they updated council members on what the group's newest initiative was.[87]

Katherine Claypole was elected president of the Women's Council; Isabella Berry became vice president. Abby Schumacher and Henrietta Chase held no leadership positions. Alice Wood, the representative from the Mary Day Nursery,[88] was elected corresponding secretary, and Lucy Bennett, who represented the Women's Foreign Missionary Society of the First Methodist-Episcopal Church (where her husband was the pastor), became recording secretary. Katherine and Isabella held their leadership positions for four terms. Both were committed to a platform of social activism and defined what the council became in Akron.

The mission of the Women's Council shifted away from familiarizing women's organizations with each other to collaboration. This was no easy task given the women's organizations affiliated with the council. Nonetheless, by appealing to women in their traditional roles as wife, mother, and caretaker of the home, the council was able to put together a platform of issues upon which the auxiliary organizations agreed. Because women were mothers, council members in 1894 pledged to agitate for free kindergartens in the schools. Because women saw the importance of education, the council and its member organizations pushed for a library reading room. Because women had the responsibility to keep their homes clean, the council members endorsed "smoke consumers," designed to keep the smoke from factory chimneys under control. And since liquor threatened so many families because of the intemperance of one or more parents, council members agitated for closing saloons in the city.[89]

That same year, Ohio women could vote in the school board elections, and council president Katherine Claypole wanted the organizational women in Akron to take advantage of the right. She ended the semiannual council meeting "by stating that she would like to see at least two women's names appear on the ballots next spring for members of the Board of Education." The names of two women did appear on that ballot; Margaret Sadler and Frances Allen, both active clubwomen in the city, were elected in their first run for public office. (Neither, however, served a second term.[90])

Each year, the Women's Council decided what it—and its member organizations—would agitate for. Each year, the reforms were conservative, easily linked to, and explained by women's traditional role within the family. In 1895, the organizations agreed to agitate for a police matron to monitor female inmates, for free kindergartens, and for a curfew. In 1896, the council organized a mothers club to train children in home life. In 1897, the council came out in favor of improving the moral tone of amusements and enhancing the sanitary conditions in the streets. In 1898, the council planned to raise money for schoolroom decorations; and the next year, the emphasis was placed on better hygiene, sanitation, and care for Akron's children and the development of a better art education program in the schools.[91]

In these early years, the Women's Council was registering successes in its rather modest goals. Kindergartens were started in each of Akron's schools. The mothers clubs flourished. By the turn of the century, there were eleven circles in Akron, including one in North Hill and one in Cuyahoga Falls. Each circle worked closely with the neighborhood teachers to be sure that schoolwork was carried into the home. The council's mothers club laid the groundwork for the Home and School League.[92]

The Women's Council's Gilded Age campaigns modestly began Akron's "municipal housekeeping" movement. The municipal housekeeping movement used the ideals of domesticity to explain women's greater involvement in bringing about reforms that improved the quality of life and health in the city.[93]

Akron women's organizations blossomed during the Gilded Age. Thousands of Akron women flocked to the church groups, the temperance crusade, the benevolent/philanthropic associations, the Women's Council, and the many other literary, musical, health, child-focused, or educational organizations in the city during the post–Civil War period. These groups sprang up in every part of Akron, from North Hill to South Akron. Every religion had its woman's organizations, from the Jewish Schwesterbund to the Catholic Altar Society, from the Universalist missionary association to the Congregational Church's Social Society. Women, rich and poor, found a special place in these organizations.

And Akron's clubwomen were better because of it. The editor of the *Beacon* perhaps captured the sentiment best: "The club furnishes a gifted and noble woman with an opportunity to say the right word at the right place." Finding that kind of outlet strengthened home life. "Many a home has been brightened by the influence of women who have had larger experience and who have spoken as only women can speak to their own; their family life has been unconsciously improved and the happiness of isolated persons increased by their kindly and helpful suggestion."[94]

The organizational women of post–Civil War Akron had built on what they had learned during the Civil War. They reached beyond a single religious denomination to build a network of committed women. Just as the women of Civil War Akron had done before them, these clubwomen used the press to reach others who wished to join their work, to raise funds, and to defend themselves against their harshest critics.

As the twentieth century dawned, new organizations started; others faded; more redefined themselves to face the conditions posed in the new century. More women—and different kinds of women—joined organizations that promised to change both the face of the city and the women within it.

Chapter 5

Religiously-based Women's Clubs in Twentieth-Century Akron

To attend Altar Guild regularly is a liberal education.
—"History of the Altar Guild, Trinity Lutheran Church, Akron, Ohio 1905–1955"[1]

The Dorcas Society does a work so important in promoting acquaintanceship among the ladies, in extending a helping hand to those in need, in being full of "good works and alms-deeds," that I should think every lady would want to be a member and regular attendant of the Dorcas Society.
—*High Street Christian Bulletin*, June 10, 1906[2]

DURING THE FIRST TWENTY-FIVE YEARS OF THE TWENTIETH CENTURY, Akron throbbed with an energy charged by expanded industrial production, a burgeoning population, and an enormous confidence in the city's future. That confidence was well placed. Although Akron had seen mills and plants shut down in the 1890s, the city also witnessed a kind of industrial renaissance when new rubber companies, such as Firestone and Kelly-Springfield, opened new factories, and older firms, such as B. F. Goodrich, Goodyear, and Miller Tire, expanded production in the new century. By 1925, Akron had truly earned its title of "rubber capital of the world."

That same year, the city had won another title, "fastest growing city in the world." Between 1900 and 1925, Akron's population increased almost fivefold. The new residents came from the south, especially from the nearby states of Appalachia. For the first time, Akron was humorously referred to as the "capital of West Virginia." No single regional reference could capture the essence of the foreign immigration into the city, however. The immigrants came from many different parts of the world, but eastern and southern Europe predominated. These immigrants brought different customs, different languages, and different religions.

The city was having problems adjusting to all the changes that marked it as an industrial center. City residents coughed their way through the pollution; a filthy gray haze hovered in Akron's skies. The city stank of rubber production. Housing was scarce, so scarce that some residents lived in garages, attics, even converted chicken coops—and paid dearly for the privilege. Immigrants crowded into ethnic enclaves on North Hill, East Akron, and "Goosetown," in South Akron.

Akron's urban problems multiplied every year. Every institution—from the police to the courts, from the schools to the churches—was taxed to its limits. Families were stressed; juvenile delinquency was up.

What the city needed was a good dose of "municipal housekeeping."

The women of Akron were ready for the chore. They had already come up with the arguments for getting involved in the community. Building on the rhetoric of domesticity, the women emphasized that their responsibilities within the home made them experts in solving the problems of the city. As mothers, they knew best how to help the schools and guide the troubled youth. As caregivers in the home, they were ideally suited to create health-care facilities tailored to children and to organize homes for senior citizens. As housekeepers, they had a unique perspective on cleaning up the pollution and filth in the city. And who was better suited to investigate the unsanitary conditions in groceries and markets? As women with a highly developed moral sense, they were uniquely qualified to provide decent housing for young workingwomen; to run facilities where women and girls could safely meet, play, learn, and pray; to make a home for women who were pregnant outside of wedlock; and to protect children from the corrupting influences of motion pictures and "obscene" billboards. As women with finely developed artistic sensibilities, they were also in tune with the community's cultural needs.

The women's organizations associated with Akron's churches during this time were ready for all these tasks. Each church and synagogue had women's organizations. Sometimes, the woman's club carried out its work independently; but, increasingly, the ladies' aid societies, the home missionary groups, and other church-related women's organizations discovered the virtues of collaboration and forged alliances across denominations to create new organizations and offer needed services.

AKRON, 1900–1925

The exuberance and confidence of the Akron women were in keeping with the city's mood. Between 1900 and 1925, Akron enjoyed boom times. Its population expanded from a respectable 42,720 in 1900 to 69,067 in 1910 and 208,435 in 1920. A depression rocked the city that year and thousands left in search of better prospects elsewhere. Nonetheless, by 1925, the city still had a population of 193,508.

It was a different kind of population for Akron, which brought fresh challenges. Beckoned by the high-paying industrial jobs, many of the new residents came from the South. This new population brought institutions and prejudices with them, including the white supremacist Ku Klux Klan (KKK). By the 1920s, the KKK became a force to be reckoned with socially and politically. Thousands of Akronites joined. By 1925, a Klan official boasted that Akron's branch, with 52,000 members, was the largest in the nation. The Klan became such a part of Akron's life that members, including those of the women's auxiliary, marched fully costumed in white in the Labor Day and Independence Day parades. The KKK supported political candidates, and in the 1920s, the Klan controlled the city's school board, helped elect a mayor, and supported several judges and county commissioners in their bids for reelection. In Akron, the Klan was suspicious of immigrants and especially targeted the growing Catholic and Jewish populations.[3]

About a third of Akron's population in the 1920s consisted of immigrants or children of immigrants. Throughout much of its history, Akron had a substantial immigrant population; but this was different. These immigrants came from different parts of the world, especially eastern and southern Europe. Many were poorly educated and could speak little or no English. They had different customs and different religions. Many were Catholic, Jewish, or Orthodox. Many were accused of being clannish, not fitting into Akron's ways. These new immigrants tended to settle in ethnic enclaves. Italian families created a city within a city on North Hill, where Italian was spoken and old ways preserved. Large numbers of Hungarian, Serb, Czech, and Yugoslavian families settled in East Akron and South Akron. For the immigrant in Akron, life could be harsh, money limited, and tensions between parents with "traditional" ways and their American-born children high.[4]

In 1925, when this photo was taken during the parade celebrating the city's centennial, Akron had one of the largest Ku Klux Klan chapters in the nation. Female relatives of those members organized an auxiliary. This float commemorates the group's goals: "Protestantism," "Womanhood," and "Public Schools." *Photo courtesy of the Special Collections Division, Akron-Summit County Public Library.*

The immigrants—from the South and from Europe—were drawn to Akron by the promise of plentiful, good-paying jobs in an industry stimulated by the First World War and America's love affair with the automobile. During the first two and half decades of the twentieth century, Akron became the home of dozens of rubber companies, from small companies producing toys to industrial giants—BFG, Goodyear, and Firestone, three of the four largest tire manufacturers in the world. It was little wonder that Akron won the title "rubber capital of the world."[5]

That was quite a change from the Akron of the 1890s. The city started that decade with a diversified economy built on clay, milling, and other manufacturing. But the depression of the 1890s had devastated the city. Match and clay production began moving out of town. Cereal and farm machinery production began moving west, closer to the agricultural heart of the nation. In their wake, Akron was left with a new industry that brought enormous prosperity to the city—and a raft of problems.

The rubber companies that had settled in Akron earlier—BFG, Goodyear, and Miller—thrived in the new century. That success was not lost on Harvey Firestone, who started his own company in Akron in 1900. By 1905, Firestone Tire and Rubber struck a deal with a new auto manufacturer, Ford Motor, to equip a new, inexpensive car with tires. That contract, which was delayed a year because of design problems at Ford, was the start of a long, lucrative business relationship between the car company and Firestone. It also catapulted Firestone from just another Akron tire company to one of the "Big Four" rubber companies in the nation. Smaller rubber companies, such as Kelly-Springfield, Anderson, Independent, Western Reserve, Summit, Mohawk, General Tire, Star Rubber, and Swinehart Tire, never equaled Firestone's success, but all thrived during this period. Rubber companies in and around the city produced everything from bicycle and car tires to children's toys, from fire hose to boots and shoes.[6]

That range of production meant that the rubber companies needed many workers. In 1910, almost one in three Akron residents—male and female—worked in the city's rubber factories. Women did the "lighter" jobs, those requiring dexterity as opposed to strength; men got the better-paid, "heavier" jobs, commonly associated with automobile tire production. Jobs in rubber factories, whether done by women or by men, were hard, dirty work. Conditions were neither safe nor sanitary, and state protective labor legislation was not always followed. Women and men often worked fifty to sixty hours a week.

Trouble was brewing in the factories. Not unionized, the laborers in the rubber factories who objected to company policies could do little. Some complained to state factory inspectors; a few walked off the job in isolated, easily contained strikes. Rubber companies easily checked any worker discontent until 1913, when the radical Industrial Workers of the World (IWW) engineered a rubber strike like none Akron had seen before. The strike, triggered by Firestone's attempt to introduce labor-saving machines and reduce the piecework pay rate, quickly spread to Goodyear, BFG, Miller, and many of the smaller rubber shops. About fifteen thousand workers walked off the job; but a month later the strike was broken, the union moved on, and the workers went back to work. Some rubber companies put into place a number of reforms to make sure that nothing like that happened again.[7]

Living in Akron at this time was a challenge. Just finding a place to live could be difficult. With thousands of new workers rushing to the city each year, Akron could not keep up with the housing demands. The housing shortage was especially acute for young women, who came to the city in search of good-paying jobs. Many came without their families. Without relatives in the city, these women were often hard pressed to find safe, clean, decent housing.

More women found jobs in the rubber factories during the twentieth century. These women worked in Department 25 of the B. F. Goodrich Company. The Zipper Girls are identified as (front row, from left) Isabel Nye, Anna Gish, Mary Riel, and Esther Swigart, (second row) Lucy Derhammer, "Big" Rose, and unknown, and (back row) Lydia Koromnow Pastor, Thelma Eaton, Minnie Horn, Margaret Rittig, and Ann "last name forgotten." *Photo courtesy of B. F. Goodrich Collection, the University of Akron Archives.*

For their part, Goodyear and Firestone tried to relieve Akron's housing short-age by building planned communities for workers and their families. Goodyear started its affordable housing first in 1912. Goodyear Heights was a short fifteen-minute walk from the rubber factory. Firestone followed suit with a community designed to appeal to both managers and workers. The housing shortage worsened as the rubber factories geared up for World War I. Rubber companies with large, lucrative government contracts needed many new workers, male and female, and those new recruits scrambled for places to stay.[8]

Akron did a better job keeping up with the religious and educational needs of its burgeoning population. By 1925, Akron had five high schools and twenty-nine elementary schools, serving more than thirty thousand students. Another group of parents kept their children from public schools and the influence of Protestants. Catholic parents sent their children to one of the eight parish-run elementary schools and the parochial high school in the city. Zion Lutheran Church contin-ued its elementary school as well.

Then, as now, Akron was a city of churches. Akron Catholic churches were especially taxed by the influx of the new immigrants. In 1901, only three churches served the Catholic population in the city. By 1920, another sixteen parishes were organized. Some served immigrant groups specifically—St. John's for the Slovak population; St. Hedwig's for the Poles; St. Joseph's for the Syrians; Holy Ghost Church, Greek Rite, for the Ukrainians; St. Michael's, Greek Rite, for the Hungarians; and St. Peter's for the Lithuanians. Others, including Annunciation and Sacred Heart of Jesus, were built to serve the growing native-born Catholic population.

The Methodists and Baptists also grew in number with Akron's shifting population. By 1925, the Methodists had nineteen churches in Akron, including three serving the growing African American population. In 1901, the Baptists had three churches in the city. By 1925, there were sixteen, including those serving the new Romanian, Hungarian, and Macedonian immigrants to the city.[9]

As had been the case the century before, priests, ministers, and rabbis realized that one of their most valuable assets was their women members. The women in these new churches, along with the long-established congregations in the city, affiliated with missionary and ladies' aid societies to bring much-needed services to the church and the community. Another generation of Akron women affiliated with already existing church associations or, more commonly, organized new groups to serve their own social/educational/cultural needs, the demands of their parish, and the challenges of the new century.

CHURCHWOMEN'S ORGANIZATIONS

Like the churchwomen before them, the women organizing in the new century opted for one of two missions—inward, focusing on the needs of the specific congregation, or outward, reaching out to the community. Those with inward missions accomplished much within their specific congregations—some helped create the church itself; others assumed responsibility for the upkeep of the altar; a few were social clubs, to cultivate a sense of community among the women of the denomination. Those with an outward mission were less parochial. Many groups worked solely with women of their specific congregation to create services within the community; others saw the value of alliances and established partnerships that crossed denominational lines to create institutions that continue today.

The women of both types of organizations were motivated by the same impulses: a commitment to traditional domestic values combined with a deep religious fervor. Those dual impulses made the churchwomen's organizations an abiding, powerful force within Akron—organizations that could accomplish much, provided that they had leaders with vision, administrative expertise, and ability to harness the energy of the members. Some women's church groups were more successful at this than others.

The West Hill Episcopalian women found the right formula in their St. Mary's Guild. Organized in November 1892, these women had an inward religious mission. The women thought West Hill, at the time not a densely populated neighborhood, needed an Episcopal church. The women had no authorization from the Diocesan Board of Missions and no apparent encouragement from the rector of the already existing Episcopal church on the other side of town. St. Mary's Guild did have a small group of West Hill women[10] committed to the mission and a president "indefatigable in her efforts for the church." Longtime president of the group Mary Hammel, wife of the proprietor of Hammel Business College, knew how to involve almost every Episcopal woman in the neighborhood to get behind her efforts. Within a year, the West Hill Episcopalians were moving toward a church of their own. A building committee (all men) was put in place, and the guild, almost a year old, was officially recognized.

Although the church looked to men for the key committees, St. Mary's Guild wielded enormous influence within the fledgling congregation at this time. When the congregation needed a parish hall, the priest turned to the guild, who agreed to pay a certain amount but only if the church could secure a loan to cover the remaining costs. The parish got the loan, and the guild paid its pledge.

These women were not all from influential or affluent families. The membership of the guild reflected the diverse economic base of the parish itself. At the time the guild was formed, Mary E. Coney was married to the owner of a furniture store on West Center Street, but Clara E. Morley was the wife of a miller. Myrt A. Billow was wed to a bookkeeper; Ann Sabin and Ida Reherd were both married to letter carriers. The socioeconomic class of unmarried sisters Mary J. and Caroline Gunn is unclear; neither their occupations nor their parents could be identified. The women of St. Mary's Guild also had a real knack for fund-raising. They did the typical things Akron churchwomen always did to raise money—sewing and giving church dinners—but they also experimented with different fund-raising techniques. St. Mary's Guild is credited with giving the first rummage sale in the city (December 3, 1900) and raising almost one thousand dollars in the process.[11] Few other organizations within the Church of Our Saviour could match the fund-raising record of the guild during the late nineteenth and early twentieth centuries. According to the Reverend Atwater, the rector of the Church of Our Saviour, St. Mary's Guild kept to its inward focus throughout this time period.[12]

Within other churchwomen's groups, that focus was not always so constant. At the First Congregational Church, for example, the APT ("all past twenty") women's group[13] started in 1890 as a social club, where young, unmarried women got together to socialize, sew, read, and do musicals. In the new century, however, the group burned with a reform spirit; the club changed its name to the Missionary Society and worked on projects to help others. Early members recalled that women of the missionary society "were on fire with ambition" and became a fund-raising machine. The women hemmed linen, tied comforters, made baby clothes, held bazaars, hosted suppers, and had teas to raise money for a wide range of activities, from a school for African Americans in the South to the Ryder Hospital in Puerto Rico, from Pleasant Hill Academy in Tennessee to the Church Building Society. The group also put together boxes for home missions. As many members of the young woman's missionary group got older, many affiliated with the senior Missionary Society. In 1913, the two groups merged.[14] That merger injected new energy into the older missionary society that had been struggling for membership.[15]

During the first twenty-five years of the twentieth century, channeling the energies of the women of the First Congregational Church became increasingly difficult. Many of the Congregational women were busy in secular benevolent, health, cultural, social, and civic organizations thriving in the city. Rather than offering a host of competing women's organizations within the denomination, the First Congregational Church experimented with a kind of "mega" churchwoman's organization, designed to appeal to all the female constituencies. Formed by a merger of the Women's Social Society and the Missionary Society, the Women's Association was made up of a number of different committees that might have been separate clubs in an earlier time. For the woman interested in social activities, the Women's Association offered a hospitality committee to organize neighborhood and church parties; for the woman who wanted to do benevolent work, the Dorcas Committee filled the bill; for the woman committed to the spiritual needs of the church, the religious education committee was ideal; for the woman interested in health and human services within the city, the social services committee had ties to the hospitals, Sumner Home for aging citizens, and the International Institute for immigrants.[16]

The group seemed to be just what the congregation needed. The association had a large membership, the majority of whom were willing to commit to the daylong

work sessions twice a month. It was a "joyful service" to the church but also an opportunity to "promote friendly acquaintance among women," one history of the
group explained. Part of that activism emanated from the highly skilled and orga-
nizationally experienced leaders of the association. These were leaders who knew
how to motivate women and keep them on task. Many were married to businessmen
who were among the most successful in the city; for example, Winifred Sperry, wife
of the president of Baker-McMillen and an active member of the Mary Day Nursery, headed the social services committee. Others were widows, like the dean of
women students at Buchtel College, Elizabeth Thompson, who was involved in a
range of women's organizations from the Woman's Club League to the College
Club and headed the religious education committee.[17]

Few other churchwomen's associations followed the First Congregational's organizational model. Most of the church groups focused on a single mission. At the
High Street Reformed Church in 1902, for example, the Reverend John C. Slayter
called for the women to replace the Ladies' Aid Society with a new group. The
women abided by his request and organized the Dorcas Society, which quickly became one of High Street's most active and most popular groups. Made up of fifty-
four women initially,[18] the new group was organized to "foster benevolence in the
church, to visit and care for the sick, and to extend a helping hand to the needy in
the church and out of the church."[19] The women sewed, quilted, folded bandages,
altered garments, packed holiday baskets, visited the sick and elderly, and did anything else necessary to help the needy and elderly in the city. Soon the Dorcas Society became known as High Street's "response to need."

The Dorcas Society drew its leadership from the most affluent members of
the congregation. Earliest officers included Martha King, the daughter of David L.
King, the sewer pipe manufacturer, and Julia Stoner, wife of the general manager
of a local manufacturing concern.[20] Leadership in the Dorcas Society could mean
a place within the power structure of the church itself. Frances Allen, president of
Dorcas in 1905, soon became one of two deaconesses within the church. It was a
natural progression for Allen. Educated at Hiram College, Frances Allen was married to one of the partners of Cummings and Allen Flour Company, which soon
merged into Quaker Oats. Indeed, much of the success of the company—and of
the breakfast cereal industry generally—has been credited to husband Miner Allen,
who may have collaborated with his wife in coming up with the oats-cooking
process used in the development of breakfast cereals. That process made Miner
Allen—and his family—very rich. By the time Frances Allen was elected president

of the Dorcas Society, she already had a long record of organizational involvement in the city and in the church. She had been one of the founders of the church's missionary society and was also involved in the county's suffrage association and the city's Women's Council. She had also tasted political power. In 1896, she was elected to the school board in Akron. She served only one term, losing in her bid for reelection.[21]

The Dorcas Society of High Street illustrated the organizational structure and strategies of the largest number of women's groups affiliated with Akron churches. In selecting their leadership, the women turned to the affluent, who had administrative and leadership experience with other clubs and organizations in the city. These groups also adopted strategies that had worked effectively for decades. However, a number of churchwomen's organizations in other denominations tried different strategies to bring about needed reforms within the city.

At Trinity Lutheran, for example, the church clubwomen tried to solve the housing crisis facing employed females in the city by opening a rooming house for women. The Hospice was designed to "furnish a Christian home for young women whose own homes are in other towns, but who find in Akron their place of employment." A former mansion located next to the minister's home was remodeled and redecorated. The rooming house was soon filled with young women working in Akron or passing through the city. It was an important work, a Lutheran publication observed: "The work of the Hospice building is a most important work and should be undertaken in the largest cities, especially for girls." But church involvement in housing for women never caught on. According to the *Lutheran*, Akron's Trinity Lutheran was the only congregation to take on sole responsibility for such a rooming house.[22]

The Hospice was popular among the tenants and Trinity's churchwomen. In its early years,[23] the Hospice was usually filled to capacity. Hospice tenants were not required to be Lutherans, and only a minority of the lodgers belonged to that denomination. Many of Trinity's organizations played a role at the boardinghouse—Sunday school Class Ruth and Class Martha, the Women's Guild, the Women's Missionary Society, Mothers' Society, Mothers' Class, and the North Hill Women were all involved. Some of these clubs even met at the Hospice as a way to include the lodgers in their work.[24]

The women's groups of Trinity Lutheran that cooperated to create and run the Hospice illustrated a strategy that became increasingly important during this period: cooperation and collaboration among women's clubs and organizations to achieve a greater goal. During the Gilded Age, women had seen the value of co-operation, as evidenced in the temperance crusade and the creation of the Women's Council. But a new era of cooperation and collaboration among women's clubs was a hallmark of the early twentieth century.

That collaboration was needed because a new generation of Akron women had ambitious plans for their clubs. These women planned lasting changes to the city and created institutions that would survive them. In the first twenty-five years of the twentieth century, Akron women restructured their groups, redefined their mission, rethought their strategies, and, in the process, extended the vision of domestic feminism.

AKRON MISSIONARY UNION AND THE EAST AKRON COMMUNITY HOUSE

The redefinition of the Akron Missionary Union illustrated these principles. Organized in 1899 as a kind of federation of Protestant women's missionary groups, the union offered a structure but only a vague purpose. By 1911, a new generation of churchwomen brought the union an ambitious new mission: to help the immigrants assimilate into their new community. Setting up its base of operations where many immigrants had settled, in East Akron, the reorganized (and reenergized) union started an array of programs and created a community house to serve those in need, regardless of religion, nationality, or race.[25]

That new union, which represented twenty-five different societies from eleven Protestant denominations in the city, needed a strong, experienced leader to get this mission started. The members selected Hallie Andrews, an ideal candidate given her credentials. Hallie was a longtime resident of the city, moving to the city with her parents in 1888. She was affluent, married to the vice president and treasurer of M. T. Cutter and Company. She also came with impeccable community credentials and experience in bringing together divergent populations. Hallie was one of the original members of the Akron YWCA, served on its board, and was one of its most energetic members. As such, she was experienced in setting up programs from scratch and with little financial support. She had been one of a small group of YWCA members who had gone into the factories and cereal mills to solicit members; worked with women from a variety of denominations, ethnicities, cultures, and classes; set up the organization's dining room; and urged companies to begin recreational programs or, at least, financially support YWCA's projects. Hallie had also been long involved with her church, Grace Evangelical and Reformed Church. There she had been president of the Missionary Society and a Sunday school teacher.[26] Thus, through her affiliation with the YWCA, Hallie had contacts in congregations across the city, was experienced in working with women from a variety of socioeconomic classes and ethnicities, and had administrative and leadership experience. She needed to draw on all of this experience as the Akron Missionary Union worked with the immigrants in East Akron.

Almost immediately, Hallie Andrews and the other Missionary Union leaders faced challenges. Most revolved around strategic issues. The group needed a clear, workable plan of action, if the union was to help immigrant families acclimate to their new land. How that was to be accomplished became the question. The Akron Missionary Union elected to work through a settlement-house model, establishing the East Akron Community House as a place where immigrants could go to get the services that the Akron Missionary Union women felt they needed.[27] Working out of a middle-class domestic ideology that did not necessarily value cultural diversity, the Missionary Union women sought to "Americanize" the immigrant family. Placing special emphasis on the children, the union opened a nursery school to inculcate the children of immigrants with the "ideals of Americanization," further aggravating tensions that already existed between the parents committed to "Old-World" values and traditions and their Americanized children.[28] The situation was worsened when the women volunteers began proselytizing to the Catholic, Orthodox, and Jewish immigrants. While such action was never endorsed by the Akron Missionary Union or its leaders, the group's underlying philosophy—that religion was a stepping-stone to better citizenship—certainly invited such action.

The volunteer structure also played a role in this. Each Protestant denomination sent volunteers to work at the community house. Those women burned with a desire to help, but few were trained to work with immigrants or women of different classes and ethnicities. The volunteers were under the supervision of the Missionary Union leadership and the paid residential director, Sarah E. Mardorff.[29]

Other churchwomen's groups simply worked behind the scenes—sewing, quilting, fund-raising for the supplies that the community house's immigrant population needed. For decades, the Missionary Union (and Sarah Mardorff) ran the East Akron Community House, offering services primarily to the needy and immigrant population.[30]

A similar collaborative effort could be seen in the launch of the Akron Day Nursery, renamed the Mary Day Nursery. What made this group so interesting was not the socioeconomic class of the founders, most of whom came from the highest strata of Akron society, but rather the age of these women. The Akron Day Nursery was a benevolent service led by a new generation of Akron women, well-educated, most under the age of thirty, and most unmarried.[31] These women brought enormous enthusiasm and fresh perspectives to the organization.

The Akron Day Nursery began in 1890 as a collaborative effort between two circles of the King's Daughters: the Heart and Hand Circle of St. Paul's Episcopal Church and the Wayside Circle of First Congregational Church. The King's Daughters was not peculiar to Akron or the Episcopal and Congregational churches. The Order of King's Daughters was a worldwide women's organization established in 1886 in New York. Although officially nondenominational, the King's Daughters was most commonly associated with Protestant churches. Each local chapter, or "circle," was to carry out service or benevolent work, and each circle determined its own focus.[32] In Akron, the circles affiliated with St. Paul's Episcopal and First Congregational churches decided to focus on children. Thus, it was natural that the two groups would collaborate on some project; the question became which one.

Helen Storer, only child of a Civil War hero who owned a jewelry store in the city, thought she had the answer—a day nursery for parents working in the factories of Akron. There was a great need for a day-care facility in the city. Akron working parents had few options; they could leave their children with friends, relatives, or neighbors or simply leave them alone to fend for themselves. Although the local need was obvious, Helen's suggestion was actually triggered by a story that appeared in the *Ladies' Home Journal,* a popular women's magazine of the day. The monthly had run a feature about the Perkins Nursery in Cleveland, underwritten by Cleveland relatives of the well-known Perkins family of Akron. That was not the only connection with the Akron Perkins family, which cast a shadow over King's Daughters at St. Paul's Episcopal Church. Mary Rawson Perkins, wife of industrialist George Perkins, had founded the St. Paul's circle; and daughter Mary Perkins Raymond, new bride of BFG executive Charles Raymond, became one of the charter members of the Akron Day Nursery.[33]

The daughters of many other prominent families were also charter members. Carita McEbright, just twenty-five and a new graduate of Cornell, was the daughter of one of Akron's leading physicians, Dr. Thomas McEbright. Julia McGregor, only twenty, was the daughter of iron manufacturer John McGregor. Sisters Julia and Mary Crouse, twenty-three and twenty respectively, were the daughters of mower-and-reaper entrepreneur George W. Crouse and his wife, Martha, a civic leader in her own right who became involved with this organization as well. Sisters Addie and Gertrude Commins, although still grieving the deaths of both their father, Alexander Commins, one of the owners of the "phenomenally successful" Akron Cereal Company, and their mother Addie, also became charter members of the Akron Day Nursery. Anna Ganter, only daughter of the longtime rector of St. Paul's Episcopal Church, the Reverend Richard L. Ganter, joined as well. Charter member Maude Watters, just twenty-two, was a daughter of mill owner Hiram Watters and his wife, Elizabeth. This was a family that encouraged daughters to make their own way in the world; Maude for a time worked as a teacher at Henry School. Lizzie Griffin was the daughter of Horace C. Griffin, a grocer in the Sixth Ward who was elected the Summit County sheriff. Alice Work, twenty-four, eldest daughter of Alanson Work, the superintendent of the Rubber Works, and his wife, Henrietta; and new bride Sadie McNeil Hitchcock, twenty-one-year-old daughter of the owner of McNeil Boiler Company, were among the twenty-four women who became the charter members of the Akron Day Nursery.[34]

Apart from their affiliation with the King's Daughters, these women had not made much of a mark for themselves in the charitable women's community of Akron. They did, however, come from families long involved in charitable organizations in the city. Thus, when these young women needed a place to house their nursery, they turned to the Union Charity Association, one of the key benevolent organizations in the city. The women of that charitable organization—many of them friends and relatives of the mothers of these day-nursery advocates—offered the young women two rooms in their headquarters. Ferdinand Schumacher's cereal mill donated food for the expected onslaught of youngsters, and the public donated clothing, beds, and other supplies. All the nursery needed was children—but Akron working parents did not rush to send their sons and daughters to this new day-care facility.

Part of the reason for the lack of enrollment may have been the rules of the day nursery. The nursery charter members adopted rules consistent with those in nurseries in other cities. Children had to be investigated before being admitted. (Board members, who were part of the "investigating committee," visited the home of every prospective student.) Mothers of the children had to work outside the home

Carita McEbright, a faculty member at Buchtel College, was a founding member and became an officer of the Mary Day Nursery. *Photo courtesy of the University of Akron Archives.*

Maude Watters (Milar) was only twenty-two when she became a founding member of the Mary Day Nursery, which is the base of today's Akron Children's Hospital. *Photo courtesy of Children's Hospital, Akron, Ohio.*

or work for wages within the home and not be able to adequately supervise their children. Parents had to pay for the nursery services—five cents a day for one child; twelve cents a day for three; fifteen cents a day for four or more. In addition, parents had to abide by the hours of the nursery—no child could come before 6:30 A.M. or remain after 7:00 P.M. No child with a contagious disease would be admitted to the nursery, nor would the nursery allow children from a home where a contagious disease existed. Finally, the matron was to see that each child was properly bathed and "neatly dressed." Children who were not adequately dressed were to change into clothing from the nursery's wardrobe. However, children were not allowed to wear those clothes home.[35]

It was a long three weeks before the first child, "Gentleman Carl" as he was affectionately called, enrolled in the day nursery. From this beginning, the nursery grew slowly; during the first year, the average attendance was only four children a day. The children got individual attention because two members of the day nursery group were on duty every day.

By 1891, the day nursery was ready for a new home, a new name, and a new organizational structure. Those changes came about because the nursery had a new patron—Col. George T. Perkins. With his wife Mary Rawson Perkins so closely associated with the King's Daughters and his daughter Mary Perkins Raymond so involved with the day nursery, it was only a matter of time before the new organization financially benefited from Colonel Perkins's generosity. By September 1891, the young women of the day nursery had proven their commitment to this new organization. The nursery, while not oversubscribed, was growing, and the rooms at the Union Charity Association headquarters no longer seemed suitable. A nursery run by the daughters of the very best families in the city deserved a more "homelike" environment. Accordingly, Colonel Perkins gave the group a house opposite the Court House on High Street. Here was the homelike environment, ideal for children separated from their parents for the day, and a more appropriate setting for young women running a thriving community organization.[36]

That donation brought about a chain of events that, in the end, assured the economic viability of the organization itself. The group formally incorporated as a "not-for-profit" group "to provide a day nursery for the care and maintenance of the children of men and women who are obliged to labor away from home during the day, and to acquire by donation or otherwise all necessary property and funds convenient therefore."[37] In the process, the nursery association formally withdrew from the King's Daughters and became an independent organization. Nonetheless, the women of the nursery did not leave the King's Daughters far behind. Any member of the Heart and Hand and Wayside circles of the King's Daughters, the groups that originally collaborated to create the day nursery, could join the new association. Any other woman could join as well, as long as she received the unanimous vote of the membership, according to the bylaws of the new organization. The nursery also got a new name, Mary Day Nursery, named for the granddaughter of donor Colonel Perkins and the daughter of charter member Mary Perkins Raymond.[38]

The new name, the new home, and the new incorporation did little to change the character of the women's organization itself. The Mary Day Nursery remained an organization of well-educated, young women from the best families in the city. As these women married and brought friends and relatives into the association, the membership aged, but the enthusiasm and creativity of the women did not abate, and the leadership of the Mary Day Nursery continued to read like a Who's Who of Akron. The population served remained the same as well. The children came from families of the laboring class. Some also came from single-parent households.[39]

By 1894, the charter members of the group began sharing leadership responsibilities with new members. That year, Mrs. William S. Chase was elected president; that election introduced the Seiberling family into the leadership of the organization. "Aunt Grace," as the Seiberling clan liked to call her, was the daughter of J. F. Seiberling, an affluent businessman in the city; sister of industrialists Frank and Charles Seiberling of Goodyear Tire and Rubber; and wife of Dr. William Sabin Chase, a physician who was one of the founders of People's Hospital (now Akron General Hospital). Like many other women associated with the Mary Day Nursery, Grace was just beginning her benevolent career. She would soon be a force in the city's YWCA and the Women's Guild of People's Hospital. At the time she was elected president of the Mary Day Nursery, Grace was only twenty-seven years old. She set an example for other Seiberling women to follow. In 1897, her older sister Harriet (Mrs. Lucius C. Miles), thirty-two, was elected vice president of the group. Harriet Miles, the wife of an executive at the Great Western Cereal Company, was more experienced than most of the leaders of the Mary Day Nursery in those early years. She had already helped to found a group that changed the cultural landscape of the city, the Tuesday Afternoon Club, an organization of young female musicians.[40]

Other young leaders of the Mary Day Nursery might not have been as well known as the Seiberlings, but they came from families long involved in the community. Buchtel College freshman Josephine Crumrine took over as secretary of the group in 1894. She was the daughter of Martin Houston Crumrine, owner of an "extensive" marble and granite works in Akron, and Olive Crumrine, who was a church and community leader. Josephine was a hands-on member of the nursery. She was part of the investigating committee that looked into conditions in the homes of children who attended the nursery. In 1897, Effie Work, twenty-three, younger sister of charter member Alice Work, stepped into the leadership of the Mary Day Nursery, initially as the secretary, and in the next two years as president of the organization.

These young leaders shared a certain pedigree: most were under thirty, all were affluent,[41] and most were just embarking on a career of benevolent work within the city. The Mary Day Nursery, then, served as a kind of training ground for this new generation of Akron clubwomen. They learned organizational techniques and honed their leadership skills. The nursery also became a kind of laboratory for new services to help the children in the city.

In 1893, for example, the Mary Day Nursery introduced Akron to the kindergarten movement that was spreading across the nation. Introduced in Germany in the 1820s and 1830s, the kindergarten movement was an outgrowth of Friedrich Froebel's view that every child was born with her/his full educational potential. What each child needed was the proper environment, a place where all children could learn through play. Building on Froebel's ideas, kindergarten became that place where all children could learn from each other in a specially crafted environment of "systematic play." Seen as especially helpful for children of poverty or special needs, kindergartens spread throughout Europe. In 1860, America got its first English-speaking kindergarten in Boston. Especially embraced by well-educated women reformers in the United States, kindergartens were often opened in conjunction with day nurseries, but they were not necessarily promoted by urban public schools. In 1892, kindergarten teachers organized their own professional association, the International Kindergarten Union (IKU), to promote early childhood education and "to elevate the standard of professional training." The next year, the organization presented a model kindergarten in the Women's Building at the Columbian Exposition in Chicago.[42]

The well-read, educated, young women of the Mary Day Nursery must have known of Froebel, the kindergarten movement, and the display at the Columbian Exposition. So it was not surprising that the women proposed a kindergarten for the Mary Day Nursery. The clientele of the nursery, sons and daughters of working-class parents, was considered the ideal population for Akron's first kindergarten. As one proponent explained,

> we must begin in the right way to educate the children of the very poor. We must pick up out of the swearing alleys and gutters of depraved neighborhoods the neglected, harshly treated, half-fed and half-clothed, unwashed and uncombed prattling child, whose greatest knowledge of language is of slang and profanity, cleanse it and cover it with wholesome garments; teach it how to play and how to talk and what truth is, and so, lovingly and carefully, plant the germ of good in its receptive mind, and fill its hopeful heart with happy dreams of doing something noble in the future that the results must be beneficial to a great degree to the race we are trying to save. It is a higher duty of society to prevent crime than to punish it. The one is ennobling and pleasant and the other harsh and deterrent.[43]

Although Akron reeled from the Panic of 1893, the women of the Mary Day Nursery went ahead with their kindergarten. This was an innovation that Akron could not afford to delay. It was soon clear that the nursery women had identified something that was sorely missing from the community; the biggest difficulties the women faced were getting the little students to the nursery—and finding the right teacher.[44]

The Akron kindergarten went through a series of teachers. At first, the association expected the nursery matron, Flora Hanchett, to handle the kindergarten in addition to all her other duties. As the nursery and the kindergarten grew, that became impractical. When the group added the "free" kindergarten in 1894, the women of the Mary Day Nursery hired Elinor Lathrop to handle the kindergarten, but it was not until Edith Barnum came on board that Akron got a kindergarten worthy of the Mary Day Nursery name.

Edith Barnum was a product of Lucy Wheelock's Kindergarten Training School in Boston. Once a kindergarten teacher herself, Lucy Wheelock, daughter of a New England minister and a descendant of John Adams, was a leader in the movement to promote the stature of kindergartens and to improve the professional training of their teachers. Her training school was one of the finest in the nation, and Lucy instilled an almost missionary spirit into each of her graduates. Certainly Edith Barnum embodied that spirit. Or, as one early organizer remembered, she "was a woman of warm heart, with a great sympathy for children and an understanding of the problems of childhood. In addition, she was a most unusual educator." Edith not only improved the quality of the kindergarten program at the Mary Day Nursery, she also educated the next generation of Akron kindergarten teachers in the Wheelock method. Further, she showed the Akron public schools that kindergartens were wanted—and needed.

Under Edith Barnum's direction, Mary Day Nursery's kindergarten flourished. The nursery and its kindergarten outgrew the home that Perkins had provided. In 1896, Perkins announced plans to build another home for the Mary Day Nursery and its kindergarten, one far grander than the house on South High Street, a place where the women of the nursery and their young charges would be comfortable for years.[45]

The new nursery opened in March 1897 in a flurry of celebration. It was a special day for the entire Perkins clan, as three generations participated in the ceremony. Young Mary Raymond, the namesake of the nursery, presented the deed and the key to her mother, Mary Perkins Raymond, president of the association. Benefactor Colonel George Perkins gave one of the speeches.[46]

Mary Day Nursery's kindergarten and Edith Barnum had a tremendous effect on the city's schools. For years, the Women's Council had pressured the schools to add kindergartens, but the Akron Board of Education had resisted. The successful kindergarten at the Mary Day Nursery forced the Akron Board of Education to rethink its position. The board of education challenged Edith Barnum and the nursery to set up an experimental free kindergarten in one of the worst neighborhoods in the city, Furnace Street at Bierce House. Mary Day Nursery provided the teachers, Edith Barnum supervised them, and the board of education provided the funding. After a year, the experiment was deemed a success, and the board of education opened kindergartens in the elementary schools and lowered the school age to allow younger children to attend.[47]

It was also a success for the women of the Mary Day Nursery, and yet it almost spelled disaster for the organization. By the early years of the twentieth century, enrollment at the nursery's kindergarten plummeted. Children were going to the kindergartens at the public schools instead. In June 1902, the executive board of the Mary Day Nursery voted to drop the kindergarten altogether.[48]

The nursery remained, and all the bills associated with the maintenance of the much larger facility had to be paid. Luckily, the women of the Mary Day Nursery had become masters in fund-raising. The women held a seemingly endless stream

Underwritten by a gift from Colonel George Perkins, this new home was built for the Mary Day Nursery and Kindergarten in 1896–1897. *Photo courtesy of Children's Hospital, Akron, Ohio.*

of linen sales, bazaars, and balls. The nursery held a special place in Akron's heart, and many of its fund-raisers became high points in the city's social season. Even schoolchildren helped support the organization. Once a year, schoolchildren brought in food to help the nursery. The campaign in 1902 was especially successful, the *Beacon Journal* reported: "The cellars of the Mary day nursery building are filled with big heaps of rosy cheeked apples, big new potatoes and great white cabbage heads, and the shelves of the pantries are loaded with hundreds of cans of jellies and numerous packages of cereals besides innumerable other articles which were donated to the institution by the children of the public schools." In 1904, the contributions were so plentiful that the *Beacon Journal* reported that the basement of the nursery looked "more like a commissary department of an army than the cellar of a charitable institution, for it would seem that there are provisions enough for a regiment stowed away there." There were so many contributions that the nursery shared its bounty with the families it served and other charitable organizations as well. All the city's schoolchildren gave and felt no undue sacrifice. The *Beacon Journal* applauded the children: "By this method of distribution no one charity, but all are benefited. There are several of the poorest families of the city taken care of by the Nursery, and these are kept supplied with provisions. . . . Many invalids are also looked after and to these the jellies, canned fruits and such articles will be given."[49]

The nursery could afford to serve as a charity warehouse because the closing of the kindergarten left a void within the association and the home. The question became what would take the kindergarten's place. Again the association turned to its members for ideas. This time, it was Alice Hill, forty-five, wife of business executive George R. Hill, who came up with the idea that energized the organization, transformed the nursery, and, eventually, redefined the organization altogether. In 1905, she suggested converting the kindergarten room into the Ward for Crippled Children.

Alice Hill's idea had a good deal of merit. No hospital in the city catered to the special health problems of children. Moreover, the proposed Ward for Crippled Children seemed to be a natural extension of the nursery's mission and was clearly within the domestic responsibilities of women generally. The idea also had merit because of the individual proposing it. Alice was a key member of the nursery organization. The wife of the president of American Vitrified Products, a sewer pipe manufacturer in Akron's Sixth Ward (Middlebury), Alice had a long history with the Mary Day Nursery. A member of St. Paul's Episcopal Church, she had been involved with the nursery since at least 1896, the same year she helped found Akron's branch of the Needlework Guild. The Hills had no children, so Alice filled her days with community work. She was on the nursery's board of trustees when the kindergarten closed, returned to the board when the ward opened, and remained there until her death in 1939. She also became an officer of the Woman's Exchange and affiliated with the Woman's Club League.[50]

Alice Hill's idea also tapped into nationwide trends. Women and women's organizations were starting children's hospitals in urban areas nationwide. Typical urban hospitals, including those in Akron, did not cater to children or their special medical problems. At a time when childhood mortality was so high (between 1850 and 1900 more than 25 percent of U.S. children died before their fifth birthday), hospitals for children were especially needed.[51]

Alice Hill did not suggest a full-fledged children's hospital. Her suggestion was more modest. She did not want to warehouse Akron's disabled children; instead the Ward for Crippled Children would help only those children who could be cured with proper medical care. Doctors from the new City Hospital would assume medical responsibility, but the ward would be located at the Mary Day Nursery in the large room vacated by the kindergarten.

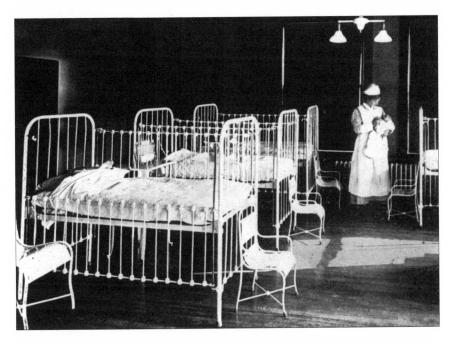

The Mary Day Nursery started its path toward creating a children's hospital in 1905 when it converted its kindergarten room into a Ward for Crippled Children, a natural progression of the nursery's mission. The idea had been suggested by Alice Hill, a community leader and longtime member of the organization. *Photo courtesy of Children's Hospital, Akron, Ohio.*

The nursery's executive board picked six doctors as the ward's first staff. Half of the doctors selected were husbands of old friends. Dr. William S. Chase was the husband of early officer Grace Seiberling Chase; Dr. James W. Rabe was the husband of Maud Rabe, a woman long active in the King's Daughters of the First Congregational Church; Dr. Harold H. Jacobs was married to the former Lizzie Griffin, a charter member of the day nursery and president of the organization when the ward was organized. Relying on husbands was not a matter of nepotism; it was a financial necessity. None of the physicians was paid for his work when the ward began.[52]

And so the women of the nursery had redefined themselves again. They had a new name, "Mary Day Nursery and Ward for Crippled Children," and new responsibilities—"the medical, surgical and hygienic treatment of . . . [children's] diseases, and to do anything necessary to further and carry out such object."[53] They relied on old patrons; Colonel George Perkins donated the $2,500 needed to transform the kindergarten room into a hospital ward. The women used old fund-raising techniques and added a few new ones: the women sold subscriptions for twenty-five dollars to buy children's beds, and a baseball game between the druggists and the doctors netted some good publicity, and money for the hospital.

The local newspaper, long an advocate of the nursery and the kindergarten, applauded the new direction and emphasized this would not duplicate efforts at the new city hospital:

> The Mary Day Nursery organization, which for the past 15 years has done a worthy work in caring for the children of mothers compelled to work for a living, will extend the work of the nursery in a direction much needed in this city.
>
> It has been decided to prepare a place for the care of injured and crippled children or those in need of surgical attention. As the city hospital has no children's ward[,] the work which will be undertaken by the nursery organization will be supplemental to that of the hospital.[54]

From its start, the Mary Day Nursery's Ward for Crippled Children assumed great importance in the medical care of the city and in the organization itself. From the beginning, Akron parents brought their injured and ailing children to the converted kindergarten room for treatment.[55]

The children came from a range of socioeconomic, religious, racial, and ethnic backgrounds. Like the nursery, the ward was open to all. Many of the children were from immigrant families who could ill afford to pay. An early patient, "Little Joey," was the son of immigrants who could not yet speak English. Afflicted with "tubercular knees," Joey had "never been well nourished," the *Beacon Journal* reported. "There were nine children in the family, all living in two rooms, including the mother and father, of course. Oh, yes, and they had one lodger." Joey and five other children slept together in one bed, "and his present condition is the result of being continually kicked." "Fair and Sweet Louis" suffered from the same malady as Joey, but his physical problems were caused by filth. The son of Hungarian immigrants, young Louis was found sleeping in a bed whose mattress was "rotted through."[56]

The ward introduced the nursery and its board to other medical shortcomings within the city. In 1909, the nursery announced plans to build a dispensary on its grounds and hire a visiting nurse. That nurse, Elsie H. Meade, a graduate of City Hospital's training school, followed up on cases of illnesses in the schools and educated the "poorer class" on caring for their sick children and improving the "sanitary conditions of the homes." Meade went into "the poorest sections [of Akron] and where children are found ill, administers the necessary care," the *Beacon* reported. Meade and the other visiting nurses also referred children to the ward for treatment.[57]

The nursery's new association with health care for children brought new prestige and opportunities for board members. Increasingly, the women of the nursery were appointed to health-related boards. Thus, when doctors formed an organization in 1909 to study city sanitation and the prevention of diseases, they selected five representatives from the Mary Day Nursery to serve on its board.

The ward, the dispensary, and the visiting nurse all came at a price, a price that the women of the nursery association found increasingly difficult to pay, no matter how adept they had become at fund-raising. As early as 1907, the nursery faced a deficit, the *Beacon* reported. The solution, the women felt, lay with the city. So in 1909 and 1910, the women of the nursery asked for financial help from Akron City Council. But that help did not come until 1911, when the city council agreed to fund two visiting nurses. The next year, the city's board of health took over supervision of the visiting nurses.[58]

That relieved the nursery/ward board of one of its responsibilities, just as it was facing another series of challenges. The Ward for Crippled Children had outgrown the kindergarten room. The women of the nursery needed to decide what to do next. Should the ward remain within the cramped kindergarten room or should the women expand their facility to a full-fledged hospital? With the support of one of their most important patrons, Colonel Perkins, the women decided on the latter and began planning for a new fifty-bed hospital wing in 1910. Perkins pledged $20,000 to $30,000 for the new venture, the estimated cost of the new addition, and the women quickly changed the name of their organization to the Mary Day Nursery and Children's Hospital.[59]

Although Mary Day Nursery was cited first in the name, the organization itself was putting much greater emphasis on the health-care portion of its mission. Nonetheless, the board never considered dropping the nursery, even though only five to seven children attended the nursery daily between 1910 and 1913. Instead, the board considered a plan to establish a branch nursery in south Akron and organized a new Babies Aid Society with members sewing for and visiting the children in the nursery. In her 1913–14 report, the secretary wrote, "It has been our endeavor not to lose sight of the importance of the Nursery work and the plans for the establishment of a Branch Nursery are already under way."[60]

Although enrollment in the nursery did increase after the group started advertising through the schools and the movies in 1916, the innovative programming of the organization was in health care, rather than day care. The centerpiece was, of course, the new hospital wing that opened in December 1911. The hospital had everything that the city's ailing children needed—an operating room ("one of the best in the city," the newspaper reported), an infant's department, and beautifully kept, clean rooms. Soon there was a x-ray machine, an isolation ward, expensive private rooms for children from affluent families, an eye clinic, and a training program for nurses.[61]

The outreach programs built upon the health-care mission. In 1916, partnering with the Women's Council, the Babies Aid Society began offering workshops on children's health. Mothers from across the city were taught new methods of caring for ill children and the basics of good hygiene.[62]

The hospital wing became an integral part of the city's medical picture. As the only location where children were treated, the occupancy rate was high and the number of operations increased dramatically. Just five years after it opened, the hospital needed more room and the day nursery moved to other quarters, closer to the "center of employment" on Locust Street.[63]

The outfitting of the new nursery, the conversion of the old nursery to a hospital, and the changes to the existing hospital wing came at a high price. Although the city began underwriting the hospital for the charity cases (the largest number of patients in the hospital), the women were facing new financial problems. As the 1920s dawned, the women of the Mary Day Nursery and Children's Hospital were managing one of the key health-care institutions in the city. Moreover, the group was doing it without the support of its two major financial patrons; as both Colonel and Mrs. Perkins had died. Nonetheless, the women leaders of the organization seemed up to the task. They had learned how to stage enormously successful fundraising events, to plan and carry out subscription and membership campaigns, and to arrange for donations from both major benefactors and small ones like the schoolchildren in the city. The women leaders of the nursery/hospital did it all while informing the public of their successes, keeping the newspapers on their side, and crafting a positive image to the city's population. The women leaders of the nursery/hospital were not just public relations experts; they had also learned other important skills. They were negotiating contracts with the city and hiring personnel. They were also deciding the direction of health care for the children in the city, as well as gaining enormous power for themselves through their appointments to the various health boards in the city.

The young women from the King's Daughters of the Episcopal and Congregational churches had grown up, and so had their organization. By 1925, the Mary Day Nursery and Children's Hospital and its auxiliary Babies Aid Society were among the largest women's volunteer associations in the city. Hundreds of Akron women joined the associations—and not all were debutantes. Many were middle-class women introduced to the cause by innovative public relations and fund-raising campaigns, especially those involving the students in the city's public schools. There was little criticism of these women, the nursery, or the hospital. The Mary Day Nursery, the kindergarten, the Ward for Crippled Children, and the Children's Hospital were the darlings of the city's newspapers, the churches, the schools, and the community. Whether the women were middle-class volunteers or leaders from elite families, they all shared a common concern for the health and well-being of children, a core element of domesticity and domestic feminism. Here was one organization that seemed to flawlessly span class and religious differences to help ailing children. In the process, the women changed the face of medical care in the city and gained power and prestige for themselves.

During the first twenty-five years of the twentieth century, thousands of women got involved with clubs and organizations through their churches or with groups that had their roots within Protestant denominations of the city. Many women gathered at their churches to repair the linen or clean the vestry as they exchanged pleasantries. More investigated cases of want and helped the destitute and ailing and their families through hard times, even as they formed lasting friendships with their benevolent compatriots. Many were beginning their benevolent careers; more were experienced, well-trained clubwomen assisting a new generation, who were venturing into their community responsibilities.

As vibrant and innovative as many of these organizations were, however, they paled in comparison to the secular women's clubs of the day. It was the secular women's organizations that took the lead in early twentieth-century Akron.

Chapter 6

Secularly-based Women's Clubs in Twentieth-Century Akron

Keep us, O God, from pettiness; let us be large in thought, in word, in deed.

Let us be done with fault-finding and leave off self-serving.

May we put away all pretenses and meet each other face to face without self-pity, and without prejudice.

May we never be hasty in judgment and always generous.

Teach us to put into action our better impulses, straight-forward and unafraid.

Let us take time for all things; make us grow calm, serene, and gentle.

Grant that we may realize it is the little things that create differences; that in the big things of life we are as one.

And may we strive to touch and know the great common woman's heart of us all;

And O, Lord God, let us not forget to be kind.

—"Akron and Summit County Federation of Women's Clubs, 1924-1925."[1]

SECULAR WOMEN'S GROUPS HAD A LONG HISTORY IN THE CITY. DURING the first twenty-five years of the twentieth century, these groups came to the fore. They took the lead in the city's "municipal housekeeping" movement and brought much-needed reforms to the city. Again building on the rhetoric of domesticity,

Akron women worked through their secular organizations to improve the social, economic, political, and environmental conditions within the city.

Some of these secular organizations had deep roots in Akron. The Woman's Christian Temperance Union grew out of the great temperance crusade of 1874, although the group was missing much of its reform zeal by the early twentieth century. The Women's Council, a federation of women's clubs, never lacked energy as it grasped the "municipal housekeeping" banner, harnessed the power of dozens of woman's organizations and hundreds of individual members, pushed for reforms to help women, the family, and the city, and, in the process, became a force to be reckoned with. Other groups evolved to meet the challenges of the new century. The Tuesday Afternoon Club started its life with a limited vision, self-improvement for its socialite members, but grew into the musical heart of the city.

A new generation of women's organizations also debuted. The Woman's Exchange, an experiment in philanthropic capitalism, offered a new model of benevolence, a store that sold the finest handiwork by women down on their luck. Akron finally got its Young Women's Christian Association (YWCA), an organization that brought enormous energy to the women's community. The new association had a wide-ranging constituency—from the daughters and mothers of the most affluent families in the city to female employees laboring in the factories and mills, from women starting their business careers in stores and offices to immigrant families just learning American ways.

These women's clubs and organizations of the new century had enormous confidence and optimism that they could cure what ailed the city. They were well positioned to carry through. Mature Akron women built on decades of organizational experience; young women brought exuberance and energy. The women's clubs of the new century adopted new strategies, built new alliances, aimed high, and accomplished much. It was a grand new day for women's organizations in Akron.

TUESDAY AFTERNOON CLUB

While the Mary Day Nursery was creating a health-care institution, another group of women from the same age group and socioeconomic class were about to bring lasting cultural changes to the city. Of course, that was not on the agenda when a dozen young women met to talk about their shared interest in music at the home of Celia Wright Ashmun Baker one Tuesday afternoon in November 1887.

Much as the Mary Day Nursery organization had evolved, so, too, did the Tuesday Afternoon Club. The club shifted from a small, inner-directed organization of affluent young women interested in perfecting their own musical skills and showing off their talents to family and friends to a cultural organization with hundreds of active and associate members who gave public recitals and brought well-known musicians from across the world to Akron. That transition took a mere ten years to achieve. Five years later, the organization was on the brink of financial ruin and needed to redefine itself again to survive. In each transition, women leaders brought the organization to enormous success, then, on the brink of disaster, repositioned the group to survive another century.

Of course, the dozen women were not thinking of the challenges ahead. They were just interested in an afternoon of socializing around music. All probably knew each other because of their interest in music and because of their families. The largest number of these women had fathers or husbands engaged in business and manufacturing endeavors. Two were related by marriage—twenty-two-year-old Harriet Seiberling Miles, wife of the young milling executive Lucius Miles, and honorary charter member twenty-eight-year-old Gertrude Penfield Seiberling, new bride of Frank Seiberling, the founder of Goodyear Tire and Rubber.[2]

Frances Robinson, only twenty-three, was the daughter of the founder of Robinson Clay Products Company. She would soon marry Frank Adams, who would make a name for himself in banking. Frank was the brother of another Tuesday Afternoon Club charter member, Zella Adams. Zella and Frank were the children of the president of Akron's waterworks.

Sarah Motz, daughter of the popular life and fire insurance agent Henry Motz, was only twenty-two. Two years later, she married John H. McCrum, who became an executive at Akron Varnish Company. Sybil Caskey, twenty-six, was the daughter of restaurant owner J. G. Caskey. She was listed as a musician in the 1880 census.

The hostess that afternoon, Celia Baker, had her own ties to business. She was married to physician George Baker, who became the president of Akron Electric Light and Power.[3]

Of course, musical ability was not limited to the families of manufacturing moguls. L. Ione Edgerton, twenty-three, was the daughter of attorney Sidney Edgerton and his wife, Mary. Her father had made quite a name for himself politically. After he moved west, he was appointed U.S. judge for the Idaho Territory and became the governor of the Montana Territory. Her mother, another strong character, penned a series of letters from the Montana frontier that became the

Celia Baker hosted the first meeting of the Tuesday Afternoon
Club (now the Tuesday Musical Club) and became the director
of the women's chorus. She was described by the *Beacon Journal* as
"a musician of deep intellectual ability." *Photo courtesy of the Tuesday
Musical Club, Akron.*

book *A Governor's Wife on the Mining Frontier: The Letters of Mary Edgerton from Montana.*[4]
Returning to Akron after their sojourn in the west, the Edgerton family especially
encouraged their daughters. Older sister Pauline became chief administrative officer
for Akron's Public Library. Ione had a career as a music teacher.

Newlywed Jessica Otis, twenty-three, was a new arrival to the city when she
joined the others that Tuesday afternoon. Born in Springfield, not far from Akron,
the former Jessica Wolfe was the daughter of a druggist. A well-known vocalist,

Jessie attended Oberlin College, where she met her husband, Edward, an immigrant from Wittenberg and an aspiring attorney. Although she was a newcomer to the city, she probably already knew Celia Baker, her neighbor on East Market Street, and the Seiberling women, who went to the same church she attended, Trinity Lutheran.[5]

These charter members had few affiliations beyond the Tuesday Afternoon Club in the 1880s, although several later became involved with the Mary Day Nursery, church organizations, and other civic groups.

In the late 1880s and 1890s, the Tuesday Afternoon Club became *the* organization for affluent Akron women with musical talent. In 1888, the club was large enough to organize a women's chorus, thirty strong, under the direction of Celia Baker, "a musician of deep intellectual ability," the *Beacon Journal* observed.[6] But the chorus never tried public concerts. The women were content with their inner-directed mission of improving their own personal musical skills and entertaining friends and relatives in private homes. Two years later, when Celia and her family moved to Denver, the baton passed to Professor Gustave Sigel, a local music teacher, and then to Professor N. L. Glover, another music instructor in the city. Both continued the limited mission of the club.

The club languished under the musical direction of the men. Only a few women frequented the weekly meetings, which had degenerated to little more than an opportunity to do fancy work while someone read aloud about music. In 1890, the group got an injection of fresh energy when Anna Berry, daughter of George C. Berry, one of the leading merchants in the city, and Isabella Berry, the WCTU and Women's Council leader, grabbed the baton and took over the group. Anna Berry, just twenty-three, burned with excitement about music. She had just returned from the Boston Conservatory of Music and was ready to introduce some new programming into the club's repertoire. Anna inaugurated composer day, which succeeded in piquing the interest of the musically talented women in the city again.[7] She spent only a season at the podium with the Tuesday Afternoon Club, and then she was off to the next stage of her life, as Mrs. Ralph Templeton of Lynbrook, New York. Luckily, the baton passed to Helen Storer, who had a vision for the group that few could have imagined when the group was formed in 1887. Helen was a woman of enormous creativity, drive, and commitment to community. Just two years before, she had pointed out to the King's Daughters of the Episcopal and Congregational churches the need for a day nursery for the mothers working in the factories of the city. It was that suggestion that led to the creation of the Mary Day Nursery.

This time Helen Storer was going to redefine and reorganize the Tuesday Afternoon Club and transform it into a cultural institution that would benefit the city. Few members dared disagree with young Helen. After all, she brought the perfect pedigree to the Tuesday Afternoon Club. Not only was she from a family with excellent business, political, and charitable connections within the city—her father James was a wounded Civil War veteran, business owner, and postmaster of the city; her mother, the former Maria Ackley, was a community organizer—but Helen also had impeccable musical credentials. She was just returned from the Wellesley School of Music in Boston.

It was Helen Storer's ability, talent, and vision that saved the organization. As one reporter observed, "Possessing both musical and business ability, an unusual combination, but one much needed for the successful conduct of such an organization, it remained for this active woman [Helen Storer] to keep the club in working order. The chorus grew in number 50 members in the following four years."[8]

Helen Storer also started an aggressive recruitment campaign among the musically talented, affluent women in the city. Women had to audition to win a place among the active members of the organization—and the chorus. Being part of the Tuesday Afternoon Club became a status symbol for cultured women in the city. Some of the new members were also involved in the Mary Day Nursery—Edith Barnum, the kindergarten teacher, Mary and Alvaretta Crouse, Mary Manton (another Seiberling sister), Mary Miller, and Julia Upson, to name but a few. Other members would go on to make their mark in the Women's City Club, the College Club, the YWCA, and a variety of literary groups. A few even got involved in the suffrage organization, but most avoided the WCTU.[9]

Building up the membership was only one part of Helen Storer's plan. From her perspective, the club could no longer be insulated from the public. Concerts had to be open to the public for the betterment of the members, the club, and the city. Four months after she took over as "directress" of the group, the newly reinstituted chorus performed in public for the first time. That concert was so popular, the *Beacon and Republican* reported, that Helen and the club created a new category of membership, the associate members, who had a deep interest in music and would, through their dues and ticket purchases, underwrite an ambitious new concert series that debuted in 1892.

That first series of concerts became the model for the club. There were to be five or six concerts, two held by the women's chorus and "home singers" and the others by artists from other locales. The first year, the Tuesday Afternoon Club brought in musicians from Chicago, Cincinnati, and New York. Associate members bought season tickets for $2.50, a reasonable price for the day. Ticket sales did not just rely on the associate members; in 1895 the *Beacon* reported that the audience exceeded one thousand, far greater than the number of associate members.[10]

Every season brought innovations and successes. The 1894 season was so successful that, in spite of extra expenses, the club donated one hundred dollars to the Union Charity. In 1895, the women's chorus teamed with the "ladies of the Buchtel College Glee club and other Akron ladies" to accompany the nationally known Theodore Thomas and his Chicago orchestra. Later that season, the club reported the largest number of season ticket sales in its history. The group planned to use profits to help underwrite scholarships for "the musical training of some Akron student having artistic possibilities."[11]

Heady with their success, in 1898 the members of the Tuesday Afternoon Club voted to change their provincial name to the Tuesday Musical Club. But this was more than a simple name change: a new constitution and bylaws changed the character of the organization, and men were allowed to join. There would be two sections to this new organization: the study section, "the same as the Tuesday Afternoon club formerly was," the *Beacon* reported, and a mixed chorus of men and women. Helen Storer remained directress of the chorus; women were to hold all the general offices of the new group for two years, so that "the club will have the guidance of the minds that have directed it before and placed the name of the Tuesday Afternoon club so high upon the list of musical organizations," the *Beacon* reported.[12]

Nonetheless, there were problems ahead for the Tuesday Musical Club. In 1901, Helen Storer married and left the organization.[13] A progression of chorus directors followed. Longtime member Katherine Parson served a year. The chorus was then left in the hands of men. Charles Clemens was brought in from Cleveland. Trained in the best German schools, Clemens was expected to bring a new standard of excellence to the chorus—and, as a consequence, more members to the group, the *Beacon Journal* predicted.

He did neither. Instead, new policies almost destroyed the organization. Ticket sales, long the responsibility of club members, were turned over to a professional agent. That was a disaster. As one member reported in the *Beacon Journal*, the agent never garnered the support of patrons, who wanted to buy their tickets from enthusiastic club members who displayed "personal interest" and "pride in the success of a local institution," not from a professional salesman.[14]

The difficulties in the Tuesday Musical Club ran deeper than a shift in subscription policies. The departure of Helen Storer, with her vision, energy, creativity, and optimism, wounded the Tuesday Musical Club deeply. The organization did not have a large reservoir of potential leaders who could keep the members committed. Few women wanted to take the leadership roles that just five years before had carried so much prestige. Former officers, including Gertrude Seiberling, refused to take on the responsibility of redefining and reorganizing the floundering organization. Without strong leadership, many members thought the group was finished and should disband. "To make no effort to resuscitate the dying cause, to let it die, and give it a decent burial!" Others, while discouraged by the low attendance at concerts and demoralized by the lack of strong, creative leadership, were not ready to give up on the group yet. Too much was at stake, including the vitality of classical music in the city. As a member observed, "What the loss would mean not only to the devoted few, but to the growth of music in Akron seemed too great."[15]

And so the women, who still had hope that the club might be revived, organized a committee and sent Gertrude Seiberling to the convention of the National Federation of Musical Clubs for some fresh ideas. There she discovered that many musical organizations across the nation were facing a similar malaise. Each dealt with it in a different manner, but the solution that Gertrude preferred was to expand the organization beyond its core of affluent, albeit talented, women. The club needed to reach out to the "byways and hedges . . . and seek those who come to our feast of music," she insisted.[16]

The committee was not entirely convinced. Nonetheless, Gertrude Seiberling volunteered to recruit a chorus of two hundred, a "people's chorus," she called it, if the committee could find someone to take over the presidency of the group. The committee looked around and thought the best candidate for the job was Minnetta Riggs, a woman known for her "executive ability." Minnetta may have honed her administrative skills in her husband's business. Spillman Riggs was the general manager of the Central Lyceum Bureau. There was a stumbling block, however. Minnetta was no longer a member of the organization. The committee persuaded her to renew her membership and run for president. Soon the committee had an entire slate that included longtime members such as charter member L. Ione Edgerton, who agreed to serve as secretary of the study section, and relative newcomers like Esther Siegrist, wife of the treasurer of the Swinehart Clincher Tire and Rubber, who volunteered to be treasurer. The new leadership committed to

Gertrude's plan and soon got excited. "The enthusiasm caught on like wild fire," the *Beacon Journal* observed. Minnetta Riggs lived up to her reputation for "executive ability" and organized a committee to solicit concert ticket sales. Gertrude got started with a publicity campaign to attract new members with musical talents from across the city. The Tuesday Musical Club had been redefined again.[17]

Gertrude Seiberling's publicity campaign did its job. Placards went up everywhere, from churches to factories. The headline, "A People's Chorus to be Organized by the Tuesday Musical Club," screamed for members. For a mere two-dollar annual dues, anyone with an interest in music and a modicum of talent could join the new chorus and work with Professor George Whitefield Andrews, director of the Musical Union at Oberlin. In addition, all members could attend the club's concerts free of charge—although the placards never revealed how many concerts would actually be staged. The $2 fee meant that the chorus was not exactly a "people's chorus." The fee effectively kept musically talented laboring-class individuals out. The poster also failed to mention the admission exam, which was still required for anyone who wanted to join the chorus. The exam, however, had been redrafted to make it easier to pass.[18] By December 1903, the club had a chorus of two hundred, "a people's chorus composed of anyone who can sing at all, read at all, or who loves music," the *Beacon Journal* reported. The new chorus rehearsed every week in preparation for a grand concert at the German American Hall in the spring. In December, the German men's choir Liedertafel agreed to join the chorus for the performance.[19]

The chorus was only one part of reinvigorating the Tuesday Musical Club. The club started an afternoon educational class as well. The "ladies" of the afternoon session were to study music, following the National Federation of Musical Clubs' two-year program. In addition, the women would conduct a "short musical program" at each of the meetings. Those afternoon sessions proved popular. The *Beacon Journal* observed that the Tuesday Musical Club was back on track. Applications for active and associate memberships were rolling in. "The club is succeeding even better than those who organized it had hoped for, and it promises to become one of the finest musical organizations in the state in an incredibly short time," the *Beacon Journal* boasted.

The newspaper was also pleased with the new, more democratic nature of the Tuesday Musical Club. "The work of the club heretofore has been rather exclusive and self-centered, but it will be the aim from now on to do work in the hospitals, the county home and the children's home, to bring pleasure to those who have no other opportunities of hearing good music."[20] The reorganized club had scored a public relations, community, and organizational victory. Or had it?

At the end of its first season as a reorganized group, the Tuesday Musical Club seemed to be on a strong financial footing. The group reported that, after paying all expenses, the club had $250 left. The *Beacon Journal* thought that laudable: "Considering the enormous expense of reorganizing and scuring [*sic*] the artists for the two concerts, this is a splendid report."[21] The club also had ambitious plans for the next year. Instead of just two concerts with the new people's chorus, there would be four, including one featuring the Cincinnati Symphony.[22] As it turned out, the reorganized club simply was not ready financially to return to business as usual.

By the end of 1905, the club was in trouble again, but this time the *Beacon Journal* came to its assistance in a campaign to raise money and save the organization. The front-page banner headline, "DON'T LET THE TUESDAY MUSICAL CLUB GIVE UP ITS CONCERTS," urged the reading public to help raise the $1,000 needed for the organization to survive. The group was too important to the cultural life of the city to die, the *Beacon Journal* argued. Moreover, a letter writer emphasized that the club had come too far to fail. "It fails not because the excellence of the musical talent has retrograded, but, on the contrary, each year has added new and splendid talent to its membership, drawn to Akron because of the musical opportunities the club offered. It is a pity that the fruit of such earnest labor is not allowed to ripen for lack of the sunshine of public spirit."[23]

A competing paper, the *Times-Democrat*, was not sure if the organization deserved to survive. Yes, the newspaper admitted, the Tuesday Musical Club had expanded its membership into groups heretofore excluded, but the organization had not welcomed those new members. According to a source purported to be a member of the group, classism reigned in the group. New members who worked for a living were not treated with civility. The *Beacon Journal*, however, branded the charges ridiculous. The club was "the best and most representative organization [that] can be gotten together in Akron now." The Tuesday Musical Club soon raised the money it needed to survive.[24]

Stabilized by that infusion of funds and later by a bequest from a longtime member,[25] the Tuesday Musical Club carried on. It did make some concessions to its critics. Membership dues went down. "This was done because of the good voices that were kept out of the chorus through singers being unable to pay . . . high dues," the *Beacon Journal* reported. The group also became more conservative in its fiscal practices. It retained the moderately priced evening concert series and added more frequent, but less expensive, concerts in the afternoon. Moreover, it no longer had problems finding women to assume the leadership roles in the group.[26]

Nor was the organization lacking in members. In 1910, the *Beacon Journal* marveled at the range of ages of the women in the study (afternoon) group. "It is an interesting body of women, who, from the young girl just taking courage from the first fruits of successful study, to the mature woman whose many years of work in music have broadened her sympathy and appreciation for all lovers of art, one and all are working hand and heart together for the success of the organization, musically as well as financially."[27]

The reorganization heralded a new cultural day for the city. On sounder financial footing, the club arranged for performances from dancers like Anna Pavlova, "one of the world's greatest dancers," to orchestras and smaller ensembles designed to draw an audience with an appreciation for classical music.[28]

The Tuesday Afternoon Club and the Tuesday Musical Club illustrated how secular women's clubs could and did make important contributions to the cultural life of the city. By offering inexpensive yet relatively high-quality classical music concerts, the club enriched the cultural life of a city better known for its industry than for its appreciation of the arts. But the Tuesday Musical Club afforded other lessons as well. It represented yet another example of how women's clubs evolved to survive; how strong women with a vision quite different from the original mission of the group forced changes; how an organization could flounder without the direction of strong, talented women with executive abilities. The women who led the Tuesday Musical Club were not professionally trained to run an arts organization. They learned the public relations, publicity, scheduling, budgeting, organizational, and executive skills on the job, so to speak.

But the story is not only about the concerts and the lessons the women learned. It is also about women who had difficulty reaching beyond their socioeconomic class. When the group first started, the affluent charter members aspired only to improve their own musical abilities and entertain a close circle of family and friends. That limited vision allowed a certain measure of personal growth but brought no cultural enrichment to those outside the members' narrow circle—and might explain why the club so quickly stagnated. The public concerts, the enthusiasm, and the gratitude of the audience and at least one newspaper allowed the group to grow and thrive again. The public presence did not necessarily bring diversity of class, race, and ethnicity to the organization itself. It was only when the organization faced yet another crisis that another strong woman, Gertrude Penfield Seiberling, offered another alternative, a "People's Chorus," that promised to break down class and ethnic lines. That promise was never fulfilled, according to the *Times-Democrat*, which reported class tensions within the group's ranks.

Achieving even a modicum of economic diversity—much less racial and ethnic variety—remained a challenge for women's clubs of Akron during that period. With the exception of the women's clubs affiliated with religious denominations (faith sometimes broke down ethnic and class divisions), Akron women preferred to join groups with like-minded individuals, neighbors, or relatives, who shared their socioeconomic class.

Two women's groups—the Woman's Exchange and the Young Women's Christian Association—tried to break that mold and form partnerships that cut across class lines. But, from the very beginning, there was a power imbalance. The organizers—affluent women—thought they knew best and imposed class-based, traditional values on working-class women. For the Woman's Exchange, that meant an experiment in retailing that would be relatively short-lived. In contrast, the YWCA weathered often public and very messy class, race, and ethnic-based difficulties and, in the end, brought needed services to all the women—but especially the workingwomen—in the city.

THE WOMAN'S EXCHANGE

The Woman's Exchange of Akron started with a simple and benevolent, albeit capitalistic idea: it offered a place where talented, needy women could sell their handiwork and affluent women from around the city would come and shop. The Woman's Exchange was a place where women of means purchased the finest quality handiwork and helped women in need, women who received only a pittance for their wares at the department stores and clothiers of the city.

In starting the Woman's Exchange, the women of Akron were joining a nationwide trend that dated back to 1832 in Philadelphia. That "Women's Depository" sold the handiwork of the "genteel poor"—women who had fallen on hard times—on commission. Thus, the women who sold their products at the depository made considerably more than the low piecerates offered by the retail establishments of the day. By the end of the nineteenth century, the Woman's Exchange movement had spread throughout the United States. By 1891, there were at least seventy-two exchanges across the nation, including three in Ohio. All operated in a similar manner—affluent women in search of the finest quality handiwork purchased what they needed at the exchange and needy women received the purchase price, less a commission to support the store.[29]

Akron came to the Woman's Exchange movement relatively late. Columbus, Cincinnati, Cleveland, Toledo, and Canton already had exchanges. In November 1903, two young, single women, apparently working on their own, opened a Woman's Exchange at 141 South Main Street, not far from O'Neil's Department Store and J. Koch clothiers, and virtually next door to one of the city's newspapers, the *Akron Beacon Journal.* The two, identified solely as Miss Owen and Miss Stratton in newspaper reports, were probably Fanny Owen and Alice Stratton, both of whom roomed with the widow Alice Daugherty at 175 West Market Street. Neither listed an occupation in the city directory of the year.[30]

Although these two started with the best of intentions, they did not have the organizational support structure needed to continue the Woman's Exchange. In spring 1904, benevolent matrons in the city met at Grace House, the home of the Union Charity, to determine how best to salvage the struggling enterprise. With the advice of the manager of the Canton Exchange, about sixty Akron women, most with long experience in benevolent organizations, decided to purchase the exchange and administer it. Neither Owen nor Stratton remained with the exchange after the acquisition.

The reorganized Woman's Exchange selected some of the most experienced benevolent women in the city as its leaders. Henrietta Work, fifty-eight, widow of Alanson Work, the former superintendent of the Akron Rubber Works and vice president of B. F. Goodrich, agreed to take on the responsibility of president. She was well-suited to the task. An experienced organizer/administrator with ties throughout the benevolent community, Henrietta Work, better known as Etta to family and friends, had been active in a range of organizations, from the WCTU, where she was a member of the finance committee, to the Women's Council, where she served as treasurer. Etta had been a board member of the YWCA and president of the New Century Club. Taking over as Woman's Exchange vice presidents were Grace T. Marvin, wife of attorney and BFG executive Richard P. Marvin and one of the organizers of the Sumner Home for the Aged and the Akron Needlework Guild, and Alice Hill, who had come up with the idea of a Ward for Crippled Children for the Mary Day Nursery. Newcomers to the benevolent community Caroline E. Bliss and Eleanor Francis served as secretary and treasurer, respectively.

Most of the forty members of the board of managers were wealthy matrons with a long history of benevolent work in Akron. Emma L. Alden, forty-seven, wife of the president of Alden Rubber, had been active in the Mary Day Nursery, the New Century Club, and the King's Daughters at the First Congregational Church. Nellie Bruner, forty-three, wife of the president of First Second Bank, was especially busy in 1904. Not only was she on the board of the exchange but she was also the president of the New Century Club and that organization's representative to the Women's Council. Her daughter Julia (Mrs. E. D. Andrews) also served on the board of the Woman's Exchange. Huldah Jacobs, fifty-nine, wife of a prominent physician, was active with the Board of Charities and the Buckley Women's Relief Corps in the 1880s and the Mary Day Nursery in the 1890s and after. Carita McEbright was among the youngest of the group. Only thirty-nine, McEbright had a long history in the benevolent community. She was one of the founders of the Mary Day Nursery, the Akron Needlework Guild, and the Little Theatre movement in Akron. Anna Miller brought the Seiberling family connection to the Woman's Exchange board. The daughter of J. F. Seiberling and the sister of the founders of Goodyear, Anna was married to the superintendent of Kelly-Springfield Tire. Robinson family ties also ran deep in the Woman's Exchange. May Robinson, wife of the president of Robinson Clay Products, and her sister-in-law Frances Adams both served on the board. Frances, forty-four, a longtime benevolent worker, brought her experience with the Tuesday Musical Club to the Woman's Exchange; May was most involved in the YWCA.[31]

Absent from the board—and from any other decision-making input—were the "needy" women the Woman's Exchange was designed to serve.

The new exchange served two groups of women—"those who can make and wish to dispose of all sorts and kinds of woman's handicraft, but cannot leave their homes to do it" (the women excluded from leadership) "and those who wish to purchase all such articles" (the affluent women who held all the positions of power within the organization).[32]

And so these women took over the exchange. They relied on one full-time employee, a "custodian," a title that lacked the prestige of "manager," the term most commonly used in exchanges across the country. Mrs. A. W. Wilcox handled the day-to-day running of the exchange for the first two years. Then the job was turned over to young, unmarried women, L. K. Thompson for one year and C. Annette Brownlees for the years that followed.[33]

The Woman's Exchange had many advantages within the city. It was widely applauded by the *Beacon Journal*, which was edited by the husband of one of the exchange's board members. It had close ties to a number of Protestant churches that provided cakes, pies, and breads for the new exchange restaurant. It had an ideal location, close to shops and not too far removed from residential areas. The organization gave up that location in 1912 when it moved to the basement of the Second National Bank at 157 South Main Street, just one block up. That might have been a cost-cutting move, since the group no doubt got preferential rental rates. After all, the president of the bank was married to a board member.

By 1912, women in Akron who needed to work were finding many more opportunities in the city—in the rubber factories, in department stores, in offices, and in households. In addition, opportunities for women in the sewing trades, working within the home, were also on the upswing at the clothiers and department stores at guaranteed, albeit low, piecerates, rather than money sent only when an item sold. In the 1920s, when the city faced yet another economic downturn, employment opportunities shrank. The Woman's Exchange could not deal with the reverses and closed.[34]

The Woman's Exchange was not the first attempt in the city to help working-women. In antebellum days, Akron women used economic pressure to wrestle higher piecerates from clothiers and tailors for all the sewing women in the city. The Woman's Exchange, however, was different. This experiment in retailing was never designed to assist the typical sewing woman in the city; it reached out to only the most-skilled, better class of women able to produce the finest handiwork, the products affluent women wanted.

How many women actually benefited from Akron's Woman's Exchange will never be known.[35] Early reports indicated that the exchange did not receive "the patronage it deserve[d]," according to the *Beacon Journal*; but the store grew into a place where affluent women shopped. By 1905, business was up and amounts sent to the women providing the handiwork "far exceeded all expectations."[36] But there were problems built into this model of philanthropy. Paydays and pay amounts were uncertain. Women were paid only when—and if—their handiwork was sold. At best, the exchange served as a source of supplemental income, certainly not as the main source of support for a family. The department stores, the clothiers, and the tailors afforded the regular, consistent income that women needed to support themselves and their families.

Moreover, this form of benevolence was especially affected by economic down-turns in the city. When business was bad generally, sales plummeted. That meant that in the early 1920s, when the city reeled from production cutbacks and men and women were thrown out of their jobs, at the very time when more women needed to sell their handiwork, the exchange could not withstand the pressure and closed.

For its brief life, the Akron Woman's Exchange provided a new model of phi-lanthropy built on capitalistic principles; it also provided needed pay for a limited number of women. But the power structure within this organization was always in the hands of the affluent; the women down on their luck had no role to play in the management, financial policies, or the direction of the exchange. Far more working-women were assisted by another organization in the city—the Young Women's Christian Association. The group opened no store. The affluent women who ran the YWCA had other things in mind for the workingwomen in the city.

YOUNG WOMEN'S CHRISTIAN ASSOCIATION

Akron came late to the YWCA movement. Started in London in 1855, the YWCA spread quickly throughout the United States after the Civil War. Ohio kept pace. Well before the turn of the century, every major city in the state—Cincinnati, Cleveland, Dayton—and even some small towns had their own chapters. Yet Akron was an ideal location for an organization pledged to "labor for the temporal, moral and religious welfare of young women dependent on their exertions for support." The city was the home of a co-ed college, a growing pool of employed women, and community activists with an interest in helping workingwomen. Those com-munity activists got a boost when, in early 1900, the powerful Women's Council, a federation of women's organizations across the city, pledged to agitate for a local chapter of the YWCA for Akron.[37]

The Women's Council did not have to agitate for long. Calista Willard Wheeler, a longtime club leader, was going to make the YWCA a reality for Akron. The wife of an executive at Citizens' National Bank, she had witnessed the benefits of the YWCA firsthand. Her daughters, Jane and Ruth, had joined the organization when they attended Hiram College in Hiram, Ohio. Calista, who had already or-ganized the Young Women's Missionary Association of the First Disciples Church, thought that Akron and its employed women would benefit from a YWCA, so she called some choice friends, representing a range of Protestant denominations, to her home in November 1900 to talk about organizing a YWCA. Also present was Helen Barnes, national secretary of the YWCA, and Nellie Adams Lowry, secretary of the Ohio state organization. With the advice of those professional organizers, these friends set about finding out how many women might be interested in joining the YWCA. They passed out pledge cards and canvassed for potential members. The group also set out to determine the number of employed women in the city.[38]

By March 1901, they had their answers. Large numbers of women worked outside the home—and, therefore, could benefit from YWCA services. The survey revealed that fifteen hundred women worked in factories, seven hundred were teachers and telephone operators, and five hundred were clerks and stenographers. The 181 pledge cards returned indicated there was widespread interest in a YWCA. Calista Wheeler could not have asked for more from the charter membership, which included the most important clubwomen in the city. Most were married, the wives of prominent business leaders, industrialists, attorneys, doctors, and politi-

Akron's YWCA was always committed to serving the needs of women rubber workers in the city. Here women workers of American Hard Rubber pose. *Photo courtesy of the Special Collections Division, Akron-Summit County Public Library.*

In the 1926, the YWCA celebrated its twenty-fifth anniversary and acknowledged some of its most active leaders. They were (top row, from left) Hallie Andrews, Isabelle Crouse, and Clara Howland and (bottom row) Grace (Seiberling) Chase, Calista Wheeler, and Harriet Wright. *Photo courtesy of the YWCA of Summit County Collection, the University of Akron Archives.*

cians. A few were single; some were employed, although not in factory jobs. No one Protestant denomination predominated, but one socioeconomic class did. Most of the charter members came from affluent families.[39]

When these women selected the leaders for their new organization, they picked women known for their administrative experience. Of course, Calista Willard Wheeler would be the president. Her enthusiasm and organizational ability had brought the Akron YWCA far.

The governing board of the YWCA was the board of trustees. Margaret Chapman Barnhart was the youngest in the group. Just twenty-seven, Margaret Barnhart was a former schoolteacher who was married to one of the city's school board executives. Ever since coming to Akron in 1893, she had been involved in community groups that helped children. Long active in the women's groups of the First Methodist Church, Margaret developed a real talent for fund-raising.

One of the eldest in the group was Isabella Berry, sixty at the time the YWCA got started. For decades, Isabella had been a familiar figure in Akron's women's community. Longtime president of the WCTU and organizer of the Women's Council, she was an outspoken prohibition advocate. She was also an experienced public speaker, who brought a religious spirit to the group. Isabella and Calista Wheeler would soon have more than an interest in the YWCA to tie them. Berry's daughter and Wheeler's son married.[40]

Harriet Sperry Wright, thirty-nine, wife of the president of First National Bank, came to the YWCA after working with the Dorcas organization. A member of West Congregational Church, Wright served as the YWCA's second president and became the organization's spokesperson in a public controversy with women employed in the rubber factories of the city.[41]

Etta Work, who figured so prominently in the Woman's Exchange, also served on the YWCA's board, as did Louisa Donsevean Upham, forty-four, wife of one of Akron's dry goods merchants. Louisa was experienced in a variety of start-ups, from the Woman's Benevolent Association to WCTU's Friendly Union. Clara Howland, wife of an executive at Akron Roofing Tile, who had been active in both the Tuesday Musical Club and the Mary Day Nursery, would also become an officer in the new YWCA. Other board members were as experienced, and the YWCA was going to draw on all that administrative talent during the first few years of organizational dysfunction.[42]

Part of the difficulty emanated from the lack of continuity in the general secretary's position. The only paid administrator in the new organization, the general secretary coordinated the enthusiastic volunteers and saw that the group carried out its primary mission—"the improvement of the social, the intellectual, the moral and the spiritual life of the young women."[43] During the first three years of its existence, Akron's YWCA had five different general secretaries.[44]

Appointed within months of the founding of the YWCA in Akron, the first general secretary, Rosella Meredith, worked well with the volunteers. She took her volunteers to the Akron Cereal Mill and the Baker-McMillen factory to recruit new members and to pray. Among the most enthusiastic of the volunteers was Hallie Andrews, who remembered, "We would sing hymns, say a prayer and then give them [the women who were eating lunch] a little talk about the Y's work to try to get them to join." There is no report of the response of the female factory workers. Rosella and her volunteers reached out to women workers in other factories as well. The volunteers put up posters inviting the women to social events at the group's headquarters in the basement of the Garfield Building on South High Street. Workingwomen in downtown Akron were already frequenting the YWCA headquarters. The dining room was a popular place for these women to stop for low-priced lunches—no men were allowed. As Rosella recalled, the YWCA rooms were special places for the group's members. "We have found in the rooms the freedom and lack of restraint that we find in our homes," she wrote. The YWCA rooms were drawing two types of women: workingwomen and young women from affluent and middle-class families in the city. Thus, the YWCA had to offer programs that cut across socioeconomic classes. One way the YWCA achieved that was through its educational programs.[45]

The YWCA headquarters became a kind of "public university" for all white Akron women. At first, the organization just offered "physical culture" (physical fitness and sports) and Bible classes, but the general secretary soon lined up volunteers to teach cooking, sewing, millinery, art, embroidery, vocal music, drawing, and other subjects that a "refined" young woman needed to know. Cooking and millinery classes were especially popular, the secretary reported. Volunteers also taught vocational classes—stenography, typewriting, and bookkeeping—designed

From its start, Akron's YWCA included girls in its program. In one of the earliest photos of Akron's YWCA—taken in 1904—girls enjoy the camaraderie that the YWCA offered. *Photo courtesy of the YWCA of Summit County Collection, the University of Akron Archives.*

Physical culture classes and athletic teams were especially popular with the women at the Akron YWCA. Here a 1915 Akron YWCA basketball team poses for a picture. *Photo courtesy of YWCA of Summit County Collection, the University of Akron Archives.*

to train women for clerical positions. The YWCA also opened an industrial school to train "poor girls," six to sixteen, household skills needed for domestic work or to run a home after they married. The education committee soon added lectures on topics the women needed to know. Dr. Katherine Kurt, one of the few female physicians in the city and a leader in the WCTU, offered a lecture on "The Human Body." It was free but open only to women and girls. The outreach, the classes, the high visibility within the community were bringing results; more and more women were joining the organization.[46]

Services to women workers stepped up in 1903 when the organization hired an extension/industrial secretary, whose primary responsibility was recruiting and programming for the workingwomen in the city. The extension secretary especially tried to serve new populations and offer programs of interest to, and in places convenient for, workingwomen, especially those employed in factories. She visited the women where they worked to find out what types of programs and services they wanted. In 1904, the YWCA started the first of its services to immigrant women, offering an English class in a factory. The group also offered classes in fancy work and "Bible talks" at factories during lunch periods and after work. The next year, the YWCA offered a wider fare at the factories. At the Akron China Works, the

YWCA offered the women literature classes; the group helped the girls open a rest room at Great Western Cereal.[47]

The pace quickened with the appointment of Sarah Scudder Lyon, a bright, young graduate of Mt. Holyoke College and the YWCA National Training School in Chicago, as extension/industrial secretary.[48] Sarah frequented the factories, recruiting and setting up new programs. In 1907, she visited six factories weekly, setting up noon meetings for the women workers. She got YWCA volunteers to come in to talk about everything from health to the Bible, from their travels to music.[49]

Sarah Lyon particularly focused the YWCA on the rubber factories and their women workers. Goodrich especially encouraged that connection, even helping to underwrite the special services the YWCA provided its women employees. In 1906, the YWCA opened a lunchroom close to the BFG plant. When deficits developed, the company covered them. By 1908, the Goodrich women had their own chapter and came directly from work to the YWCA headquarters for Bible lessons. Later, the BFG branch met at the factory, making it, according to press reports of the day, the only YWCA organization in the country in which the work was done completely in the factory. BFG would also be the first rubber company to establish a rooming house—in collaboration with the YWCA—for its "shop girls" in 1909.[50]

Women of the Goodyear Tire and Rubber Company came to the YWCA fold a little later. In 1912, they reorganized their "What's It To You Club" into the Goodyear branch of the YWCA. From a group of twenty-five, including more women from the office than from the factory, the branch grew to more than one hundred in four short years. YWCA members from Goodyear took advantage of the classes at the group's convenient downtown headquarters. According to the company newspaper, the physical culture and domestic arts classes were the most popular with the factory women. The YWCA had cultivated a kind of sisterhood among the "Goodyear girls." The company newspaper reported:

> The Branch feels that the value of club life is too great to be missed by any of the girls at Goodyear. The jolly, good times, the opportunities for educational work, and the possibility of making the Goodyear Branch take its place beside the largest branches of the [Industrial] Federation— in short the tremendous value of an organized group of girls with varied interests but one aim, should be enjoyed by all.[51]

The Akron YWCA fostered close connections with the rubber companies and even started branches within the factories. By 1916, Akron's YWCA started an industrial federation to afford more leadership opportunities for workingwomen. *Photo courtesy of YWCA of Summit County Collection, the University of Akron Archives.*

The close connections developing between the workingwomen and the YWCA encouraged the organization to offer new services. In 1908, the YWCA opened an employment bureau for women. (The group had established a nursing registry in 1903.) The YWCA provided all the pertinent information prospective employers in the city needed to know: name of the woman, address, kind of job sought, wages expected, religion of the woman seeking employment, her nationality, appearance, and work history. Women paid only a small fee for the services; perspective employers paid more.[52]

To help women deal with the housing shortage in the city, the YWCA kept a list of "desirable boarding places" for workingwomen, beginning in 1904. As more and more women inquired about that list, the board of the YWCA debated if the organization should start a boardinghouse of its own. Although the need was great, the board—all affluent women—decided the finances were inadequate. Another decade passed before the YWCA started its own dormitories for workingwomen in the city.[53]

YWCA President Harriet Wright was optimistic about the organization's ability to provide services to workingwomen. In 1911, Wright predicted more clubs and branches convenient to the workingwomen in the city:

The extension department plans to have more clubs and branches similar to those in the Goodrich and Werner factories, to secure a room in South or East Akron to use as a club room for girls in the neighborhood, who cannot or do not come to the [YWCA headquarters] building; to organize a volunteer workers class to acquaint its members with the life of industry and methods employed to benefit it, and either independently or in connection with the churches of the city, to bring a trained woman here to devote some time to the investigation of the needs of foreign girls in the city, with a view to organizing English classes among them.[54]

This kind of attention was gaining results. YWCA membership increased more among the two populations that the organization hoped to serve: the daughters of affluent and middle-class families and workingwomen. While the affluent women remained the foundation of the Akron YWCA, serving as its leaders and volunteers, workingwomen represented a growing percentage of the membership. By 1911, the YWCA had more than sixteen hundred members, making it one of the largest women's organizations in the city. Drawn by the special programming at the factories and the YWCA headquarters, the opening of a new building ("beautiful, cozy and homelike, a refuge to the tired and weary, and a place where counsel and comfort can always be had merely by asking," the *Akron Press* reported), and new low membership rates, workingwomen of all stripes were joining. In 1911, 47 percent of the YWCA's membership consisted of employed women, divided by occupation—7 percent were teachers, 6 percent were factory workers, 14 percent were clerical/stenographic workers, 5 percent were saleswomen, 5 percent were nurses, 1 percent were milliners, 5 percent were telephone operators; 2 percent were domestics, and another 2 percent were dressmakers.[55]

The increasingly close connection between the workingwomen and the YWCA posed special challenges for the organization. It was not simply programming for women of a different class, with different interests and needs. It was also defining the role the YWCA should play in ameliorating the problems women faced where they worked. Should the YWCA be an advocate for employed women and risk losing the financial support of the companies and the goodwill of its affluent membership? Or should the group keep above all the labor questions? Keeping above the fray became increasingly difficult as the industrial secretary, who worked directly with the female workers, reported problems in the factories to the board of trustees. In 1908, for example, the industrial secretary at the time, Sarah

Women workers at Goodyear Tire and Rubber Company and all the rubber factories faced difficult working conditions. Akron's YWCA worked behind the scenes to convince employers to provide rest rooms and lunchrooms for their women workers. *Photo courtesy of the Goodyear Tire and Rubber Company Collection, the University of Akron Archives.*

Lyon, told board members that a number of factories were requiring their women workers to work irregular hours.[56] The continuing problems at the rubber factories forced the YWCA's hand in 1912—and the organization landed squarely on the side of the employers, against the extension secretary and the women workers, some of whom were members. The issue revolved around low pay, inadequate housing, and substandard working conditions. Much to the embarrassment of the YWCA, industrial secretary Berenice Brown took the issue to the public in the pages of the *Akron Press,* accusing the rubber manufacturers of being unconcerned about the "moral and mental welfare" of their women employees. Berenice pleaded for better wages, rest rooms in the rubber shops where women might find some respite from the grueling work in the factories, and clean, safe dormitories. Although the early YWCA had long supported rest rooms for women in every factory and clean, safe dormitories, the group did not appreciate her public assertions. The YWCA always preferred less public tactics, working behind the scenes so as not to embarrass corporate contributors or wealthy patrons. Now, Berenice's disclosures had to be dealt with publicly. Harriet Wright, president of the YWCA at the time, responded with a stinging denunciation of the charges. The women working in Akron factories were "well paid, the average wage far exceeds that of most cities," Harriet wrote in a letter to the editor of the *Akron Times.* Yes, she admitted, there was a housing shortage. "It is true it is difficult for out of town girls to find enough rooms to supply the number entering Akron, and a Boarding Home would be an acceptable addition to the city life," but, she continued, "Such difficulties arise in any growing city." Employers have been working to improve conditions for women in their factories, she insisted:

> The Y.W.C.A. and the employers work hand in hand. The employers provide sanitary conditions, rest rooms, restaurants, trained nurses, etc. The Association seeks to supplement the employer's efforts after working hours by furnishing wholesome recreation, educational classes, club activities and the like, providing those things which the girls themselves ask for and enjoy.

One workingwoman was not satisfied with that response and invited Harriet Wright to come to work in a rubber shop and "see how she would like to work for 10 cents an hour and work 10 hours. And then pay $4 a week to board in a respectable place."[57]

That exchange set the tone for the remainder of Harriet Wright's administration. In January 1913, Professor Rauschenbusch of the Rochester Theological Seminary told the Akron YWCA that women deserved less pay than the men because they were less skilled and had no families to support.[58]

The Akron organization took no public stand during the monthlong IWW strike against the rubber shops the same year. Women strikers continued to frequent YWCA programs, but there must have been some tension. After the strike, a YWCA report explained that "all 'Red Ribbons' and hard words were forgotten, as it were, and only the association spirit ruled."

The public disagreement, the speech, the lack of support during the disastrous IWW strike did not stop the growth of the YWCA in the factories or its popularity among workingwomen. By World War I, almost every rubber shop in the city had some connection with the YWCA, and many factory women frequented the organization's dining rooms, classes, socials, vesper services, and "physical culture" programs. Moreover, the Akron YWCA, then under general secretary Sarah

During the 1913 Industrial Workers of the World (Wobblies) strike, Akron's YWCA provided no public support of the strikers. Women strikers continued to frequent YWCA programs. After the strike, the YWCA reported, "all 'Red Ribbons' and hard words were forgotten . . . and only the association spirit ruled." *Photo courtesy of the B. F. Goodrich Collection, the University of Akron Archives.*

Lyon, tried to give the workingwomen more power within the organization by creating in 1916 an "industrial federation" of YWCA clubs based in factories. The idea, she explained, was to give the workingwomen more opportunities within the association and within the city. Modeled after the Federation of Women's Clubs, this industrial union brought together women from the rubber factories and the female department store workers to develop coordinated programming and services. It also afforded leadership opportunities for workingwomen who were excluded from the executive positions of the general YWCA.[59]

Sarah Lyon, who had started her career in Akron as the group's industrial secretary, remained an advocate for the city's workingwomen during her nine years as general secretary of the city's YWCA. One thing she especially wanted was a YWCA-run dormitory where workingwomen could find affordable, clean, safe housing. She thought she could achieve that goal in 1910 when benefactor Colonel George Perkins left fifty thousand dollars to the YWCA. She hoped that money would underwrite an expanded lunchroom and start a dormitory as well as set up a permanent endowment for the association. The board had other plans for the money, and the dormitory was delayed.[60] She tried again in 1912, when she pointed out to the board and the public that workingwomen needed a "clean, safe place, within the reach of their pocketbooks." Those pleas were ignored as well. Finally, in 1915, she opened the top floor of the Grace House as a dormitory for ten to twelve women, and, in 1916, she planned a "cot dormitory" in the gymnasium of the headquarters. Those moves were designed to provide *temporary* housing, while the women looked for permanent places to live in the city.[61] The situation became even more desperate during World War I, when more and more women—recruited by rubber factories to produce life jackets, gas masks, and other war-related products—poured into the city and found an abysmal housing shortage.[62]

Things were going to change, however. Part of this was due to administrative changes within the YWCA. The group had a new president, thirty-four-year-old Anna Case, a trained social worker who had given up her career when she married and moved to Akron. The YWCA also had a new general secretary. Sarah Lyon had accepted a job at Wooster College, a temporary stop on her way to a position at the national YWCA organization in New York. Taking her place was Edith Nash, a YWCA administrator from Wilmington, Delaware. Eager to return to the Cleveland area where her mother still resided, Edith, a graduate of Oberlin College, became general secretary of Akron's YWCA in January 1917.[63]

It was under Anna Case and Edith Nash that the YWCA cooperated with Firestone to create the "Firestone Branch in East Akron." Harvey Firestone, president of Firestone Tire and Rubber, offered a furnished building to "house industrial girls from Firestone plants," and the YWCA agreed to maintain and manage the dormitory. To great fanfare, the Firestone dorm opened in 1918, at the height of war production. The dormitory had room for seventy-five to eighty women, and the facility quickly filled to capacity, primarily with Firestone workers.[64]

It was also under Anna Case and Edith Nash that the first dormitories owned and operated by the YWCA were planned. The dormitories opened in 1920. The YWCA patched together a "Blue Triangle" of dormitories from three houses on South Union Street (Numbers 129, 143, and 149). Designed to accommodate thirty-three permanent residents initially (that capacity was doubled in 1923), the houses also provided rooms for transients, women who had just moved into the city and needed a little time to locate decent housing. Rent was determined by wages. The more the woman earned, the more she paid in rent. Preference was always given to the youngest women applying, who usually earned the least. Most

The YWCA's "Blue Triangle" dormitory provided a homelike environment for the resident women workers and students. Here women residents relax in the shared living room. The women had to live by the YWCA rules that included strict curfews. Matron Emma Buchtel interviewed each potential resident. *Photo courtesy of the YWCA of Summit County Collection, the University of Akron Archives.*

women in the dormitory were between the ages of eighteen and twenty-one, the YWCA reported. Not all the residents were factory workers. In fact, the dormitories housed a cross-section of young Akron women. Some were students at Buchtel College; others worked in rubber factories; a few were junior office girls; and others were waitresses and clerks. But they all got along well at the dormitories, the YWCA reported. All residents ate dinner together and then went to the living room for a "home evening of a large and happy family of young people." The congenial atmosphere was due, no doubt, to the women selected to reside in the dormitories. All shared YWCA's values; dormitory matron Emma Buchtel saw to that when she interviewed each potential resident. The women also had to abide by YWCA rules that included strict curfews. If a resident did anything that reflected badly on the dormitory or the YWCA, she was turned out.[65]

The "Blue Triangle," the cots in the Grace House attic, and the rooms in the Firestone branch illustrated how the YWCA, sometimes working in collaboration with a sponsor and other times alone, provided needed housing to the young

In 1920, Akron's YWCA opened its "Blue Triangle" dormitory, a combination of three homes on South Union Street. Here was a place where women who came to Akron to find work or to go to school could find clean, safe, reasonably priced housing. *Photo courtesy of the YWCA of Summit County Collection, the University of Akron Archives.*

women in Akron. The YWCA would expand its housing in 1931 when it opened a new headquarters in Akron.

In its quiet reforms, its unpublicized cajoling of employers to provide rest rooms and other improvements to the workplace, its lunchrooms, its educational program, and its socials, the YWCA improved the working and living environments for many workingwomen in the city. But the relationship between workingwomen and the YWCA could be an uneasy one. In deference to its corporate patrons and its affluent members, the YWCA could not—would not—be a public advocate for the workingwomen, at least not in the first twenty-five years of the twentieth century. That stance sometimes put the board of trustees at odds with the YWCA staff. The situation was most clearly manifested in 1911 when the industrial secretary went public, urging the very reforms that the YWCA did privately. The YWCA president castigated the staff member and her assertions publicly. The dormitory issue was yet another example. Although the talented general secretary Sarah Lyon pushed hard for a dormitory when the YWCA received a substantial amount from the Perkins estate, the board rejected the recommendation, preferring to commit the funds to projects that benefited a greater number of members.

Likewise, during the IWW strike of 1913, the strikers—many of whom were members of the YWCA—received no public organizational support. Two factors explained these stances: the class chasm that separated the YWCA leadership from its working members and the age gap between the older, affluent, matronly leaders wedded to conservative, middle-class, traditional expectations of women and the younger working members facing quite a different socioeconomic future. Times began to change with the partnership of new YWCA president Anna Case and new general secretary Edith Nash, which brought about results for workingwomen in Akron. That collaboration also brought about an International Institute and other innovative programs in the city.

Workingwomen were not the only constituency that the YWCA had to serve in Akron. In 1914, the YWCA formed its first teen organization, Censowe, for female students at Central, South, and West high schools, and the group expanded its structured youth activities in 1918 with the formation of the Girl Reserves. By 1920, the YWCA extended its structured reach to younger girls through the Triangle Girls clubs in the grade schools of the city. These were the only *organized* efforts of the YWCA to include girls in its activities. From its start, daughters of affluent and middle-class families affiliated with the organization and used the group's facilities, even if the formalized association had not been organized.[66]

By 1925, Akron's YWCA had become the heart of the women's community in the city. Young girls and adults took part in various physical culture programs in the gymnasium and the pool. Young girls participated in the "Penny Savings Program" that the Union Charity insisted the YWCA continue. Fewer went off to the YWCA summer camp that the Akron and Cleveland chapters jointly ran.

No age group was immune from the touch of the YWCA. Under Sarah Lyon, Buchtel College got a YWCA branch for its co-eds, and under Edith Nash, the branch flourished. Also under Sarah's tutelage, alumnae created their own College Club, where well-educated women in the city could exchange ideas. That group usually met at the YWCA headquarters along with other women's clubs and organizations. Even the venerable WCTU, which during the late nineteenth century served as the central meeting ground for women's clubs in the city, gave up its Main Street rooms and met at the YWCA. Only a few women's organizations, like the Woman's Exchange and the Mary Day Nursery, retained their independence, meeting at their own headquarters. Edith Nash and subsequent YWCA general secretaries saw the important relationship between the meeting place of a club and opportunities for collaboration and influence.

Ys and other Ys

Young Womens Christian Association

Our Motto: *"I am come that they might have life, and that they might have it more abundantly."*

Vol. II   AKRON, OHIO, 1926   OCTOBER-NOVEMBER   No. 1

By 1925, the staff of Akron's YWCA was large enough to start a bimonthly newsletter to keep the membership informed of everything the organization was doing. *Newsletter courtesy of the YWCA of Summit County Collection, the University of Akron Archives.*

WOMAN'S CHRISTIAN TEMPERANCE UNION

In 1900, the WCTU was the dominant woman's organization in the city. From its rooms on South Main Street, the group's full-time employee worked with the volunteers who ran a "noon rest" for workingwomen, programs for the incarcerated, and assistance for those in the infirmary. By 1925, the WCTU could no longer afford a separate headquarters or a full-time matron and held its meetings at the YWCA. Notwithstanding these reverses, the WCTU carried on its mission of helping women and families and attempting to keep Akron morally grounded.

By 1900, the WCTU had a new generation of leaders. Isabella Berry, the long-time president, and Henrietta Chase, her vice president, gave up their offices and got involved with other organizations in the city. Beloved treasurer Dr. Katherine Kurt died in 1910.[67]

The new generation of WCTU leaders was not as experienced as the women who came before; and, while financially privileged, the new officers did not have as high a status in the community. A few, like Flora Barnett Adamson, had excellent resumés, in terms of both family connections and benevolent records. Flora was the wife of Alexander Adamson, an immigrant from Scotland who settled in Akron in 1883 and ran the successful Adamson Machine Company. Of all the new officers of the WCTU, she had the strongest record of benevolent work. A Universalist, Flora was a member of the Buckley Women's Relief Association, lifetime

Katherine Kurt, one of the few female physicians in the city, served as treasurer of the Woman's Christian Temperance Union for many years. *Photo courtesy of the Summit County Historical Society, the University of Akron Archives.*

member of the Summit County Woman Suffrage Association, trustee of the Sumner Home for the Aged, and member of the Women's Guild of People's Hospital. She was president of the WCTU from 1901 through 1906.[68]

The background of Jennie Fish was more typical of this new generation of WCTU leaders. Taking over as WCTU president from Zelia Walters, the wife of a corporate executive at McIntosh-Baum, Jennie Fish was the wife of Perry Fish, a mechanical engineer in the city. While financially comfortable, she certainly was not of the same socioeconomic stature of Flora Adamson, Isabella Berry, Henrietta Chase, or Zelia Walters. A lifetime member of the Summit County Woman Suffrage Association, Jennie also got involved with the Woman's Club League. She served as president of the Akron WCTU from 1910 to 1915.

Rose Keller Cartmell stepped in as treasurer after the death of Katherine Kurt and found it difficult to keep the organization financially steady. The daughter of a carpenter, she worked as a teacher before her marriage. After she moved to Akron with her husband, Rose got involved with the WCTU, the county suffrage association, and the Woman's Club League.[69]

In the early years of the twentieth century, a full-time employee, called a matron, supervised the day-to-day work of the WCTU in Akron. From the late nineteenth century to the early twentieth century, Mary A. Moore, a widow, held that position. Little is known about Mary or her circumstances, but newspaper accounts suggest that she aligned herself with the leadership on controversial topics. When Flora Adamson, WCTU president at the time, applauded the saloon-busting tactics of Carrie Nation in 1901, Mary agreed, saying "The time has come for action. . . . Right here in Akron, we would be justified in starting . . . another crusade against the saloon keepers who defy the law by keeping their places open after hours and on Sunday. I believe that Mrs. Nation is all right and hope she will succeed in stirring up such a movement as will deal the liquor traffic a death blow." (Nonsense, countered Sue S. Sargent, an active member of Akron's WCTU. Carrie Nation was insane. "Such depredation cannot do the cause any good, and I am afraid it will do it incalculable harm," Sargent emphasized.) After Mary gave up her position as matron, she remained active in the group and in 1916 was elected the WCTU president; it was rare in Akron for a former staff member to make such a transition.[70]

The rift in the Akron WCTU over Carrie Nation was not deep, long lasting, or disruptive. The local branch carried on its various programs from rooms at 164 S. Main Street and later 70 S. Main Street. Both locations were close to Yeager's Department Store, making the WCTU rooms ideally located, close to shopping, and not too far removed from stores and offices where many women worked. That was perfect, because one of the WCTU's more popular programs was the "noon rest," "the place where young women employed in stores and offices may comfortably spend the noon hour eating the lunch which they bring with them, upon tables provided, or supplementing it with hot dishes, tea or coffee, or if they prefer obtaining a full meal at mere cost." Increasingly, however, the "noon rest" found competition from the YWCA lunchroom around the corner on High Street.

The WCTU faced no competition in some of its other programs, like temperance education, one of the group's top priorities. According to Flora Adamson and the WCTU leaders, the local branch was doing well with its temperance education, among both the young and the older in the community. Few other women's groups competed with the WCTU in its work with drunkards and the criminals in the jails and among the sick and ailing in the infirmary. The WCTU also lobbied for the enforcement of the Sunday Closing Law (the so-called Blue Laws that forbade labor, business, and commercial work on the Sabbath), fighting the "billboard nuisance," or protesting baseball games held on Sunday.[71]

During the early twentieth century, the Akron WCTU was also heavily involved with the campaign for suffrage. In this, the WCTU was ahead of the YWCA. Beginning in the late nineteenth century, the Akron WCTU had collaborated with the local suffrage association to push for the right to vote, especially in local elections. In this collaboration, the Akron WCTU was ahead of many branches in Ohio. It was not until 1906 that the state organization called for all branches in Ohio to collaborate with the suffrage leagues to pressure the legislature to award the vote to women. The state organization echoed the pleas the Akron WCTU had used decades earlier. Harkening back to woman's traditional domestic roles, the state group beseeched, "Let wives plead for the power to protect the home, mothers for the protection of the children and maidens for the power that young men will feel bound to respect."

Whether the state organization was pushing for suffrage or not, the women of the WCTU in Summit County continued their campaign. The various branches in the Akron area brought in speakers and held meetings to keep their members committed to the cause. In 1910, Mrs. Florence Richards told the women that politics is, indeed, rotten, so women needed to vote. "The politics of today . . . are as low and as rotten as they can get and why is it? Because only the men vote." If women had the vote, she argued, the women "would soon enter into the field, armed with a ballot and clean the place out." Moreover, one of the first things the women would do was get rid of the greatest evil facing society—liquor. Meetings revealed that WCTU members were never discouraged—disappointed, perhaps, but never discouraged. As the *Beacon Journal* reported in 1912, "While the ladies were somewhat disappointed that the liquor license carried, and woman suffrage was defeated, they have not given up, nor will they until woman is given the ballot." No doubt their spirits brightened when the *Beacon Journal* editorially supported the right to vote for women.[72]

The biggest problems facing Akron's WCTU in the early twentieth century revolved around organizational issues. While creating branches across the city made sense from a recruitment standpoint and certainly increased leadership opportunities for women in different neighborhoods and from a wide range of socioeconomic classes, it watered down the power of the central Akron organization. Each branch had its own meetings, elected its own officers, sponsored its own events, and defined its own mission within the wider temperance goal. Thus, the central Akron WCTU had to compete with its own branches at the very time the organization was facing pressure from other women's clubs in the city.

WOMEN'S COUNCIL

As the WCTU struggled, the Women's Council of Akron emerged stronger than ever. Representing more than ten thousand Akron women individually or as members of affiliated clubs, the Women's Council had truly become the federation of women's clubs that its founders had hoped. During the first twenty-five years of the twentieth century, the council faced none of the difficulties that the WCTU did. It faced another set. The council had to channel the energies, interests, politics, and personalities of dozens of women's organizations and hundreds of individual members into ambitious municipal housekeeping campaigns to change the city.

The Women's Council could never accomplish that balancing act without an extraordinary set of leaders with vision, experience, skill, and prestige. The council looked to its affiliated groups for those leaders. Although the WCTU had figured so strongly in the council's founding, the organization seldom figured in that selection. Only one council president in the early twentieth century—Sarah Day Seymour Parsons—had discernible WCTU ties. Fifty-three at the time of her election in 1899, Sarah, the mother of six grown children and wife of an executive at Aultman, Miller and Company, had a rich organizational history. She had been involved with the Women's Council from its start, representing an organization from St. Paul's Episcopal Church. She was the first president of the New Century Club,[73] an educational and social group, and continued her activism in that organization after her tenure as president of the Women's Council.

The New Century Club, the Mary Day Nursery, and the Tuesday Musical Club produced the largest number of Women's Council presidents in the years from 1900 to 1925. The organizational backgrounds of Rhea Hugill Adam and Eva Proctor Heintelselman were typical. A native of Akron who was active in her church, St. Paul's Episcopal, Rhea was married to E. Reginald Adam, an executive at Saalfield Publishing at the time of her election in 1914. By the time she took over as president of the council, she had administrative experience from the Mary Day Nursery and Children's Hospital. Eva Proctor Heintelselman brought both a Tuesday Musical Club and a New Century connection to the presidency of the Women's Council. Eva Heintelselman, who was the wife of an executive at Akron Extract and Chemical, had just completed a successful term as president of the New Century Club when she was elected president of the Women's Council in 1907. After she ended that term, she was elected president of the Tuesday Musical Club.[74]

Rhea Adam and Eva Heintelselman were representative of other trends within the leadership of the Women's Council. Both were married; of the presidents of the Women's Council from its founding in 1893 until 1925, only two were single— Helen Wolle, thirty-five at the time of her election in 1919, and Isabel Bradley, forty-eight at the time of her election in 1912. Helen Wolle was the niece of Frank

In 1919, Akron's Women's Council changed its name to the Akron and Summit County Federation of Women's Clubs. In 1925, like so many other women's organizations, the federation participated in the city's centennial parade. *Photo courtesy of the Special Collections Division, Akron-Summit County Public Library.*

Seiberling, founder of Goodyear Tire and Rubber, and women's club organizer and leader Gertrude Seiberling. Helen followed a Seiberling-family tradition when she got involved with the Akron Garden Club and later organized a women's club of her own, the Women's City Club of Akron. Isabel Bradley differed from the Women's Council mold in a number of different ways. She was a physician at a time when few women practiced medicine. The daughter of a farmer in Kent, Ohio, she taught in that town's local schools before going on to Buchtel College and then the medical school at the University of Michigan. In 1911, she moved to Akron to practice psychiatry. Before her election to the presidency of the council, Isabel had relatively little women's club experience in Akron; her only affiliation had been with the woman suffrage organization. After her tenure as council president, she became a kind of *cause célèbre* for the organization. The group pushed hard to get Isabel appointed to the Board of Health in 1914. Women's Council treasurer Flora Adamson argued, "Women understand matters relating to cleanliness better than men." As a physician and a woman who understood housekeeping, Isabel was the ideal candidate for the job. Council President Rhea Adam argued, "Dr. Bradley is a woman of training, intelligence and civic spirit." But Mayor Frank Rockwell did not see it that way and appointed a local business owner to the board, in what was interpreted as a slap against the Women's Council and its "clean up campaign" undertaken during Isabel's tenure. Soon after, Isabel left Akron, transferring her medical practice to the State Mental Hospital in Columbus in 1917.[75]

Rhea Adam and Eva Heintelselman also shared a privileged socioeconomic class. The matron leaders of the Women's Council through 1925 were from the highest reaches of Akron society, married to men who were members of the business or professional elite. Of the thirteen husbands of Women's Council presidents during this time period, twelve were definitively identified. The greatest number of these husbands (seven) were business owners and/or corporate executives. The remainder were professionals, typically educators (most affiliated with Buchtel College) or physicians.

These women reflected the composition of the greatest number of groups affiliated with the Women's Council. The members of these clubs were, primarily, white, Protestant, and middle class or higher. The organizations represented in the Women's Council ranged from the WCTU to ladies' aid/missionary societies of the larger Protestant churches in the city, from the thriving YWCA to the various women's "hives" of the Maccabees, a group committed to helping women and children,[76] from the suffrage association to the Fortnightly Club, a study group.[77]

As time passed, the Women's Council grew to represent different types of organizations; by 1923, sixty-five clubs were affiliated with the group. Class lines were crossed with the Federation of Industrial Clubs, representing the YWCA branches at the various factories. Jewish women joined the council in the clubs affiliated with Temple Israel and the Schwesterbund Society, a benevolent organization of Jewish women that dated back to the nineteenth century in Akron.[78]

During the Gilded Age, the Busy Bee Hive of the Maccabees in Akron pioneered insurance for women and organized girls clubs. Here the Maccabees take part in the 1925 parade that celebrates Akron's centennial. *Photo courtesy of the Special Collections Division, Akron-Summit County Public Library.*

The might of the Women's Council was not just in its affiliated groups. In 1909, the council admitted individual members and hundreds of women joined. That move accomplished two things: it tied the group *directly* to Akron women, and it strengthened the financial resources of the organization. Now, the council had two revenue streams, one from the affiliated organizations and the other from individual women. The additional revenue was needed because the Women's Council was going to embark on ambitious campaigns to clean up the city.

From the first days of the twentieth century, the council focused on issues that fell within the traditional purview of women—child welfare, cleaning and health maintenance, and the welfare of women and families, which were also key areas of municipal housekeeping nationwide. In 1903, for example, the council pushed for a separate juvenile court. At the time, the mayor determined what cases would be tried outside of the regular police court. The council wanted to strip the mayor of that discretion. The *Beacon Journal* reported, "[O]ccasionally young boys are seen on the prisoners' bench along with the worst types of the vicious criminal, and the women believe that the matter should be definitely determined by ordinance." Early campaigns also sought to eliminate billboards ("a menace to life and limb . . . and a most unsightly disfigurement of the city streets"); to stop spitting on the sidewalks ("filthy practice"); and to push for the strict enforcement of the law against selling liquor on Sunday. The women also worked to reintroduce manual training in the schools after the Board of Education voted to eliminate it, expand the mother's library, and start a beautification project that would also enhance the health of schoolchildren ("The children are to take care of whatever they plant, thus serving a double purpose of employing the children in this healthful work, and in beautifying the city").[79]

These early campaigns were not always successful. Beautification worked; the billboard campaign did not; the library expanded; but the juvenile court stalled. In 1909, the Women's Council, under new president Nona Sippy, wife of a prominent Akron physician/surgeon, unveiled another ambitious action agenda, with new strategies, new alliances outside the women's community, and a new attitude toward politics and pressuring city hall. The issues remained the same—women, children, family, cleanliness, and health—but the means to those ends changed. Many noticed the reinvigorated council. The *Beacon Journal* observed in 1909 that "the Women's council [*sic*] is a thriving and very important organization in this city and that it is coming to be a big factor in civic and social affairs."[80]

The Daughters of America, one of the many women's organizations in Akron in 1925, joined the other organizations parading during the city's centennial celebration. *Photo courtesy of the Special Collections Division, Akron-Summit County Public Library.*

The Women's Council worked through a labyrinth of committees. That organizational structure accomplished two things—it allowed women to volunteer for specific areas where they had expertise and interest, and it meant no one woman or group of women was overtaxed in campaigns. Nona Sippy—and subsequent council presidents—and the executive board channeled the committees.

In 1909, the educational committee under Margaret Barnhart was one of the most active of the council's subgroups. Margaret was the secret of the educational committee's success. A former teacher married to the secretary of Akron's Board of Education, she had a passion for children and improving the conditions they faced. She was also an astute politician who knew how to build alliances. This was best seen when Margaret reactivated the council's push for a juvenile court. She brought the prosecutor and the probate judge into the campaign and even tried to include Akron's mayor. The pressure, alliances, and publicity worked. The juvenile court was soon established and a probation officer appointed. Two years later, in response to the educational committee's continuing pressure, the city created a detention home for youthful offenders, instead of housing youthful offenders in jails with adult criminals.

Margaret Barnhart and her committee could not build alliances when it came to the new children's home for Akron. Margaret and her group backed the "cottage

Members and leaders of the Akron chapter of the Daughters of the American Revolution (DAR) pose at the dedication of the boulder at the northern terminus of Portage Trail in 1925. The dedication was part of the city's celebration of its centennial. *Photo courtesy of the Summit County Historical Society, the University of Akron Archives.*

plan," a series of small cottages, instead of one large institutional home for the displaced children, the less-expensive alternative backed by the board of trustees. Margaret emphasized that the cottage method had been adopted in the new children's homes. "It is more home-like and is better in every way," she argued. The board of trustees, however, would not be swayed.[81]

Issues related to children were not the only focus of the Women's Council in 1909 and subsequent years. The council especially emphasized health-related issues during the presidency of Nona Sippy (1908–10). During that time, the council got involved with the Summit County Health Protective Association, aided in the fight against the "white plague" (tuberculosis), pushed for medical inspections in the schools, and pressured the city to reduce pollution. The council built many important alliances in these campaigns but risked them all in its attempt to control pollution and convert Akron to a "smokeless town." Council members monitored where the smoke and pollution came from and reported their findings to the sanitary officer—and the newspapers of the city. According to the council, all the rubber factories, sewer pipe works, twelve school buildings, one church, and others were responsible for the smoke and pollution in the city's skies. In a letter to the city's sanitary officer, the council urged that all the polluters be fined. The sanitary officer compromised with the women. There would be no closings and no fines, but the offenders would be notified. "I will not cause any of our factories in this city to be shut down because of the smoke, but I will notify every firm, corporation or individual whose name appears in the list, and have them take steps to stop the nuisance."[82] The smoke continued to billow, and the haze lingered over the city for decades to come.

In 1914, the Women's Council tried another health initiative. This time the council was under Dr. Isabel Bradley, and the target was the disease-carrying fly. The campaign was designed to educate the public, clean up the city, and get rid of the flies. The campaign enlisted a range of groups, including the Boy Scouts, who delivered "Safety First" booklets to every house in the city, the Summit County Health Protective Association, the Federation of Jewish Societies, Children's Hospital, and the Akron Chamber of Commerce. The campaign publicized the filth in the city and embarrassed Akron's Board of Health. During the council's 1914 summer of housekeeping, Akron homes, bakeries, groceries, alleys, and backyards got a good cleaning; but members of the health board stewed. According to the *Beacon Journal*, employees of the health board were "decidedly peeved" over the council campaign. Those sentiments were not revealed until the next year, when the mayor passed over the council's candidate, Isabel Bradley, and appointed someone else to the advisory board. Notwithstanding this slight, the Women's Council refused to give up its clean-up campaigns, which were repeated in 1915 and 1916, embarrassing the health board each time.[83]

The Women's Council even exercised its economic muscle in 1916, when it urged Akron women to join the nationwide food boycott to force prices down. As Mrs. W. J. Gelink, chairman of the Housewives' Committee, and Mrs. Hermine Z. Hansen, president of the Women's Council, wrote to Akron women, prices would come down if Akron housewives boycotted certain foods. "The women are quite stirred up about this matter and are ready to act on it," Hermine said.[84]

The Women's Council scored some of its greatest successes from 1909 to 1916, a time of great activism in the nationwide municipal housekeeping movement. The juvenile court was created, a probation officer appointed, and a detention home established. The group started its ambitious clean-up campaigns to improve the health and beauty of the city, pushed for a "sane fourth" to make July 4 celebrations safer for children and the entire community, set up a Housewives' League to inspect the markets, and started a Baby Week that highlighted the need for consistent medical monitoring of newborns and toddlers.[85]

Several things coalesced to make these campaigns so successful. During this period, an extraordinary team of women led the Women's Council. Nona Sippy, Marie Ellene Olin,[86] Isabel Bradley, and Rhea Adam were women of vision, with energy, connections, and organizational ability. These women were backed up by a talented board and committee members who worked hard to bring improvements to the city. Affiliated organizations got firmly behind the campaigns that fit so neatly into women's domestic roles.

The gains came at a price, however. Although it had become a force in the community, the Women's Council made enemies. Mayor Frank Rockwell's rejection of the council's candidate for the health board was only the most obvious incident. As the most visible women's organization in the city, the council became the target of criticism for the entire women's club movement. When Rabbi Philo warned the women that their clubs might be equivalent to the snake in the Garden of Eden, luring the women from their obligations at home, he was talking to the council and every clubwoman in the city. When council president Zelia Walters responded by pointing out that club work made women better wives and mothers,[87] she spoke for every clubwoman in the city.

And there were *thousands* of clubwomen in Akron in the first two decades of the twentieth century. Many enjoyed afternoons with friends where they talked about books, history, culture, and social developments in small neighborhood literary clubs. But there was something different about the women's clubs of the first twenty-five years of the twentieth century. Certainly there were more of them—hundreds of them. There was a club to suit every woman's interest, age, socioeconomic group, race, creed, ethnicity, and neighborhood. And, if one was not quite right for a particular constituency, women organized yet another.

That reflected the enormous confidence that early twentieth-century Akron clubwomen possessed. The more mature clubwomen built on decades of organizational experience; the younger women brought a raw enthusiasm, a can-do attitude, imagination, and energy to every task.

That translated into results. Certainly, many women's clubs in Akron carried on the traditional benevolent and social activities that had proved so beneficial to the city during the nineteenth century. However, other women burned with the reform impulses of the Progressive Era and started more ambitious programs. They reorganized their old groups, redefined their goals and missions, and took the club in different directions. Others started from scratch, creating organizations ready to face any challenge. They found many challenges as they created health institutions that continue today, transformed the city's cultural picture, built churches, and delivered needed services to workingwomen.

The women of this new century were practicing their own brand of domestic feminism. There were limitations to feminism, however. The largest number of clubwomen in Akron—especially those of these secular organizations—suffered from the same prejudices that afflicted the city. Immigrant, African American, and less affluent women who desired the sense of belonging that only a woman's club could provide were not usually welcomed into the organizations of white, middle-class women. Instead, they organized associations of their own.

Chapter 7

Other Perspectives on Women's Clubs in Twentieth-Century Akron

In our club work for next year we hope to dovetail the women's work with the girl's work so that the gap between the foreign mother and her American daughter may be more easily bridged and that there may be a common basis of understanding.

—Helen E. Miller, Monthly Report 1925[1]

The Daughters of Jerusalem treat their guests as they do everything else, that is, just right, at the right time, in the right place. They have shown the intention of doing things properly.

—*Akron Beacon Journal*[2]

WHILE THE NATIVE-BORN, FINANCIALLY COMFORTABLE, WHITE WOMEN busied themselves creating the great cultural, educational, health, and social institutions that transformed the city, the "unempowered"—the factory women, the immigrants, and the African Americans—were generally excluded from these worthwhile pursuits. Only a limited number of clubs, primarily those affiliated with churches with memberships that cut across economic and ethnic boundaries, welcomed women of different classes and ethnicities on an equal footing. Most Akron clubwomen in the early twentieth century preferred to get involved in civic organizations with like-minded individuals—women who shared the same values, spoke the same language, enjoyed the same socioeconomic advantages, came from the same cultural heritage, and were members of the same race.

Benevolent women were more than willing to help those less fortunate—workingwomen, the poor, immigrants, and African Americans—but seldom (if ever) did they see the disadvantaged as *partners* in these endeavors. Even if factory women, immigrants, and African Americans were committed to the goals of a specific woman's club, they were seldom welcomed into the association. Thus, when African American women expressed an interest in temperance work, they had to organize their own "colored" branch of the WCTU.[3]

Nonetheless, a large number of female factory workers, immigrants, and African Americans burned with the same desire to organize clubs that drove the white, financially comfortable women in the city. These women craved the friendships built upon the sense of accomplishment that only a women's club could provide during this time. However, the aims, missions, goals, and strategies of some of the women's clubs organized by the female factory workers, immigrants, and African Americans stood in contrast with the more traditional models employed by the white, affluent clubwomen in the city. Other organizations had much in common with the clubs run by white, middle-class women. The women's organizations at Goodyear Tire and Rubber illustrated both principles. The Girls' Relief Association, one of the early women's clubs formed by and for women workers at the Goodyear rubber factory, followed an organizational model more closely associated with the aims, missions, goals, and strategies of men's groups than with those of traditional women's organizations, while the Wingfoot Girls and the Goodyear Women's Club had more in common with the other women's organizations in the city.

WOMEN'S ORGANIZATIONS OF GOODYEAR TIRE AND RUBBER COMPANY

A relief association headed by men to benefit male employees had been in existence for some time at Goodyear. In 1917, the women decided to start their own group. The timing was ideal. Goodyear was hiring more and more women to produce war materials in the period leading up to America's entrance into World War I. These women, many of whom had come to the city without their families, needed the security that a relief association could offer—the same organizational impulses that had led to the development of the male group. Like the women's groups in the city, this relief association depended on one well-organized, networked individual to get the organization started. In the case of the Goodyear's Girls' Relief Association, the moving spirit was Miss Lura Close, who had been with the company two years, working in the office—in the mail room—where she came in contact with clerical workers from throughout the plant. She was also involved in other Goodyear-based organizations, including the company's branch of the YWCA.[4] Thus, she had friends across the plant, not just in the office. To get corporate approval for the organization,[5] Lura had to demonstrate widespread interest in the relief organization. Thirty Goodyear women, organized by Lura, circulated a petition around the office and factory. More than 80 percent of the women working in the factory and the office signed the petition, so the company let the women go ahead with their plans.[6]

This relief association looked to the men's organization as its model. Like the men's organization, the women's association required low dues and a relatively small initiation fee. In return, the group promised benefits in times of sickness or injury. Dues were only twenty-five cents a month and the initiation fee was one dollar; all fees were deducted from the woman's paycheck. Benefits were high, five dollars a week, slightly less than a woman earned at Goodyear at the time, but much lower than the benefits paid by the men's group.

Within two months, the Girls' Relief Association had 160 members at Goodyear and was on its way to becoming the welfare center of the female community at the factory. The women of the relief organization, however, did not rely solely on dues; they also drew on fund-raising strategies commonly employed by women's clubs in the city. They organized dances and socials to build up their treasury and to establish a sense of camaraderie, a key element for every women's organization in the city.[7]

The Girls' Relief Association had a good deal of prestige at Goodyear, partly because of the women who agreed to lead the group. Clara Bingham, the first female employee at Goodyear and by then head of the company's welfare work, agreed to serve as president; Lura Close became treasurer; and Lillie Murphy, a sixteen-year veteran of the factory who had worked her way up to "forelady" and an "active worker among the organizations for the girls of the factory," agreed to serve on the board of trustees. All but one of the other officers were single. That leadership, the continuing series of socials and dances, and the sound principle of a relief organization caused more and more Goodyear women to join the group. By 1918, twelve hundred women were members of the relief association.[8]

Clara Bingham was a key figure in getting most of the early women's organizations started at Goodyear Tire and Rubber Company. *Photo courtesy of Goodyear Tire and Rubber Company Collection, the University of Akron Archives.*

Membership peaked just as the influenza epidemic swept the city. In its wake, the Girls' Relief Association was left on the verge of financial ruin. By December 1919, the group had paid out more than two thousand dollars in benefits, the largest amount going to the victims of the influenza epidemic. The group reported that others receiving benefits had tonsillitis, "nervous breakdowns," rheumatism, and operations. By 1920, the relief association had to raise dues and find new members if it was to recover. By 1921, the Goodyear women, trying to recover from the influenza epidemic and the general economic downturn in the city and at the company, proposed merging with the men's relief organization. The women were to get the same benefit as before (by then, eight dollars per week, less than the twelve dollars per week that the men received), but the men were to take over the women's resources and assume its obligations. The Goodyear women's attempt to maintain a distinct relief organization had died.[9] Subsequent Goodyear women's organizations would take quite a different shape.

The Goodyear Women's Club and the Wingfoot Girls, established in 1922 and 1925 respectively, followed the organizational pattern most commonly followed by women's organizations in the city. On the surface, the two seemed to have duplicate functions—promoting the "better and broader" acquaintance among Goodyear women. Yet, in reality, the two groups served distinctly different constituencies and revealed a class division within the women's organizations of Goodyear.

Established first, the Women's Club became the organization for the wives, sisters, mothers, and daughters of Goodyear employees, typically executives, managers, or those who aspired to those positions. It was founded by a well-connected woman, Clara Bingham, the same woman elected president of the Girls' Relief Association. She called together nine women to organize a club committed to promoting "a better and broader acquaintance among Goodyear women and to bring together women interested in literature, art, music, science and civic problems."[10]

Women workers apparently were not welcomed into the group. Thus, three years later, Clara Bingham started an organization specifically for the women who worked in Goodyear's office and factory. Organized "to promote a broader acquaintance among Goodyear girl employees, to cultivate the social, intellectual and physical development of its members, and to be of service," the group offered an opportunity for women "to become acquainted in a clean, wholesome, social environment." It is unclear if African American women were invited to join the organization. Nonetheless, by 1933, Goodyear had its own Colored Women's Club with an array of dances, parties, and musicals.[11]

The Girls' Relief Association was quite different from the Goodyear women's organizations that followed. The Wingfoot Girls, the Women's Club, and the Colored Women's Club were social/literary/benevolent organizations, not so different in form and function from other women's clubs across the city. Although a certain amount of socializing took place at its various fund-raisers, the Girls' Relief Association was, at its heart, an organization designed to provide a measure of security—that is, financial benefits—to its members at times of illness and injury, times that could bring disaster to any workingwoman. Here was an example of workingwomen attempting to protect *themselves* financially. These women would not have to rely on the ladies' aid societies of their churches, on benevolent groups, or on city charity if they became ill or were injured.

DAUGHTERS OF JERUSALEM

African American women, excluded from the power structure within the city, organized their own clubs. Many mirrored the middle-class women's organizations of the city—garden clubs, sororities, mother's groups, and literary societies;[12] but one club, in particular, built on the African American cultural history as the central focus of its mission. The Daughters of Jerusalem was the first and the longest lived of the African American women's organizations in the city.

As a national organization, the Daughters of Jerusalem dated back to antebellum days, although its structure, membership, and goals were quite different in those days. The club grew out of the American Mysteries organization and the auxiliary women's organization, the Daughters of Zion. In the early days of the organization, both women and men, black and white, joined. They were united in the goal of helping slaves escape to Canada via the Underground Railroad. After the Civil War, the organization reorganized as a society of African Americans, primarily women. The reconstituted group had two missions: to create a home for "aged colored women," at the organization's headquarters in Springfield, Ohio; and to preserve "traditions and memories of the trying days of race." The society was composed of forty to fifty councils across the nation and was especially strong in Ohio, where eleven of the councils were based. The Daughters of Jerusalem carried all the trappings of a fraternal organization, with a uniform of sorts (white dresses with purple sashes for officers), a proclivity to parade, and exotic titles for its leadership (there was no president, but there was a "grand princess royal"), not far different from the fraternal organizations of the day.

Established in Akron in 1886 as a woman's organization, the Daughters of Jerusalem had religious, benevolent, and social underpinnings. Like other women's organizations in the city, the Daughters of Jerusalem owed its existence to one woman—in this case, Mary J. Pickett. Mary was part of the elite within Akron's African American community. She was married to Henry Pickett, a whitewasher, who had moved north from Kentucky. With Charles Alexander, Henry Pickett eventually opened Excelsior White Washing Company, one of the few African American–owned companies in nineteenth-century Akron. Mary had been born in Indiana; her father was from Virginia and her mother from North Carolina. Little is known about her early life or education. By 1880, the Picketts had married, had at least one child, Alexander, and settled in Akron. Six years later, Mary, fifty-one, organized the Daughters of Jerusalem. From the beginning, she was a key leader in the city's Daughters of Jerusalem; she even served as the group's representative to the local Women's Council. Mary also moved up to leadership in the regional and national Daughters of Jerusalem organization, serving as grand chaplain, pro tem, of the group.[13]

In Akron, the Daughters of Jerusalem was most closely aligned with two churches in the city, the A. M. E. Zion Church and the Second Baptist Church, both African American congregations. Several of its most active members were married to or were relatives of ministers of those congregations. Rhoda Simmons was the wife of the Reverend Charles W. Simmons, pastor of the A. M. E. Zion Church; Mattie Jones was the wife of the Reverend Royal A. Jones, the longtime pastor of the Second Baptist Church; and Susie Strothers was the daughter of the Reverend Robert J. Strothers, another pastor at A. M. E. Zion, and his wife, Nannie. A familial connection with a minister was not required for membership or leadership. Many other Akron African American women were active in the Daughters of Jerusalem, which, during the early twentieth century, was said to be "one of the best orders of color in the city," according to the *Beacon Journal.* A number of members came from families long active in Akron's African American community, an elite group, although not necessarily drawn from the highest reaches of socioeconomic classes. (Opportunities for upward socioeconomic mobility for African Americans in Akron were limited in this period.) May V. Dandridge, twenty-four, was the daughter of Joseph and Sarah Dandridge. Joseph, identified as an engineer in the 1880 census, joined the Union League and served on the committee to assist Akron's black population in gaining justice in the city. Leah A. Lancaster was married to Frank, another engineer, who served as chairman of the executive committee of the Colored Citizens Club in Akron. Others seem to have been new arrivals in the city. Isadore Hyman, twenty-three, had moved up to Akron from Pickaway County, in south-central Ohio. Isadore worked as a domestic in the household of Charles and Mary Henry on East Buchtel. Eva Hawkins also worked as a domestic, in the home of Henry A. and Ludie Robinson, 847 East Market Street. Some mothers and daughters joined the group. Jessamine Simpson, just eighteen, and her mother, Ella, forty-three, both were active in the group in the late nineteenth century.[14] In some instances, the Daughters of Jerusalem served as the training ground for African American women about to start a career in fraternal, civic, and benevolent activism. Pearl V. Heath, Mattie Jones, Julia Pinn, and Irene Rideout all became charter members of the women's auxiliary of the Knights of Pythias. Mary Pickett, Pearl Heath, and Irene Rideout were charter members of the "colored" branch of the WCTU in Akron.[15]

Akron's Daughters of Jerusalem offered its members many opportunities, including the chance to socialize with those from across the city. The *Beacon Journal* observed that meetings ended with "pleasant conversation" and applauded the group because it treated "their guests as they do everything else, that is, just right, at the right time, in the right place." The club also gave black Akron women leadership opportunities. Limited financial means did not curtail a woman's access to elected positions in the Daughters of Jerusalem. Mary Pickett, the wife of a business owner, held many positions nationally and locally, but Emily J. Morrison, the wife of a laborer, also won a leadership role within the organization. She served as grand messenger in 1902; Julia Pinn, wife of teamster Levi Pinn, held the same position in 1911. Katie Wooldridge, wife of another teamster, was the group's deputy for all of northern Ohio in 1906. In this regard, the Daughters of Jerusalem had far greater economic diversity in its leadership than most organizations run by white women in the city.

There were also ample opportunities for African American women to hone their communication and musical talents. Most meetings included speeches, recitations, and music. Young members especially were featured in the musical offerings. Lula Hamilton, Susie Strothers, and Mamie Thomas were the trio of singers at the 1895 feast. Pearl Heath, the daughter of laborer Robert B. Heath and wife Victoria, was a featured soloist in 1906, and Florence Johnson, who could not be identified in the city's directories, offered an instrumental solo at one of the meetings in 1905. Older members read essays or papers they had researched, thereby improving their communication skills. Capitola Robinson Dyson, the first African American woman to graduate from Central High School, read a paper at a 1906 meeting; Leah Lancaster, the wife of a leader of the Colored Citizens Club, gave an address at the 1906 meeting.[16]

Like many women's organizations in the city, the Daughters of Jerusalem invited outside speakers. But unlike the other clubs in the city, the Daughters of Jerusalem heard speakers address issues of cultural heritage and ways to improve the race or keep alive the "memories of the trying days of race." In 1905, the group brought in Jason Brown, son of abolitionist John Brown, who led the abortive uprising at Harpers Ferry before the Civil War. Brown briefed the women about his father and about his own involvement in the Kansas uprising. James Coleman, the husband of one of the members, spoke about his life as a slave before the Civil War, and Dr. James Bradfield offered his perspectives on the need for hospitals and senior citizen homes for African Americans. He emphasized that once African Americans showed the "proper progressive spirit," whites would help them.[17]

Bradfield's comments about senior citizen homes for African Americans were in keeping with the number one benevolent project of the Daughters of Jerusalem. The Akron branch was an important fund-raiser for a senior citizen home for African American women. At each meeting, the group took up a collection for the "home for aged women." Although the proceeds were often limited, the Akron group was ever hopeful that it would soon have enough money to build the home; prospects seemed good because Mary Pickett was serving as a trustee for the home. The local group also helped other black Akron women who were down on their luck, by holding socials to benefit the women. In 1896, for example, the local council held a benefit to assist "Mrs. Howard," who had been ill. The *Beacon Journal* reported that the event was a great success: "a neat sum" was raised and everyone had a good time. ("Dancing was the principal amusement.")[18]

The Daughters of Jerusalem was the start of a vibrant African American women's club movement in Akron. Excluded from most female-run civic organizations in the city, African American women found a home in the Daughters of Jerusalem, a group that combined social aspects with fraternal trappings and benevolent, educational, and cultural goals. Started at a time when the African American population of the city was small, the organization flowered as more black women emigrated to Akron. The Daughters of Jerusalem proved to be an important training ground for African American women. In this club, the women learned organizational skills, honed their communication talents, and improved their networking abilities. The Daughters of Jerusalem became a kind of launching pad for other African American women's organizations in the city. Daughters of Jerusalem members helped start the women's auxiliary of the Knights of Pythias, the "colored" branch of the WCTU, and other women's organizations as well. By 1932, there were so many African American women's groups in the city that the Akron Council of Negro Women, a federation of women's clubs, was started. It was the first such council started in the United States.[19]

Immigrant women faced formidable challenges in organizing their clubs in Akron in the first twenty-five years of the twentieth century. The women had to adjust to so much—living in a new country, learning a new language and new customs, and achieving a measure of financial security. Within the immigrant enclaves in the city, women organized clubs associated with the churches.[20] Outside of the church, the International Institute served as the important organizational meeting ground for immigrant groups in the city.

Although Akron had always been a city of immigrants, the International Institute was not organized there until 1917, when the YWCA formally opened the International Institute in South Akron. The YWCA had made overtures to immigrants earlier, primarily through the classes offered. In 1904, for example, Estelle Musson, a music teacher at Buchtel College, volunteered to teach immigrant women English at one of the factories. The next year, the YWCA added more English-language classes to its repertoire at the YWCA headquarters. Those classes, offered in the evening so more immigrant women and girls could attend, were under Carita McEbright, a well-known community organizer and educator.

English-language classes were in keeping with YWCA trends nationwide. In 1910, following a U.S. Immigration Commission report that highlighted the difficulties new immigrants were facing in adjusting to American life, the YWCA in New York began a program designed to protect immigrant women who were coming into the United States unaccompanied. The YWCA sent employees to meet immigrants when they arrived in Ellis Island, the major entry point into the eastern United States for immigrants in the late nineteenth and early twentieth centuries, and helped them find their families. In 1911, the New York YWCA started the first International Institute to assist immigrants as they adjusted to American life. YWCA chapters were not required to establish an International Institute. However, with its large foreign-born population and the lack of other resources for immigrants in the city, Akron was an ideal location for the creation of such an institute.[21]

In 1916, the Akron YWCA moved in that direction by hiring its first immigration secretary, Shirley Leonard, who had the responsibility of overseeing the YWCA's programming for immigrants. Shirley Leonard did not wait for the immigrants to get to the city. She arranged for the government to send regular reports with the names of foreign-born women landing in Ellis Island who planned to settle in

Akron. Shirley reported to an Immigration Committee, which had a broad mandate of easing the plight of immigrant women. Anna Case, a former social worker in Cleveland with experience working with Hungarian and Polish populations, headed that Immigration Committee. In Anna, Shirley had an ally. With the input of Edith Terry Bremer, who had started the YWCA's first International Institute in New York, Shirley, Anna, and the Immigration Committee built the argument in favor of the creation of an International Institute in Akron. In November 1916, the Akron YWCA board agreed and approved the money to create a new branch. The International Institute opened in 1917 on South Main Street.[22]

From its start, the institute provided a wide range of services to foreign-born women and men. (Unlike other YWCA branches, the International Institute served both women and men.) Institute volunteers and staff members visited new arrivals to the city and helped the families sort out American life. That could be as simple as helping a mother care for her children. If a baby needed to see a doctor, an institute volunteer or staff member took the mother and child to infant welfare clinics and translated for them. If there was tension between a mother and her Americanized daughter, an institute volunteer helped the pair work through the problem. Or, as one staff member observed, "The mother must be helped to understand what the young daughter wants and why instead of being left to submit to despair to the unknown monster of 'American ways,' which the daughter is constantly flinging at her." During the influenza epidemic of 1918, which hit the Akron immigrant population hard, institute staff and volunteers translated for physicians and explained medical orders in ways that non-English-speaking residents could understand.

Institute personnel also had to unravel government red tape. During World War I, institute staff workers explained army induction orders to non-English-speaking draftees. Interpreters explained citizenship and residency requirements. When immigrants ran into difficulties with the government, the institute sorted out the problems, filed the necessary paperwork, and contacted the proper government offices.[23]

The International Institute also took over the YWCA's English-language classes and started offering citizenship courses. This was no easy task. Immigrants settling in Akron came from many parts of Europe—Italy, Yugoslavia, Czechoslovakia, Russia, Poland, Hungary, Germany, Austria, the Ukraine, Serbia, and Lithuania. In its early years, the institute served more than two dozen different nationalities, many of them non-English speaking. That meant Shirley Leonard had to hire staff or find volunteers who could serve as interpreters for one or more of those languages. Shirley found some gifted translators, individuals who could speak four or more languages. The institute's services were long overdue. As one longtime YWCA officer recalled, the International Institute was the "only agency in the city dealing exclusively with the foreign born and their children of all nationalities and religions, who constitute nearly one-third of our population, with a staff of workers who speak their languages."[24]

The International Institute was probably the most complex branch of the YWCA to administer. Shirley Leonard, as immigration secretary, was the titular head of the institute, and the "Committee of Management," a semiautonomous group of twenty-one women, determined the programs that the organization offered its constituency. The composition of that committee differed considerably from the typical board that directed a large women's club at that time. The committee itself was a blending of cultures and perspectives of what the International Institute should be. A portion of the committee was made up of representatives of the institute's constituencies, immigrants and/or daughters of the foreign-born; the other members were YWCA leaders, well-meaning, affluent, native-born matrons. In general, the YWCA contingent wanted the emphasis to be on Americanization, while the representatives of the institute's constituencies—immigrants and/or daughters of the foreign-born—wanted to provide a safe environment where new residents could retain their native culture, even as they adjusted to American life. In its programming and policymaking for the institute, the Committee of Management had to find a balance between Americanization and the retention of cultural and ethnic diversity.

The International Institute achieved this by offering English-language and citizenship classes, before the city's schools took over the responsibility, thereby achieving the Americanization that the YWCA valued,[25] and it nurtured cultural heritage by hosting events that showcased different ethnicities and by serving as the home for many ethnically based women's organizations. Those clubs served as a place where women spoke their native tongues, talked about shared problems in their new home, and kept traditional customs alive.[26] For immigrant girls and daughters of the foreign born, the institute offered special Girl Reserve clubs, country-specific girls clubs, and "cosmopolitan" clubs (described as a "melting club for many nationalities").[27]

From the start, the International Institute served as a safe haven for immigrants in the city. Here immigrants found staff and volunteers who did not judge them in a city too often critical of its foreign-born population. Many International

Institute staff members and volunteers understood precisely what these immigrants faced, for most were immigrants themselves or daughters of the foreign born. As the institute reported, staff and volunteers were "trained, cultured people . . . who know the crises through which their people pass, such as language helplessness, change of occupation, change of diet, housing, custom, laws, etc., in which physical life is cast."[28] The institute provided much-needed services to immigrant women and men—English-language classes, citizenship instruction, assistance to work through the maze of American bureaucracy, family counseling, organizational opportunities along ethnic lines—not available elsewhere.

The International Institute contrasted with the general YWCA. The most obvious was the diverse ethnic base. The YWCA remained an organization run by well-educated, affluent women wedded to traditional perspectives on municipal housekeeping and domestic feminism. The dormitory for workingwomen, the classes designed to teach students domestic skills or to prepare them for clerical positions, the Bible lessons, the lunchroom, the employment bureau that handled only jobs in traditional female occupations—all illustrated how the YWCA leaders were taking their domestic responsibilities into the city by creating safe housing for young women, teaching the next generation the skills needed for household duties and traditionally female jobs in the workplace, strengthening their religious foundation, and feeding women (and later men) nutritious but inexpensive meals. Those services, though badly needed in the city, never stretched the bounds of traditional gender roles.

The International Institute worked from a different perspective. Run by staff and volunteers who were immigrants or daughters of the foreign born, the institute respected cultural diversity and offered programming that cultivated and nurtured that variety. Each ethnic group was free to organize its own women's clubs and cultivate its own support network. Each ethnic group turned to a specific staff member or volunteer who served as its advocate to government agencies. As *advocates*, institute workers were free to veer from the YWCA's traditional expectations within the municipal housekeeping model of benevolence. Of course, some of the programs fit neatly into the municipal housekeeping model—the translation program during the influenza epidemic, the family counseling, the women's clubs, the Girl Reserves—but others expanded it. The work with government agencies and the citizenship classes were services more commonly associated with professional social work. It is unclear why and how the women of the International Institute were able to expand their role. No doubt part of the reason may have been the autonomy of the branch. Run by a separate Committee of Management and by a staff and volunteers from ethnic groups excluded from YWCA leadership, the institute became a public advocate for immigrants, when few others wanted that responsibility. The immigrants responded with loyalty so strong that during the Depression and after, the central YWCA questioned the institute and its programs and attempted to rein in the group's autonomy.[29] This advocacy differed greatly from the YWCA and its programs for workingwomen during the first twenty-five years of the twentieth century. In the International Institute, immigrant women became *partners* in the organization; as the International Institute mission statement outlined, its goals were

> TO WORK with the foreign born so that they may adapt themselves to a new country and share in its growth and development.

> TO HELP both Americans and Foreign-born to become better acquainted and to understand the cultures of the many who are participating in our national life.

> TO KEEP before us the mutual benefits gained from the contributions of the different nationalities in our city.[30]

Thus, the club movement of Akron was not just the purview of white, middle-class women. Workingwomen, African Americans, and immigrants organized their own clubs and organizations. Within these forums, these women—excluded from many of the social and economic opportunities in the city and traditionally defined as "unempowered"—discovered the fellowship of club work and found new ways to resolve the difficulties they faced in the city.

Within these clubs, "unempowered" women defined their own missions, goals, organizations, and strategies. These were not necessarily the same as the ones that middle-class white clubwomen employed. The immigrant, workingwomen, and African American clubwomen were not able to create the great health, welfare, educational, and cultural institutions that more affluent white women did; but, through clubs and organizations, "unempowered" women were discovering the power of united action.

Chapter 8

Conclusion

Such is her destiny; to visit the forsaken, to attend the neglected, amid the forgetfulness of myriads to remember.

—*American Democrat*[1]

They were like all girls "just looking for something to do." It is doubtful if any of the dozen had the slightest idea that from their informal gatherings would spring a city wide musical organization.

—*Akron Beacon Journal*[2]

ONCE UPON A TIME IN AKRON, THERE WERE NO WOMEN'S CLUBS—and there was not much of a town either. A few adventuresome souls eked out an existence in a town that promised much but delivered little. By 1842, Akron had all the makings of a mercantile center—two canals running through it, growing prosperity, a small but optimistic population, a few churches, vice, disease, violence—and its first woman's organization. From these humble beginnings, Akron women launched a club movement that improved the city—and transformed its female members.

On paper, the earliest of those women's organizations were simply auxiliaries to the male temperance groups, merely appendages, "supporting" husbands, brothers, and fathers in their battles against alcohol. The designation "auxiliary" belied the true nature of these groups. Like the men, Akron women had come together in a spirit of reform to eliminate the sin of inebriation. But the women, with their finely tuned sense of morality and duty, expanded their mission, identified those in need, and extended help to women and families in crisis, even if liquor did not figure into their dilemma. In the process, the temperance women discovered a network of friends, bound together by a sense of mission and satisfaction in a job well done.

By 1925, tens of thousands of Akron women had enjoyed that special sense of belonging that only a woman's club provided. Through their clubs and organizations, Akron women had helped countless families, crusaded against liquor, cared for children, built hospitals, created cultural institutions, and much more.

Women's clubs felt right to Akron women. The clubs and organizations fit neatly into the middle-class social expectations of women as wives, mothers, and caregivers. In fact, the women's clubs of Akron used the bonds of domesticity to their advantage. They used its rhetoric in recruitment appeals and fund-raising, in explanations of the problems facing women and families in need, and in rationales for leaving the home to help the community. Yes, domesticity and the separate sphere for women in the home, on the surface, seemed constricting and limiting; but the Akron clubwomen discovered those bonds could be stretched and molded to their liking as they defined and redefined their responsibilities to the city. In their clubs and organizations, Akron women were displaying all the characteristics of what historians label "domestic feminism," using "ladylike" characteristics to rationalize reforming the community, the "public world," traditionally the sphere of men.[3]

Between 1842, the year of the earliest discernible women's organization in the city, and 1925, the ending point of this book, Akron women formed hundreds of organizations. Three, in particular, were especially important in illustrating the evolution of women's clubs in Akron generally and the furtherance of "domestic feminism" in particular. These three clubs taught Akron women skills upon which to build as they organized.

The first was the giant of the Civil War, the Akron Soldiers Aid Society. Here was a group that differed greatly in size, scope, and responsibility from the women's organizations that preceded it. The Akron Soldiers Aid Society built upon the conservative ideological, organizational, and strategic model of the antebellum ladies' committees. But the aid society women added a larger mission, the care of Akron men away at war; that, in turn, forced the aid society women to rethink the scope of their activities. The Akron Soldiers Aid Society shipped countless boxes to the hospitals via the U.S. sanitary commission in Cleveland, collected thousands of dollars, and staged a series of successful fund-raising extravaganzas. The Soldiers Aid

Society taught valuable lessons that Akron women applied to other groups after the Civil War. It was in the aid society rooms that women learned organizational skills. They learned how to recruit members and work with women from different neighborhoods, religious denominations, and, in some instances, ethnic backgrounds. Upper- and middle-class women worked together.

Women of the working class seldom, if ever, entered the sanctum of the Soldiers Aid Society rooms; this inability to welcome women of the lower class remained a shortcoming that plagued clubs organized by white women in the city and domestic feminism generally. The women of the Soldiers Aid Society also learned how to set goals, strategize, and come up with plans to reach those goals. Perhaps as important, aid society women learned how to use the press for the best possible coverage. The newspapers in the city became their partners and their champions, reporting events both before and after, encouraging the community to continue to donate to the group and to attend aid society get-togethers, and editorially supporting the organization and its work. Certainly, the Akron Soldiers Aid Society was at an advantage here; two of its members were the wives of the owners of the *Summit County Beacon.* However, this type of coverage would not have been possible if the "communication committee," yet another innovation of the aid society, had not mastered valuable public-relations skills. The women of the Soldiers Aid Society grasped early the role that the press played in advancing the organization's cause and building community support. Aid society communication committee members kept the newspapers informed of their activities by creating circulars and letters that served as early press releases. These releases were quite sophisticated. Aid society women crafted these pieces so as to employ social conventions of the day. Events were held at a *man's* home, without reference to the wife, the aid society leader or member; the contributions of men were always highlighted. In the process, the aid society shared the prestige of the male patrons, gave the impression of male support, and got publicity for its cause.

The second turning point that furthered domestic feminism and the club movement in Akron was the temperance crusade and the organization that grew out of it, initially the temperance league that grew into the various branches of the Woman's Christian Temperance Union in the city. Akron women did not come up with the crusade; they merely used it to their own advantage, to publicize their goal of eliminating liquor from the city. On the surface, the temperance crusade seemed a radical departure from ladylike behaviors expected in domestic feminism. In reality, however, the crusades were carefully orchestrated events that played to the fundamental values of domestic feminism. The crusaders cast purity to the fore, in sharp contrast to the corrupting influence of the saloons that they protested. The crusade also demonstrated the great organizational ability of the temperance women, as well as a fine-tuned understanding of public relations and special-event planning. The crusades were carefully staged events designed to capture maximum publicity and community attention. Providing that its aims were high and its members acted like "ladies," even a temperance crusade furthered the end of domestic feminism. Moreover, the leagues and the WCTU branches carried the temperance discussion—and the rhetoric of domestic feminism—into the halls of government. Akron women gained a voice in the temperance debate in city hall and state government. The sweet, soft, feminine voice of temperance always spoke of the idealized role of women in society and how temperance improved society and enhanced family life. The WCTU's influence could be found in other ways as well. Its Friendly Union served as a kind of intellectual incubator for future women's clubs as well as a central meeting place where Akron clubwomen talked mission, goals, strategies, and alliances in late-nineteenth-century Akron. The WCTU's reach was long and could be found in many of the benevolent groups of nineteenth-century Akron.

The WCTU also taught the perils of over-organization. This group stumbled in the late nineteenth and early twentieth century by establishing too many branches within the city. Every neighborhood seemed to have its own union. While that strategy increased membership and opened leadership opportunities to a more diverse group of Akron women, in the end, it diluted the ability of the central WCTU to speak as a single, strong, powerful voice.

The third group demonstrated the exuberance—and power—of youth within the domestic feminism framework and introduced fresh strategies into Gilded Age and Progressive Era women's clubs in Akron. The Akron Day Nursery (later the Mary Day Nursery), a collaboration of King's Daughters from two denominations, was a group of young women, most of them under the age of thirty, committed to both the tenets of domestic feminism and improving life for working-class women and youth. Although charter members came from families in which women had long made benevolent and civic contributions to the city through other clubs, the Akron Day Nursery advocates themselves had only limited organizational experience, so the women brought fresh perspectives to their club work. This organization illustrated how women's clubs evolved and redefined their mission to survive. The women began by creating a nursery for the children of working mothers, then expanded that mission to include a kindergarten. When kindergartens were introduced into the public schools of the city, the nursery organization redefined itself and expanded its mission to health care for children. These young clubwomen were soon running the only children's hospital in the city. This was a new, expanded brand of domestic feminism, one comfortable with business and personnel issues at Children's Hospital, an institution that continues today. These young women were also quite adept in their public relations and fund-raising duties. The women of the nursery and hospital introduced innovative methods of fund-raising. The most successful—from a public relations standpoint—was the yearly food drives involving children in the city's public schools. This gave every child in the city, rich and poor, immigrant and native born, black and white, the opportunity to help less fortunate and ailing children—and a sense of ownership in the nursery and hospital. It was a brilliant campaign that not only brought much food to the nursery (which was distributed to other charitable organizations in the city), but tied the *entire city* to the Mary Day Nursery and Children's Hospital organization through the students. It also served as a valuable recruitment tool, committing many mothers of these students to the organization. Finally, it represented a perfect publicity device; the newspapers reported on the contributions of the children and commented (positively) about the amount of public support for the institution, thereby further strengthening sentiment toward the nursery and the new hospital.

These three organizations illustrated the evolving, expanding scope of the women's organizations in the city.

The clubwomen of this period accepted the separation of spheres—the men in the business world; the women with their more refined moral sensibilities at home. But that did not make women powerless. By working within their clubs and organizations, these women had a sense of mission—and belonging. Together, the clubwomen were able to accomplish much and bring many improvements to the city—by transferring their traditional domestic responsibilities to the community. Thus, the clubwomen did fund-raising for their churches, assisted families who had fallen on hard times, tended to youngsters of the working class, planned the city's first (and only) children's hospital, started an International Institute to help integrate the immigrants into a new country, and created a musical heritage for the city.

The middle-class women of Akron were not the only ones who longed for a sense of belonging and accomplishment. Workingwomen, immigrants, and African Americans, who wished to share the sense of sisterhood as equal partners, organized on their own and felt their own sense of accomplishment as they achieved their own goals.

The city benefited greatly from the women's clubs that worked so tirelessly to bring improvements to the cultural, health, benevolent, and family life of the city; but so, too, did Akron women. The women's clubs offered enormous opportunities to their members. Where else could Akron women develop finely tuned organizational skills, perfect their public relations talent, display their fund-raising acumen, earn their financial stripes, and cultivate their leadership gifts, all within a supportive environment of like-minded women?

Where else could Akron women exert such influence? Within clubs and organizations, Akron women determined the mission, goals, and strategies. These clubs and organizations allowed certain women—by virtue of their family ties, organizational skills, leadership talents, community vision, or sheer will—to emerge as formidable, albeit forgotten, characters in Akron's history. During the Civil War, Pamphila Wolcott and Elizabeth Abbey were characters of influence and import through their work in the Akron Soldiers Aid Society. In the heat of the temperance crusade, Angelina Manley kept a cool head and a sharp mind as she sent crusading bands of women to Howard and Market streets to pray outside the unruly and corrupting saloons. After the crusading spirit ebbed, Isabella Berry took over as leader during the group's most dynamic period. Isabella cast a long shadow over Akron women's clubs. She, along with Katherine Claypole, was the moving force behind the Women's Council. Helen Storer in the Mary Day Nursery and the Tuesday Musical Club, Calista Wheeler and Anna Case in the YWCA, Mary Pickett in the Daughters of Jerusalem, Lura Close in the Girls' Relief Association, Gertrude Seiberling in the Tuesday Musical Club, and so many other women had the sheer force of will, organizational skill, vision, and networking to create organizations and refocus groups that had grown old, tired, and obsolete.

These women had allies in their organization work. During the Gilded Age and after, a whole new class of women joined the club movement. These were paid, professional administrators. Overworked and underpaid, these well-educated women had the job of harnessing the enthusiasm of energetic volunteers, carrying the group's mission forward, and tending to the day-to-day administrative chores of the organization. The first generation of paid staff in Akron—Florence Savage and Lou Lusk—kept the WCTU and the Woman's Benevolent Association on track. Women's organizations came to see the benefit of a paid staff and started hiring professional women administrators to keep the groups going. Working with an exceptional volunteer leadership, Sarah Lyon and Edith Nash transformed the YWCA. Shirley Leonard brought a strong administrative vision to the International Institute.

An administrator was not always enough to salvage an organization. C. Annette Brownlees lacked the influence, leverage, and authority to make a difference at the Woman's Exchange. Indeed, without a supportive volunteer leadership and board, no administrator, no matter how talented, could save an organization.

The professional administrators point to another aspect of club life in Akron: these clubs and organizations served as a training ground for the next generation of women workers. Edith Barnum, head teacher of the Mary Day Nursery's kindergarten, trained the first generation of Akron kindergarten teachers. Shirley Leonard turned to immigrant women to find the translators she needed at the International Institute. The head nurse at the Ward for Crippled Children supervised a staff of young pediatric nurses.

Thus, the influence of the women's clubs ran deep through Akron. The groups provided needed services to the community, assisted underserved populations, built great institutions, and opened more and different types of employment opportunities to women. Through their work in these organizations, Akron women gained enormous power, prestige, responsibility, and a sense of accomplishment within a supportive environment. The women's clubs of Akron humanized the city and did so much more.

Notes

CHAPTER I

1. "How Women Are Banded Together," *Akron Beacon Journal*, August 21, 1907, 27.

2. "Akron Is Organized to Death—Mrs. Brookover," *Akron Beacon Journal*, January 22, 1911, 5.

3. Building on the work of Carroll Smith-Rosenberg ("Beauty, the Beast, and the Militant Woman: A Case Study in Sex Roles and Social Stress in Jacksonian America," *American Quarterly* 23 [Winter 1971]: 562–84) and Nancy Cott (*The Bonds of Womanhood: Woman's Sphere in New England, 1780–1835* [New Haven, Conn.: Yale University Press, 1977]), Karen J. Blair argued that the clubwomen were feminists, although from the "domestic feminism" branch. Domestic feminists used "ladylike" characteristics to rationalize reforming the community—the public world—traditionally the sphere of men. "Despite public criticism, thousands of nineteenth-century women effectively employed the lady's traits to justify their departure from the home to exert special influence on the male sphere. By invoking their supposed natural talents, women took the ideology of the home with them, ending their confinement and winning influence in the public realm. Domestic Feminism resulted when women redefined the ideal lady." Clubwomen—including Akron's clubwomen—"transformed ladydom by providing an intellectual and social self-improvement program outside the realm of the household . . . to demand reforms for women and for all people in a society that relegated them to the sidelines." Karen J. Blair, *The Clubwoman as Feminist: True Womanhood Redefined, 1868–1914* (New York: Holmes and Meier, 1980), 4–5.

4. Arthur M. Schlesinger, "Biography of a Nation of Joiners," *American Historical Review* 50 (October 1944): 1.

5. Alexis de Tocqueville, *Democracy in America, the Henry Reeve Text as Revised by Francis Bowen*, edited by Phillips Bradley (New York: A. A. Knopf, 1960), 2:106, 108–9.

6. James Bryce, *The American Commonwealth* (London: Macmillan, 1889), 2:239, 240.

7. De Tocqueville, *Democracy in America*, as quoted in *Images of Women in American Popular Culture*, edited by Angela Dorenkamp, John F. McClymer, et al., 72 (New York: Harcourt Brace Jovanovich Inc., 1985).

8. Bryce, *American Commonwealth*, 2:598.

9. Barbara Welter, "The Cult of True Womanhood: 1820–1860," *American Quarterly* 24 (Summer 1966): 151–74.

10. John Angell James, *The Marriage Ring; or, How to Make Home Happy* (Boston: Gould, Kendall and Lincoln, 1842), 104, 115.

11. Rev. F. B. Fulton, *Woman as God Made Her: The True Woman* (Boston: Lee and Shepard, 1869), 41–42.

12. Mrs. John Sandford, *Woman, in Her Social and Domestic Character* (Boston: Otis, Broaders and Co., 1842), 173; Catharine E. Beecher and Harriet Beecher Stowe, *The American Woman's Home, or, Principles of Domestic Science; Being a Guide to the Formation and Maintenance of Economical Healthful, Beautiful, and Christian Homes* (New York: J. B. Ford, 1869), 18.

13. See, for example, Barbara L. Epstein, *The Politics of Domesticity: Women, Evangelism, and Temperance in Nineteenth-Century America* (Middletown, Conn.: Wesleyan University Press, 1981); Nancy A. Hewitt, *Women's Activism and Social Change: Rochester, New York, 1822–1872* (Ithaca: Cornell University Press, 1984); Agnes Hooper Gottlieb, *Women Journalists and the Municipal Housekeeping Movement, 1868–1914* (Lewiston, N.Y.: Edwin Mellen, 2001); Karen J. Blair, *Clubwoman as Feminist*; Elizabeth Hayes Turner, *Women, Culture and Community: Religion and Reform in Galveston, 1880–1920* (New York: Oxford University Press, 1997).

14. "Woman," reprint from *Blackwood's Magazine*, in *American Democrat*, April 4, 1849, 4.

15. Catharine Beecher, "The Peculiar Responsibilities, and Difficulties, of American Woman," as reprinted in *Roots of Bitterness: Documents of the Second History of American Women*, edited by Nancy F. Cott, Jeanne Boydston et al., 134 (Boston: Northeastern University Press, 1996); Beecher and Stowe, *American Woman's Home*, 245.

16. "Rules for Wives," *Glad Tidings and Ladies Universalist Magazine*, February 12, 1840, 140.

17. Porcia, "Hap-Hazard Ideas," *Akron Offering*, August 1849, 109.

18. "American Females," *Glad Tidings and Ladies Universalist Magazine*, June 17, 1840, 380.

19. David L. Sills, "Voluntary Associations: Sociological Aspects," in *International Encyclopedia of the Social Sciences*, edited by David L. Sills, 16:362–79 (New York: Macmillan and Free Press, 1968); David L. Sills, *The Volunteers: Means and Ends in a National Organization* (Glencoe, Ill.: Free Press, 1957).

20. Gottlieb, *Women Journalists*, 19–20.

21. "Rabbi Philo Tells What He Meant by 'The American Club Woman,'" *Akron Beacon Journal*, December 13, 1905, 6; Mrs. Zelia M. Walters, letter to the editor, "Club Woman Protests," *Akron Beacon Journal*, December 13, 1905, 6.

22. "The Club Woman," *Akron Beacon Journal*, December 19, 1905, 4.

CHAPTER 2

1. "The Seamstresses," *Summit Beacon*, April 5, 1854, 3.

2. "The Firemen's Celebration," *Summit Beacon*, June 6, 1849, 3.

3. Dr. W. S. Chase, "Yesterdays with Akron Doctors," in *A Centennial History of Akron, 1825–1925* (Akron: Summit County Historical Society, 1925), 212–13.

4 Samuel A. Lane, *Fifty Years and Over of Akron and Summit County* (Akron: Beacon Job Department, 1892), 57.

5. Laurine Schwan, "Amusements and Meeting Places," in *Centennial History of Akron*, 371; Lane, *Fifty Years*, 59.

6. Father Scullen, "Story of the First One Hundred Years, 1837–1937, of St. Vincent DePaul Church, Akron, Ohio" (no date, no publisher, no location); Rev. George Atwater, "Akron's Churchs," in *Centennial History of Akron*, 279–92, and Elizabeth A. Thompson and Susannah C. Cole, "Akron's Schools," in *Centennial History of Akron*, 256. The first school built in the area still stands on Broadway near Buchtel Avenue. See also George W. Knepper, *Akron: City at the Summit* (Tulsa, Okla.: Continental Heritage, 1981), 30–32, 38.

7. Lane, *Fifty Years*, 66–68.

8. Many well-known Akron merchants, including Benjamin Stephens, Henry Allen, Benjamin Meacham, and Delos Smith, filed for bankruptcy during these years. See, for example, "Bankruptcy," *Summit Beacon*, March 16 and 23, 1842, 3; "Bankrupt Notices," *Summit Beacon*, May 4, 1842, 3. On the failing of Akron businesses, see also Lane, *Fifty Years*, 65.

9. *New York Tribune* as reprinted in Lane, *Fifty Years*, 447, and Schwan, "Amusements and Meeting Places," *Centennial History of Akron*, 371.

10. "Rules for Wives," *Glad Tidings and Ladies Universalist Magazine*, February 12, 1840, 140; "Model of a Wife," *Akron Buzzard*, January 27, 1838, 3; "Good Wives," *American Democrat*, March 25, 1847, 1. These views were not all that different from those held by the large national women's publications of the day. Barbara Welter, "Cult of True Womanhood."

11. Lori D. Ginzberg, *Women and the Work of Benevolence: Morality, Politics and Class in the Nineteenth-Century United States* (New Haven: Yale University Press, 1990); Carroll Smith-Rosenberg, "Women and Religious Revivals: Anti-Ritualism, Liminality and the Emergence of the American Bourgeoisie" in *The Evangelical Tradition in America*, edited by Leonard I. Sweet, 199–231 (Macon, Ga.: Mercer University Press, 1984); Nancy A. Hewitt, "The Perimeters of Women's Power in American Religion," in Sweet, *Evangelical Tradition*, 233–56.

12. Antebellum groups did not always update newspapers about their activities. Moreover, social customs of the time probably worked against such a notification during the antebellum period. Typically, names of women appeared in print only at their birth, at their marriage, and at their death.

13. "A Washingtonian," *Summit County Beacon*, January 19, 1842, 2; Ian R. Tyrell, *Sobering Up: From Temperance to Prohibition in Antebellum America, 1800–1860* (Westport, Conn.:

Greenwood, 1979), 159–99; Jack S. Blocker Jr., *American Temperance Movements: Cycles of Reform* (Boston: Twayne, 1989), 30–44; Kenneth W. Povenmire, "The Temperance Movement in Ohio, 1840 to 1860" (master's thesis, Ohio State University, 1933), 123–36; Knepper, *Akron*, 38.

14. "Temperance," *Summit County Beacon*, December 1, 1841, 2, and December 22, 1841, 2; "The Washingtonians," *Summit County Beacon*, December 29, 1841, 2; "Temperance Movements," *Summit County Beacon*, January 5, 1842, 2; "A Washingtonian," *Summit County Beacon*, January 19, 1842; "County Washingtonian Total Abstinence Society," *Summit County Beacon*, February 23, 1842, 2.

15. Tyrell, *Sobering Up*, 179–81 and Blocker, *American Temperance Movements*, 30.

16. See, for example, "Temperance Pic-Nic," *American Democrat*, December 26, 1844, 3; "Temperance," *Summit Beacon*, December 1, 1841, 2; "Temperance Lecture," *American Democrat*, January 18, 1843, 3; "Washington's Birth-Day," *American Democrat*, February 15, 1843, 3; "The Washington Total Abstinence Society of Summit County," *American Democrat*, March 8, 1843, 3; "Temperance Meeting," *Cascade Roarer*, November 4, 1845, 2.

17. "Notice," *American Democrat*, November 14, 1844, 3.

18. "Mr. King's Address," *American Democrat*, March 29, 1843, 1; "The Ladies and Temperance," *Summit County Beacon*, April 5, 1843, 2.

19. Knepper, *Akron*, 38, 41; "Akron—Rum and Morality," *Akron Buzzard*, September 2, 1845, 2. The *Cascade Roarer*, a temperance newspaper in the city, complained that, by 1846, the Washingtonians had lost all energy, and attendance at the annual meeting was slim. See "Annual Meeting," *Cascade Roarer*, January 6, 1846, 2. In contrast, the Sons of Temperance had taken over the temperance activism in the city. "Sons of Temperance," *Cascade Roarer*, January 20, 1846, 2.

20. "Sons of Temperance," *Summit County Beacon*, April 4, 1849, 3. "Constitution, By-laws and Rules of the Cascade Division, number 88, of the Sons of Temperance of the State of Ohio: Instituted September 7, 1846" (Akron: Bro. H. Canfield, 1848), no page number, Summit County Historical Society Collection, University of Akron Archives.

21. Blocker, *American Temperance Movements*, 49–50, and Tyrell, *Sobering Up*, 211–17. "Great Temperance Demonstration of Summit County," advertisement, *American Democrat*, October 12, 1848, 3.

22. "Temperance Festival," *Summit County Beacon*, October 24, 1849, 3; "The Temperance Festival," *Summit Beacon*, October 31, 1849, 3; "Dedications," *Summit County Beacon*, October 31, 1849, 3.

23. "To the Benevolent of Akron," *American Democrat*, October 29, 1849, 2.

24. Certain churches did provide some welfare services to their members.

25. "Indignation Meeting," *Cascade Roarer*, March 3, 1846, 2.

26. See, for example, Mary Ryan, "The Power of Women's Network: A Case Study of Female Moral Reform in Antebellum America," in Nancy F. Cott, *History of Women*

in the United States: Historical Articles on Women's Lives and Activities, vol. 17, *Social and Political Reform,* pt. 2, 26–45 (Munich: K. G. Saur, 1994).

27. "Seamstresses' Rally," *Free Democratic Standard,* April 4, 1854, 1; "The Summit County Female Labor Association," *Summit County Beacon,* April 4, 1854, 2.

28. "Report of the Traveling Committee of the Summit County Female Labor Association," *Summit County Beacon,* June 21, 1854, 3.

29. Ibid.

30. "The Seamstresses," *Summit County Beacon,* April 5, 1854, 3.

31. "Report of the Traveling Committee," *Summit County Beacon,* June 21, 1854, 3.

32. Ibid.

33. "The Twenty-Second," *Free Democratic Standard,* February 13, 1851, 3.

34. Lane, *Fifty Years,* 330–31; "The Firemen's Celebration," *Summit Beacon,* June 6, 1849, 3 and "Firemen's Festival," *Free Democratic Standard,* February 12, 1852, 3.

35. "Firemen's Festival," 3.

CHAPTER 3

1. Mrs. E. T. Chapman to Miss M. C. Brayton, February 5, 1864, Middlebury, container 14, vol. 10, U.S. Sanitary Commission Papers, Western Reserve Historical Society (hereafter cited as U.S. Sanitary Commission Papers).

2. Mrs. E. T. Chapman to Miss M. C. Brayton, August 17, 1865, container 14, vol. 10, U.S. Sanitary Commission Papers.

3. *Centennial History of Akron,* 89; Knepper, *Akron,* 43–44; and P. Wolcott to Mrs. R. Rouse, October 2, 1862, container 11, vol. 1, U.S. Sanitary Commission Papers.

4. Mrs. F. Adams to Mrs. R. Rouse, April 24, no year, container 14, vol. 10, U.S. Sanitary Commission Papers.

5. Mrs. C. P. Wolcott to Mrs. R. Rouse, October 2, 1861, container 11, vol. 1, U.S. Sanitary Commission Papers.

6. Mrs. C. P. Wolcott to Mrs. R. Rouse, June 10, 1861, container 11, vol. 1, U.S. Sanitary Commission Papers.

7. See, for example, A. M. Coburn to Mrs. R. Rouse, March 14, 1862, container 11, vol. 1, U.S. Sanitary Commission Papers; Mrs. E. Chapman to Mrs. R. Rouse, July 8, 1863, container 14, vol. 10, U.S. Sanitary Commission Papers; Mrs. S. H. Coburn to Mrs. R. Rouse, January 16, 1862, container 11, vol. 1, U.S. Sanitary Commission Papers.

8. "Obituary," *Summit County Beacon,* April 16, 1863, 2.

9. Mrs. P. Wolcott to Mrs. R. Rouse, May 31, 1862, container 11, vol. 1; Pamphila Wolcott to Mrs. R. Rouse, October 9, 1861, container 11, vol. 1; and Mrs. P. Wolcott to Mrs. R. Rouse, October 17, 1861, container 11, vol. 1. All in the U.S. Sanitary Commission Papers.

10. Adeline Coburn to Miss M. C. Brayton, February 19, 1863, container 11, vol. 1, U.S. Sanitary Commission Papers; "Obituary," *Summit County Beacon*, April 16, 1863, 2. After the war, Pamphila Wolcott worked for a time in the pension office in Washington, D.C. She died in Akron in 1899. For additional details on Wolcott, see Kathleen L. Endres, "Pamphila Stanton Wolcott, 1827–1899," Akron Women's History website, http://www3.uakron.edu/schlcomm/womenshistory/wolcott_p.htm, retrieved August 8, 2004.

11. *Summit County Beacon*, February 18, 1864, 3; May 19, 1864, 3; and October 19, 1865, 3. See also Janelle Baltputnis, "Adeline Myers Coburn, died 1887," Akron Women's History website, http://www3.uakron.edu/schlcomm/womenshistory/coburn_a.htm, retrieved August 8, 2004.

12. Adeline Coburn to Mrs. R. Rouse, January 16, 1862, container 11, vol. 1, and Adeline Coburn to Mrs. R. Rouse, March 14, 1862, container 11, vol. 1. Both in U.S. Sanitary Commission Papers.

13. Adeline Coburn to Miss M. C. Brayton, April 25, 1862, container 11, vol. 1, U.S. Sanitary Commission Papers.

14. Isabella Green to Mrs. R. Rouse, July 21, 1862, container 11, vol. 1, U.S. Sanitary Commission Papers.

15. "An Appeal," *Summit County Beacon*, January 8, 1863, 3. See also "Vegetables for the Army," *Summit County Beacon*, January 29, 1863, 3; "Reached Its Destination," *Summit County Beacon*, February 5, 1862, 3; "A Complete Success," *Summit County Beacon*, February 12, 1863, 3; "Report of the Akron S.A.S.," *Summit County Beacon*, February 12, 1863, 3. For additional details on Abbey, see Angela Abel, "Elizabeth Smith Abbey, 1807–1874," Akron Women's History website, http://www3.uakron.edu/schlcomm/womenshistory/abbey_e.htm, retrieved August 8, 2004.

16. "Vegetables for the Army," *Summit County Beacon*, January 29, 1863, 3; "The Girls Dime Party," *Summit County Beacon*, December 11, 1862, 3.

17. Sarah Peck to Miss M. C. Brayton, March 7, 1863, container 11, vol. 1; Sarah Peck to Miss M. C. Brayton, February 14, 1863, container 11, vol. 1. Both in U.S. Sanitary Commission Papers.

18. No membership lists exist for the Akron and Middlebury societies. Names were gleaned from monthly reports published in the *Summit County Beacon* and individuals named in letters available in the U.S. Sanitary Commission Papers at the Western Reserve Historical Society. See, for example, "Report of the Akron S.A.S.," *Summit County Beacon*, February 12, 1863, 3. Names were then traced through census, city directories, marriage and death records, church archives, and city directories to obtain a profile of the women involved with the aid societies. With the exception of the marital status, findings are incomplete.

19. All this may have been a limitation of the records used.

20. "School Girls Dime Party," *Summit County Beacon*, December 4, 1862, 3.

21. Sills, "Voluntary Associations: Sociological Aspects," 262–70.

22. See, for example, Adeline Coburn to Mrs. R. Rouse, January 16, 1862, container 11, vol. 1, U.S. Sanitary Commission Papers.

23. Amanda Merrill to Mrs. R. Rouse, February 24, 1862, container 14, vol. 10, U.S. Sanitary Commission Papers.

24. "Dime Party," *Summit County Beacon*, October 30, 1862, 3.

25. *Summit County Beacon*, December 29, 1864, 3; "Dime Meeting," *Summit County Beacon*, September 15, 1864, 3; and "Dime Party," *Summit County Beacon*, November 17, 1864, 3.

26. "Dime Party," *Summit County Beacon*, February 16, 1865; "Dime Party," *Summit County Beacon*, November 17, 1864.

27. "Go and See the Elephant," *Summit County Beacon*, April 16, 1863, 3; "A Complete Success," *Summit County Beacon*, February 12, 1863, 3; "Dinner at Grace Park," *Summit County Beacon*, July 2 and 9, 1863, 3.

28. "A Complete Success," *Summit County Beacon*, February 12, 1863, 3.

29. A. W. Coburn to Miss M. C. Brayton, April 12, 1862, container 11, vol. 1, U.S. Sanitary Commission Papers; "Fruit for the Soldiers," *Summit County Beacon*, September 10, 1863, 3; "Pillows for the Soldiers," *Summit County Beacon*, October 22, 1863, 3; "Hospital Soldiers' Letters," *Summit County Beacon*, April 2, 1863, 3.

30. Amanda Merrill to Miss R. Rouse, March 4, 1862, container 14, vol. 10, U.S. Sanitary Commission Papers.

31. "An Appeal," *Summit County Beacon*, January 8, 1863, 3.

32. Mrs. E. T. Chapman to Miss M. C. Brayton, May 17, 1865, container 14, vol. 10, U.S. Sanitary Commission Papers.

33. Mrs. W. B. Raymond to Miss M. C. Brayton, May 13, 1868, container 11, vol. 1, U.S. Sanitary Commission Papers.

34. Mrs. E. T. Chapman to Miss M. C. Brayton, May 22, 1865, container 14, vol. 10, and Mrs. Bottsford to Miss M. C. Brayton, October 4, 1865, container 14, vol. 10. Both in the U.S. Sanitary Commission Papers.

CHAPTER 4

1. "Fifth Annual Report," manuscript no. 1334, Woman's Missionary Society Collection, Trinity Lutheran Church, Akron, Ohio. Hereafter referred to as Trinity Lutheran Church Archives, Akron.

2. "Report of Trinity," *Grace Church Reformed Herald*, June 1891, 1.

3. Editorial, *Akron Beacon and Republican*, March 17, 1891, 4.

4. The "second class" designation was not a comment on the quality of the city. It was a legislative designation based on population. *Centennial History of Akron*, 91, 93–108.

5. *Centennial History of Akron*, 294–323.

6. Lane, *Fifty Years*, 621–39; *Centennial History of Akron*, 442–52, 468–75; Knepper, *Akron*, 48, 51, 54.

7. Helga Eugenie Kaplan, "Century of Adjustment: A History of the Akron Jewish Community, 1865–1975" (PhD diss., Kent State University, 1978), 67–72.

8. It is difficult to say precisely which church had the first organized women's organization. The local newspaper did not always report that information, and histories of the churches do not always include information about the women's organizations. Based on published accounts of the churches, histories of the congregations, and manuscript collections, it does not appear that Akron churches started formally organized women's organizations until after the Civil War.

9. "German Catholic Fair," *Summit County Beacon*, December 22, 1864, 3; "Congregational Fair," *Summit County Beacon*, March, 1, 15, and 22, 1866, 3.

10. "Fifth Annual Report," manuscript no. 1334, Trinity Lutheran Church Archives, Akron.

11. The Congregational Church was the denomination of the families of many of the leaders in the city. Histories of women's groups of the Congregational Church tend to emphasize those families. Because full membership records have not been retained, it is impossible to determine if others were part of these organizations. "The Beginnings of the Local Missionary Society, June 21, 1934," Folder: Church Histories for 1984 Sesquicentennial, First Congregational Church Archives, First Congregational Church, Akron, Ohio.

12. "Centennial Souvenir," no page number, Folder: Centennial Celebration, First Grace United Church of Christ Archives, First Grace United Church of Christ, Akron, Ohio.

13. It is unclear when this organization started. One account (Harold J. Taylor, "135 Year History of the High Street Christian Church, 1839–1974" [Akron: High Street Christian Church, 1974], 11) gives that starting date at 1882. Gerald Bright, writing more than twenty years earlier, gives the starting date of the Home Society as 1871. Gerald D. Bright, "History of the High Street Church of Christ, Akron, Ohio, 1839–1942" (PhD diss., Butler University, August 1952), 28. High Street's women's missionary group was especially active in the 1870s and 1880s. For a fuller discussion, see Bright, 52.

14. Ruth Simon, "Heritage: A Centennial History 1868–1968" (Akron: Evangelical Lutheran Church of the Holy Trinity, no date), manuscript no. 799, and John Seiberling, "Memorial of the Twenty-Fifth Year" (Akron: Trinity Evangelical Lutheran Church, 1896), manuscript no. 280, Trinity Lutheran Church Archives, Akron.

15. "Woman's Missionary Society," Woman's Missionary Society, manuscript no. 1334, Trinity Lutheran Church Archives, Akron.

16. The Dorcas Committee of the First German Reformed Church should not be confused with the Dorcas Society, a civic organization that had close ties with a number of different Protestant denominations in the city and that will be discussed later in the chapter. "Dorcas Committee," *Grace Church Reformed Herald*, February 1896, 3.

17. 1880 Federal Census, U.S. Census Office, 10th Census, 1880. *Akron City Directory, 1887–1888* (Akron, Ohio: Burch Directory Co., 1887).

18. In 1928, the congregation became known simply as the First Reformed Church. "Centennial Souvenir" (Akron: First Evangelical and Reformed Church, Akron, 1953).

19. *Akron Official City Directory* (Akron, Ohio: Burch Directory Co., 1896).

20. Church records in the archives of the Grace United Church of Christ do not include the annual reports or minutes of the Dorcas Committee during this period.

21. "Woman's Missionary Society Minutes," March 6, 1889, 25; April 6, 1890, 39; March 1891, 60; March 2, 1892, 90; "Fifth Annual Report," 96, manuscript no. 1334, all in the Trinity Lutheran Church Archives, Akron.

22. B. R. Cowen, *Our Beacon Light* (Columbus, Ohio: F. L. Patrick, 1884), 351–61.

23. See, for example, "Temperance," *Summit County Beacon*, February 11, 1874, 2; "Temperance Tidings," *Summit County Beacon*, February 25, 1874, 2; "The Women's War on Whiskey," *Akron City Times*, February 25, 1874, 2.

24. From the beginning, the "women's war" against liquor had been opposed by the Catholic Church. See, for example, "Catholic Opposition to the Women's War—What the Church Is Doing," *Summit County Beacon*, March 4, 1874, 2.

25. Ibid.

26. "Temperance Call," *Summit County Beacon*, March 4, 1874, 3; "Temperance Rally," *Summit County Beacon*, March 4, 1874, 2.

27. "Temperance! The Grand Mass Meeting at the M. E. Church," *Summit County Beacon*, March 11, 1874, 3; "The Temperance Movement," *Akron City Times*, March 11, 1874; "Temperance Meeting," *Summit County Beacon*, March 11, 1874, 1; "Temperance," *Akron City Times*, March 18, 1874, 2; "Street Work," *Summit County Beacon*, March 18, 1874, 3; *Summit County Beacon*, March 25, 1874, 2.

28. "Temperance," *Akron City Times*, March 18, 1874, 2; "Street Work," *Summit County Beacon*, March 18, 1874, 3; *Akron City Directory, 1873–1874* (Akron: A. R. Talcott, 1873); *Akron City Directory, 1875–76* (Detroit: Burch and Potter, 1875).

29. "Temperance," *Akron City Times*, March 18, 1874, 2.

30. "The War in Akron," *Akron City Times*, March 25, 1874, 3; *Akron City Directory, 1873–1874*; *Akron City Directory, 1875–76*.

31. *Summit County Beacon*, March 25, 1874, 2; "Sixth Ward Notes," letter to the editor, *Akron City Times*, April 1, 1874, 3.

32. "Sixth Ward," letter to the editor, *Akron City Times*, April 1, 1874, 2; "The Outcome, So Far," editorial, *Akron City Times*, April 15, 1874, 2; "Croakers," *Summit County Beacon*, June 23, 1874, 2.

33. "City Council," *Summit County Beacon*, April 8, 1874, 3; "The Temperance Movement," *Akron City Times*, April 8, 1874, 3.

34. "Croakers," 2; "The Out-come," 2.

35. Manley's last name is found spelled with an e and without it.

36. "The Days of the Crusaders of the State of Ohio," *Akron Beacon Journal*, October 10, 1903, 9.

37. "The Cincinnati Convention and Its Lesson," *Summit County Beacon*, April 29, 1874, 2.

38. Pamelia Goodwin was elected president and Anna Hollinger was elected secretary. Each church sent a delegation of four teens/young women to the meeting. Representing the Congregational Church were Mattie Steward, Lizzie Berry, Ida B. Foote, and Lucy Alexander; representing the Baptist Church were Maggie Bender, Louisa Thomas, Mary Payne, and Nellie Wilcox; representing the Universalists were Susie Chamberlain, Clara Weaver, Effie Danforth, and Inez Shipman; representing the First Methodist-Episcopal Church were Ada E. Frank, Nellie Snyder, Mattie Tibbals, and Agnes Buckley; representing the Episcopalians were Mary Shook, Belle Taylor, Mary Bennett, and Susie King; representing the Disciples Church were Minnie Allen, Lois White, Ida Bender, and Ida Benson; representing Grace Reformed were Mollie Bolender, Maggie Oberholtz, Louisa Oberholtz, and Pauline Cranz. "Young Ladies Temperance Meeting," *Summit County Beacon*, May 27, 1874, 3. See also "Young Ladies' Temperance Organization," *Akron City Times*, May 27, 1874, 3.

39. Lane, *Fifty Years*, 787; "The Days of the Crusaders of the State of Ohio," *Akron Beacon Journal*, October 10, 1903, 9; "The Cincinnati Convention and Its Lesson," *Summit County Beacon*, April 29, 1874, 2.

40. "Dr. Kurt, First Woman Physician in Akron, Is Dead," *Akron Beacon Journal*, September 13, 1910, 3.

41. It is difficult to say precisely how many organizations had cross-membership with the Akron and/or Summit County WCTU. The membership lists of the WCTU have not been preserved.

42. "The Friendly Inn," *Summit County Beacon*, October 27, 1875, 3; "A Decade of Good Deeds," *Summit County Beacon*, March 19, 1884; "The Akron W.C.T.U.," *Summit County Beacon*, March 27, 1889.

43. "Prohibition's Failure," *Summit County Beacon*, October 17, 1883, 2.

44. "Women Who Would Vote," *Summit County Beacon*, April 8, 1885, 1; "The Ladies Vote," *Akron Beacon and Republican*, November 8, 1892, 4; Mary Margaret Stanton, "The Woman Suffrage Movement in Ohio Prior to 1910" (master's thesis, Ohio State University, 1947).

45. "A Decade of Good Deeds," *Summit County Beacon*, supplement, March 19, 1884; "The Akron W.C.T.U.," *Summit County Beacon*, March 27, 1889.

46. "Excellent Reports," *Akron City Times*, May 29, 1889, 8; "The Akron W.C.T.U.," *Summit County Beacon*, March 27, 1889.

47. "Earnest Women," *Akron Beacon and Republican*, November 21, 1893, 1; "Particularly for the Ladies," *Akron Daily Beacon*, April 11, 1890, 1.

48. "Earnest Women," 1; "Particularly for the Ladies," 1.

49. Akron, like many other cities across the country, placed great emphasis on "worthy poor," individuals who lacked food, fuel, clothing, or a home, because of unfortunate circumstances, unrelated to vice or liquor. See, for example, Ginzberg, *Women and the Work of Benevolence,* and Marvin Olasky, *The Tragedy of American Compassion* (Washington, D.C.: Regnery Gateway, 1992). *Centennial History of Akron,* 403.

50. "Jottings," *Akron City Times,* December 23, 1874, 3.

51. For a general discussion of women and religion, see Epstein, *Politics of Domesticity.*

52. In 1875, the officers of the Dorcas Society were president: Mrs. H. L. Carr; vice presidents: Mrs. Emma Leland of Congregational Church, Mrs. Louise Meacham of First Methodist-Episcopal Church, Mrs. Frances Kohler of Baptist Church, Mrs. Laura Barber of St. Paul's Episcopal Church, Mrs. S. J. Weaver of Universalist Church, Mrs. Helen Scott of Disciples Church, and Mrs. J. F. Fahs of the Lutheran Church; secretary: Mrs. D. C. Tomlinson; and treasurer: Mrs. J. H. Chamberlin.

53. Leaders were not always identified with the husband's first name or their own. For example, "Mrs. Dempsey" was on the visiting committee for the Sixth Ward. Without additional information, the specific "Mrs. Dempsey" involved with Dorcas could not be positively identified. See, for example, "Systematic Benevolence," *Summit County Beacon,* December 8, 1875, 3.

54. Lane, *Fifty Years,* 164 and 545, and *A Portrait and Biographical Record of Portage and Summit Counties, Ohio* (Logansport, Ohio: A. W. Bowen, 1898), 560.

55. "Systematic Benevolence," 3; "Akron's Aid," *Akron City Times,* September 18, 1878, 3; "The Dorcas Society," *Akron City Times,* December 17, 1879, 3; "The Dorcas Society," *Akron City Times,* December 8, 1880, 3; "Dorcas Donations," *Akron City Times,* April 12, 1881, 3; "Six Years of Good Work," *Summit County Beacon,* December 8, 1880, 1.

56. "Systematic Benevolence," 3; "Akron's Aid," 3; "The Dorcas Society," December 17, 1879, 3; "The Dorcas Society," December 8, 1880, 3; "Dorcas Donations," 3; "Six Years of Good Work," 1.

57. "The Dorcas Society," December 17, 1879, 3.

58. "Akron W.C.T.U. Work," *Akron Daily Beacon,* March 20, 1886, 1; "Helping Hands," *Summit County Beacon,* December 13, 1876, 3; "Free Dispensary a Fact," *Summit County Beacon,* September 5, 1883, 3.

59. "Poverty at the Door," *Summit County Beacon,* December 3, 1884. "Akron W.C.T.U. Work," 1.

60. "Poverty at the Door"; "G.A.R. Ladies Organizing," *Summit County Beacon,* March 5, 1884.

61. "Poverty at the Door."

62. Such conclusions are based on a search of the newspapers of the day, church archives, obituaries, and city directories.

63. This is in keeping with earlier studies. David L. Sills pointed out that socioeconomic status was a major correlate in participation in voluntary organizations. He concluded that the majority of people in lower socioeconomic classes did not participate in voluntary organizations. David L. Sills, *Volunteers,* 18. See also David L. Sills, "Voluntary Associations," 364–65.

64. Federal Census, U.S. Census Office, 10th Census, 1880. *Akron City and Summit County Directory, 1884–1885.* (Akron: Burch Directory Co., 1884).

65. "History of the Buckley Post, No. 12 and its Auxiliaries, Department of Ohio, G.A.R." (Akron: Beacon Publishing Co. 1885), 43–46, in folder: Community Organizations: Veterans Groups, GAR, Buckley Post History, box E7, Summit County Historical Society Collection, University of Akron Archives.

66. "Mrs. Sarah Battels Before the Court of Inquiry at Akron," *Akron City Times,* March 23, 1887, 1; "G.A.R. Versus W.R.C.," *Akron City Times,* March 16, 1887, 3.

67. "Board of Charities," *Summit County Beacon,* January 21, 1885, 3.

68. "Let Us Have Peace," *Akron Daily Beacon,* March 1, 1886; "Board of Charities;" Lane, *Fifty Years,* 129, 182, 191, 245, 261, 273, 366, and 546.

69. "Local Charity Work," *Summit County Beacon,* February 13, 1886.

70. "A Pen Picture of Want," *Summit County Beacon,* January 21, 1885; "Local Charity Work."

71. "Local Charity Work," "In the Ladies' Behalf," *Summit County Beacon,* February 20, 1886; "A Statement Soon to Come," *Summit County Beacon,* February 23, 1886; "Card from Judge Tibbals," *Summit County Beacon,* February 24, 1886; "Let Justice Be Done," *Summit County Beacon,* February 25, 1886.

72. "To Help the Poor," *Akron Daily Beacon,* January 20, 1886.

73. "The W.B.A. Organized," *Summit County Beacon,* February 3, 1886; "Winter 1884–5" *WBA,* May 25, 1887, 10, folder: Woman's Benevolent Association, Summit County Historical Society Collection, University of Akron Archives.

74. The full list of the charter members is found in the WBA newsletter, May 25, 1887, 10, folder: Woman's Benevolent Association, Summit County Historical Society Collection, University of Akron Archives.

75. "Rules for the Work Room of the Woman's Benevolent Association," *WBA,* May 25, 1887, 6, folder: Woman's Benevolent Association, Summit County Historical Society Collection, University of Akron Archives.

76. "In the Ladies' Behalf," *Akron Daily Beacon,* February 27, 1886; "Card from Judge Tibbals"; untitled editorial, *Akron Daily Beacon,* March 6, 1886; "Peace Treaty Ratified," *Akron Daily Beacon,* March 8, 1886.

77. "All About the W.B.A.," *WBA,* May 25, 1887, 5, folder: Woman's Benevolent Association, Summit County Historical Society Collection, University of Akron Archives.

78. B. R. Cowen, *Our Beacon Light* (Columbus, Ohio: F. L. Patrick, 1884), 352.

79. "Helping the Needy," *Summit County Beacon*, February 12, 1889; "Charities," *Akron City Times*, May 15, 1889, 7; "A Kitchen Garden," *Summit County Beacon*, June 5, 1889, 1.

80. "Home for Girls," *Summit County Beacon*, June 30, 1889, 5; Lane, *Fifty Years*, 1095–96; *Centennial History of Akron*, 404–5.

81. Exact figures are not known because the group's records have not been preserved. Newspapers did not report membership figures of this particular organization. Lane, *Fifty Years*, 139, 155, 179; *Centennial History of Akron*, 274; "The Woman's Suffragists Organize," *Summit County Beacon*, May 29, 1889; "Gentlemen Admitted," *Akron City Times*, June 6, 1889, 6; "Woman Suffrage," *Akron City Times*, October 15, 1890, 5; "Satisfactory Progress," *Akron Daily Beacon*, May 10, 1890, 5.

82. "Woman Suffrage Club," *Akron Daily Beacon*, April 25, 1890, 3; *Cleveland Press* editorial, as reprinted in the *Akron Beacon and Republican*, February 9, 1892, 2.

83. "The Ladies Vote," *Akron Beacon and Republican*, November 8, 1892, 4; "A Suffrage Meeting," *Akron Beacon and Republican*, February 2, 1893, 1.

84. "A Woman's Council," *Akron Beacon and Republican*, February 10, 1893, 2.

85. The following groups were represented: First Congregational Church, Henrietta Chase and Hannah Monroe; First Baptist Missionary Society, Mrs. R. E. Abbott and Mrs. A. E. Scoville; Ladies' Aid Society of First Baptist Church, Mrs. D. A. James and Mrs. H. D. Cole; King's Daughters, Mrs. Chase; Tuesday Afternoon Club, Mrs. H. B. Manton and Mrs. Frank Adams; The Atticans, Miss Flora Hanchett and Miss Hattie Phillips; High Street Disciple's Missionary Society, Miss Santom and Miss Blackman; Columbian Association, Mrs. Parsons; St. Paul's Church Auxiliary, Mrs. Parsons; West Congregational Church Ladies' Aid, Mrs. Beck and Miss Goepfert; High Street Church Aid Society, Mrs. Weston and Mrs. Allen; North Hill Methodist Episcopal Church Aid, Mrs. Rittenhouse and Mrs. Warden; Woman's Suffrage Club, Miss Claypole and Miss Agnes Kuleman; Woman's Relief Corps, Mrs. Koplin and Mrs. Warburton; UVRC, Anna E. H. Clark and Anna R. Taneybill; First Methodist Episcopal Church Home Missionary Society, K. W. Cory and Mrs. Emma Farrar; Isabella Club, Mrs. Trowbridge and Mrs. Wells; Ladies' Aid Hospital League, Mrs. K. W. Cory; Pythian Sisterhood, Mrs. L. E. Williams and Mrs. O. L. Sadler; Crescent Commandery, Order Red Cross, Miss Emma Mengensdorf and Miss Anna Vanderhoof; Daughters of Rebekah, Columbian Lodge, Miss Metta Kulke and Miss Mary Von Alt; Daughters of Liberty, Miss Amanda Butz and Mrs. M. R. Gridley; Daughters of St. George, Mrs. Stansfield and Mrs. A. E. Moon; Women's Missionary Alliance, Mrs. A. E. Moon; Daughters of Jerusalem, Mrs. Ella Simpson and Mary J. Pickett; Huse Lodge, Mrs. Chapman and Mrs. Rockwell, and WCTU, Mrs. Berry and Mrs. James. "A Woman's Council," *Akron Beacon and Republican*, March 4, 1893, 8.

86. "A Woman's Council," *Akron Beacon and Republican*, March 4, 1893, 8; "A Woman's Council, *Akron Beacon and Republican*, April 15, 1893, 1; "Council of Women," *Akron Beacon*

and Republican, November 10, 1893, 1; "Interesting," *Akron Beacon and Republican,* November 10, 1894, 6; *Akron Evening Journal,* November 10, 1896, 1.

87. "A Woman's Council," March 4, 1893, 8; "Council of Women," 1; "Interesting," 6; "The Woman's Council," *Akron Beacon and Republican,* November 26, 1895, 2.

88. The Mary Day Nursery will be discussed in the next chapter.

89. "Interesting," 6; Scott Dix Kenfield, ed., *Akron and Summit County, 1828–1928* (Chicago: S. J. Clarke, 1928), 1:167.

90. "Interesting," 6.

91. Kenfield, *Akron and Summit County,* 1:167–69.

92. Ibid.

93. For a complete discussion of municipal housekeeping and its role in urban life in the Progressive period, see Maureen A. Flanagan, "The City Profitable, the City Livable: Environmental Policy, Gender and Power in Chicago in the 1910s," *Journal of Urban History* 22 (January 1996): 163–90; Maureen A. Flanagan, *Seeing with Their Hearts: Chicago Women and the Vision of the Good City, 1871–1933* (Princeton: N.J.: Princeton University Press, 2002); and Suellen M. Hoy, *Chasing Dirt: The American Pursuit of Cleanliness* (New York: Oxford University Press, 1995).

94. "Women's Clubs," *Akron Beacon and Republican,* February 15, 1896, 2.

CHAPTER 5

1. "History of the Altar Guild, Trinity Lutheran Church, Akron, Ohio 1905–1955," manuscript no. 1244, Trinity Lutheran Church Archives, Akron.

2. "Dorcas Society," *Christian Bulletin,* June 10, 1906.

3. *Centennial History of Akron,* 109–22; Hugh Allen, *Rubber's Home Town: The Real-Life Story of Akron* (New York: Stratford House, 1949), 111–81; Daniel Nelson, *American Rubber Workers & Organized Labor, 1900–1942* (Princeton, N.J.: Princeton University Press, 1988), 99–104; Knepper, *Akron,* 100, 104, 119; *Akron Official Directory . . . 1925* (Akron: Burch Directory Co., 1925), 26.

4. *Centennial History of Akron,* 109–22; Allen, *Rubber's Home Town,* 111–81; Frances McGovern, *Written on the Hills: The Making of the Akron Landscape* (Akron: University of Akron Press, 1996), 124–27; Knepper, *Akron,* 70–71; "Report of the International Institute, 1928," Akron, folder 16: Annual Reports, box 1, International Institute Collection, University of Akron Archives.

5. United States Rubber was the fourth of the "Big Four" rubber companies; it was based in New Jersey. For a fuller discussion of the early rubber companies in Akron, see Nelson, *American Rubber Workers,* 8–76.

6. *Centennial History of Akron,* 318–41; Allen, *Rubber's Home Town,* 158–59.

7. The machinists who went out on strike in 1916 were more successful. Although many never were hired back at Goodyear and Firestone, the machinists found other jobs

in the rubber factories in the city and won the forty-eight-hour week. Nelson, *American Rubber Workers*, 41–42 and 68–69; Kathleen L. Endres, *Rosie the Rubber Worker: Women Workers in Akron's Rubber Factories during World War II* (Kent, Ohio: Kent State University Press, 2000), 25–26.

8. Allen, *Rubber's Home Town*, 172–73; McGovern, *Written on the Hills*; "Neighborhoods," Ohio Dot Com, Akron Celebrating Our Heritage, http://www.akron175.com/back/neighborhoods/, retrieved December 9, 2003.

9. *Akron Directory* (Akron, Ohio: Burch Directory Co., 1901), *Akron Official City Directory* (Akron, Ohio: Burch Directory Co., 1920), and *Akron Official City Directory . . . 1925.*

10. The first members of St. Mary's Guild were Mrs. Peter Hammel, Mrs. George W. Billow, Mrs. Charles Billow, Mrs. John Sabin, Mrs. Arthur Morley, Miss Mary J. Gunn, Miss Caroline Gunn, Mrs. Ida Reherd, Mrs. Douglas Jarvis, and Mrs. Mary E. Coney. George Parkin Atwater, *Annals of a Parish; A Chronicle of the Founding and of the Growth and Development of the Church of Our Saviour, Akron, Ohio, Together with a Personal Narrative by the Reverend George Parkin Atwater, Who Served the Parish as Pastor, Priest and Rector, from November 20, 1897 to October 1, 1926* (privately published, 1928), 2.

11. Atwater, *Annals of a Parish*, 2, 25, 39, 44–45.

12. Atwater, *Annals of a Parish*, 44–45.

13. The first members were all unmarried and all members of the same Sunday school class at the First Congregational Church. The original members were Clara Smith (Mrs. Wilfred H. Collins), Lulu Parker (Mrs. P. King Crawford), Julia White (Mrs. Leonard Craft), Blanch Blanchard (Mrs. Thomas Read of Marion, Ohio), Ethel Wright (Mrs. Frank Peabody), Jane Sargent (Mrs. Harold Barnhardt), Maude Newberry (Mrs. LaVeqa of Detroit), Mabel Goodwin (Mrs. F. Koons), Theresa Alexander (Mrs. G. H. Barber of W. Orange), Flora Goodwin (Mrs. William H. Evans), Ethel Foster, Metta Dagus (Mrs. Joseph Weller), and Mrs. Joseph W. Kelly, the wife of the teacher of the Sunday school class. Mrs. W. A. Means and Mrs. Flora Goodwin Evans, "The Young Women's Missionary Society of the First Congregational Church of Akron, 1910–1913," typescript manuscript, folder: Church Histories for the 1984 Sesquicentennial, First Congregational Church, First Congregational Church Archives, Akron.

14. Means and Evans, "The Young Women's Missionary Society of the First Congregational Church."

15. A history of the association of the group reported that the early twentieth century had been lean years for the senior missionary group—"These were hard years. Nearly always there was a plea to interest more of our members as we are anxious to increase our membership. Ask some of our friends to join our society." "Missionary Society, 1890–1920," handwritten manuscript, no author, 6, folder: Church Histories of the 1984 Sesquicentennial, First Congregational Church, First Congregational Church Archives, Akron.

16. Chloey Naef, "Women's Association," typed manuscript, folder: Church Histories for 1984 Sesquicentennial, First Congregational Church Archives, First Congregational Church, Akron.

17. Naef, "Women's Association," 1.

18. It is unknown who the original members were, since the Dorcas Society's records were destroyed in a church fire in 1975. "Dorcas Service Circle" (Akron: High Street Christian Church, 2002).

19. Barbara Garman and Linda Wilson, "Women of High Street Christian Church, 1876–1974: 98 Years of Study and Service."

20. A complete list of leaders is not available; see note 18. "Dorcas Service Circle."

21. Harold J. Taylor, *135-Year History of the High Street Christian Church, 1839–1974* (Akron: High St. Christian Church, 1974), 27–29; Frank E. Rowe, ed., "History of the High Street Church of Christ, 1839–1942, Akron, Ohio," folder: Church of Christ, Box E4, Summit County Historical Society, University of Akron Archives.

22. "A Garden Spot in Akron, Ohio," *Lutheran,* August 25, 1921, 12; "A Questionnaire Concerning Our Hospice," *Trinity Luther Leaguer,* November 3, 1929, 6; "Hospice Will Observe Its 9th Birthday," *Akron Times Press,* no date or page noted, and "Plan Anniversary Entertainment at Lutheran Hospice," *Akron Beacon Journal,* no date or page noted, both in Scrapbook General, 1929–1930, file number 1501, Trinity Lutheran Church Archives, Akron.

23. The Hospice opened in 1920.

24. "Hospice," *Trinity Luther Leaguer,* December 5, 1920, 1; "Hospice Number," *Trinity Luther Leaguer,* November 6, 1921, 1; "News from Our Hospice for Young Women," *Trinity Luther Leaguer,* November 5, 1922, 1; "Lutheran Hospice for Young Women," *Trinity Luther Leaguer,* November 4, 1923, 1.

25. Carol Cole, "Educational Groups Meet Regularly in Community Center," *Akron Beacon Journal,* November 9, 1928, clipping; "Fifty Years of Helping," *Akron Beacon Journal,* March 12, 1961, clipping; Joe Rukenbrod, "East End Community House Management Reorganized," *Akron Beacon Journal,* June 6, 1948, clipping; all in East Akron Community House file, morgue file, *Beacon Journal* editorial office, Akron.

26. Helen Geib, "A YWCA Director 50 Years," *Akron Beacon Journal,* March 27, 1951, 20, and Jane Neely, "Akron Y.W.C.A. Founder, 86, Only Active Charter Member," *Cleveland Plain Dealer,* June 6, 1955, clipping, in local history file, Akron Public Library.

27. East Akron Community House still functions in Akron today, although it serves different populations and offers different services.

28. Shirley Leonard, immigration secretary of the International Institute, saw the tension between American-born children and their immigrant parents as one of the greatest challenges facing these families in the city. International Institute clubs and organizations specifically attempted to ease that stress of the cultural chasm developing

between immigrant parents and their children. *Akron Times*, undated clipping, scrapbook, box 46, YWCA of Summit County Collection, University of Akron Archives.

29. Mardorff was the resident director for more than twenty years. She was the first and last woman to act in that capacity. "East Akron Community House Trains Pre-School Children," *Akron Beacon Journal*, February 18, 1940, clipping, East Akron Community House file, morgue. *Beacon Journal* editorial offices, and David B. Cooper, "A Plus for East Akron Much to Be Proud of at EACH," *Akron Beacon Journal*, January 30, 1986, A4.

30. In 1948, shortly after a new, male director (Homer Pettengill) took over at the community house, the management of EACH was reorganized. The Missionary Union was replaced by a Board of Managers, a group open to any church organization or association interested in working with the Community House. "Fifty Years of Helping," *Akron Beacon Journal*, March 12, 1961, clipping; "East Akron Community House Trains Pre-School Children," *Akron Beacon Journal*, February 18, 1940, clipping, and Joe Rukenbrod, "East End Community House Management Reorganized," *Beacon Journal*, June 6, 1948, no page number. All in East Akron Community House file, morgue, *Beacon Journal* editorial offices.

31. The members of the two circles of the Daughters of the King that formed the Akron Day Nursery in 1890 were Mrs. Mary Perkins Raymond, Anna S. Ganter, Carita McEbright, Belle Adams, Gertrude Commins, Addie Commins, Julia M. Crouse, Mary R. Crouse, Rose Day Christy, Belle Green, Helen Humphrey, Maude Watters, Mary A. Buell, Lizzie Griffin, Martha W. Henry, Julia H. McGregor, Mary Miller, Helen A. Storer, Harriet Wise, Alice Work, Mattie E. Pettibone, Sadie McNeil Hitchcock, and Jessie O'Brien Marvin. Patricia M. Zonsius, *Children's Century: Children's Hospital Medical Center of Akron, 1890–1990* (Akron, Ohio: Children's Hospital Medical Center of Akron, 1990), 206.

32. "International Order of King's Daughters and Sons," *The New International Encyclopaedia* (New York: Dodd Mead, 1902).

33. Zonsius, *Children's Century*, 6–9, and *The Story of the Children's Hospital, Akron, Ohio* (Akron, Ohio: undated), 2.

34. Federal Census, U.S. Census Office, 10th Census, 1880; *Akron City Directory* (Akron, Ohio: Burch Directory Co., 1890/91); Lane, *Fifty Years*, 152, 200, 266, 284.

35. Zonsius, *Children's Century*, 5–10; *Story of the Children's Hospital*, 21–24.

36. *Story of the Children's Hospital*, 30–31, and Zonsius, *Children's Century*, 9–10.

37. See "State of Ohio Articles of Incorporation, Mary Day Nursery of Akron, Ohio, Sept. 18, 1891," as reprinted in Zonsius, *Children's Century*, 9.

38. "Constitution and By-Laws of the Mary Day-Nursery Organization," "Annual Report of the Mary Day-Nursery Organization of Akron, Ohio . . . Record of the Work for the Year 1894–1895, with the Officers and Standing Committees for the Year 1895–1896," Archives, Children's Hospital.

39. The leadership of the 1891–92 group was president Mary Perkins Raymond, daughter of industrialist George Perkins and wife of BFG executive Charles Raymond; vice president Ann Ganter, daughter of the Episcopalian priest; secretary Carita McEbright, daughter of a prominent Akron physician; and treasurer Bessie Raymond, daughter of banker William B. Raymond and his wife, Helen, and sister-in-law of Mary Perkins Raymond. Subsequent leaders showed the evolution of the organization. The 1892–93 leaders were president Helen A. Storer, daughter of a jewelry store owner; vice president Miss Julia Crouse, daughter of industrialist/politician George W. Crouse and Elizabeth (Alden) Crouse; secretary Julia McGregor, daughter of an iron manufacturer; and treasurer Mrs. Kenyon Conger, the former Anna Ganter. In 1893–94, Raymond, Crouse, Conger, and McGregor held the positions president, vice president, secretary, and treasurer, respectively. In 1894–95, there was a shift in the leadership of the group. Julia Crouse, the only charter member elected that year, remained as treasurer; Mrs. William S. Chase became president. Grace Pitkin, daughter of the Reverend Caleb J. Pitkin and Flavia Pitkin, was elected vice president; and Josephine Crumrine, daughter of Martin Houston Crumrine, owner of a marble and granite works in Akron, and his wife, Olive. In 1895–96, charter member Carita McEbright, then a faculty member at Buchtel College (now the University of Akron), was elected president. New member Clara Howland, wife of Charles Howland, a young Akron business executive, was beginning her activist career as the vice president of the Mary Day Nursery. She would go on to make her mark in the Tuesday Musical Club, the YWCA, and the People's Hospital Woman's Guild. New member Mrs. E. A. Oviatt took over as secretary. Oviatt would remain active in the nursery and Children's Hospital for decades. In 1896–97, Mary Perkins Raymond returned to the presidency. She kept that position the next year as well. The leaders of the group in 1896–97 were president Mary Perkins Raymond, who kept this position for the next year as well; vice president Emma Phinney, twenty-five, daughter of a boot-and-shoe merchant in Akron; and secretary Lora Alden, just twenty, daughter of the president of Alden Rubber. In 1897, Mrs. Lucius Miles, wife of an executive at Great Western Cereal and one of the Seiberling sisters, was elected vice president of the organization. That same year, Effie Work, younger daughter of the superintendent of the Rubber Works, took over as secretary. Emma Phinney remained as treasurer, and Bessie Raymond was her assistant. The next year Effie Work took over as president and Mrs. Charles C. Goodrich, wife of the son of the founder of the B. F. Goodrich Co., became vice president. Helen Storer, secretary; Emma Phinney, treasurer; and Bessie Raymond, assistant treasurer, returned to serve as leaders of the nursery again. In 1899–1900, Effie Work returned as president; Mrs. E. A. Oviatt was vice president; Elizabeth Alden was secretary; and Mrs. George C. Kohler was treasurer, with Gertrude Mason as her assistant. Zonsius, *Children's Century*, 212–13.

40. The Tuesday Musical Club was the organization most closely identified with the Seiberling family in Akron.

41. At least all those who could be positively identified through city directories, census, and marriage records.

42. Association for Childhood Education International, "A Brief Look at Our History," http://www.udel.edu/bateman/acei/history.htm, retrieved January 27, 2004; see Mrs. Virginia Thrall Smith, "The Kindergarten," in *The Congress of Women: Held in the Woman's Building, World's Columbian Exposition, Chicago, U. S. A., 1893*, edited by Mary Kavanaugh Oldham Eagle, 178–79 (Chicago, Ill.: Monarch Book Company, 1894).

43. Smith, "The Kindergarten," 179.

44. Zonsius, *Children's Century*, 12–14. *Story of the Children's Hospital*, 33–35.

45. Barnum stayed in charge of kindergarten work in Akron for many years and then moved on to Teachers College at Columbia University. Zonsius, *Children's Century*, 13–15; *Story of the Children's Hospital*, 33–35; "Report of the Mary Day-Nursery and Kindergarten Organization of Akron, Ohio . . . Record of the Work for the Year 1897–1898" (Akron: Werner Co.), no page number, folder: Mary Day Nursery, Summit County Historical Society Collection, University of Akron Archives.

46. Zonsius, *Children's Century*, 15.

47. *Story of the Children's Hospital*, 35–36; Zonsius, *Children's Century*, 15–18; "Report of the Mary Day Nursery and Kindergarten Organization of Akron, Ohio, 1897–1898," folder: Mary Day Nursery, Summit County Historical Society Collection, University of Akron Archives.

48. *Story of the Children's Hospital*, 38; Zonsius, *Children's Century*, 15–19.

49. Zonsius, *Children's Century*, 18–19; "Mary Day Nursery Bazar will be held Wednesday and Thursday," *Akron Beacon Journal*, November 29, 1904, 7; "Donation Day," *Akron Beacon Journal*, November 20, 1902, 7; "Helping the Poor People," *Akron Beacon Journal*, February 9, 1904, 3; "Food for the Poor of Akron," *Akron Beacon Journal*, November 26, 1904.

50. Lane, *Fifty Years*, 476–77; *Centennial History of Akron*, 309–12; Zonsius, *Children's Century*, 221; Federal Census, U.S. Census Office, 10th Census, 1880.

51. It was not until the 1880s that pediatrics was established as a medical specialty. Edmund Burke, "Abraham Jacobi, MD: The Man and His Legacy," *Pediatrics* 101 (February 1998): 309–12; "Committee Report: American Pediatrics: Milestones at the Millennium," *Pediatrics* 107 (June 2001): 1482–91.

52. "Help Needed," *Akron Beacon Journal*, May 2, 1905, 3; "Mary Day Nursery," *Akron Beacon Journal*, May 5, 1905, 10.

53. State of Ohio, Articles of Incorporation, "Mary Day Nursery and Ward for Crippled Children of Akron, Ohio, 1906," as quoted in Zonsius, *Children's Century*, 25.

54. "A New Work," *Akron Beacon Journal*, May 4, 1905, 3.

55. "Successful Year," *Akron Beacon Journal*, July 24, 1907, 3.

56. "Pity the Poor Mary Day Nursery Children," *Akron Beacon Journal*, May 1, 1909, 10.

57. Zonsius, *Children's Century*, 31; "Mary Day Dispensary and Visiting Nurse," *Akron Beacon Journal*, September 30, 1909, 3; "Mary Day Nursery Asks Help," *Akron Beacon Journal*, June 8, 1909, 2.

58. Zonsius, *Children's Century*, 34.

59. "Perkins Gift to Cut Death List," *Akron Beacon Journal*, September 26, 1910, 1; Zonsius, *Children's Century*, 32–33.

60. "Annual Secretary's Report for 1911 and 1912, Mary Day Nursery and Children's Hospital," Secretary's Book 1911–1917, 47 and "Annual Secretary's Report for 1913–1914," Mary Day Nursery and Children's Hospital, Secretary's Book 1911–1917, 97, Archives, Children's Hospital.

61. "Hospital for Little Ones Will Be Dedicated Sunday," *Akron Beacon Journal*, December 7, 1911, 7; "Children's Hospital at Mary Day Nursery Is a Fine Institution," *Akron Beacon Journal*, July 26, 1912, 16; "Secretary's Annual Report, 1915–1916," 146, and March 5, 1917, 5, Mary Day Nursery and Children's Hospital, Secretary's Book 1911–1917, Archives, Children's Hospital.

62. Zonsius, *Children's Century*, 37.

63. "Secretary's Annual Report, 1915–1916," 147; September 11, 1916, 148, and September 16, 1918, 149, Mary Day Nursery and Children's Hospital, Secretary's Book, 1911–1917, 147, Archives, Children's Hospital, Akron, Ohio.

CHAPTER 6

1. "American and Summit County Federation of Women's Clubs, 1924–1925," sixth edition, folder: "Akron Federation of Women's Clubs," box E1, Summit County Historical Society Collection, University of Akron Archives.

2. Gertrude Penfield Seiberling has always been included as an honorary charter member, even though she was not at that first meeting. She and Frank Seiberling did not marry until 1888, and Gertrude did not move to Akron until then. Nonetheless, most histories of the city as well as of the Tuesday Musical Club itself note that Gertrude Seiberling was a charter member or an honorary charter member. See, for example, Kenfield, *Akron and Summit County*, 1:200. See also Howard Wolf, "Tuesday Musical Club Founded 40 Years Ago," *Akron Beacon Journal*, October 1, 1927, and Donald Rosenberg, "The Troublesome Ladies Who Make Akron Get Culture," *Beacon Magazine*, October 29, 1978; photograph, Tuesday Musical Club headquarters, Akron, Ohio.

3. *Centennial History of Akron*, 307; *Akron City Directory* (Akron: Burch Directory Co., 1888/89).

4. The book was edited by James L. Thane Jr. and published by the University of Utah Library, Salt Lake City, 1976.

5. Rounding out the other founding members were Martha Herrold, twenty-seven, a music teacher in the Fifth Ward of Akron; L. May Burnham Saunders, a singer who would remain active in the club for decades; Alma Little; and Dorothy Bell. Kenfield, *Akron and Summit County*, 1:200, and photograph, Tuesday Musical Club headquarters, Akron, Ohio.

6. Mrs. M. H. Fullington, "Music . . . has done for Akron," *Beacon Journal* clipping, no date, vol. 3, Tuesday Musical Club Collection, University of Akron Archives.

7. "Matter of Pride," *Akron Beacon and Republican*, April 4, 1896, 3; Federal Census, U.S. Census Office, 10th Census, 1880.

8. "Matter of Pride," *Akron Beacon and Republican*, April 4, 1896, 3; "Devotees," *Akron Beacon Journal*, January 7, 1899, 9; Kenfield, *Akron and Summit County*, 1:200–201; "Music . . . has done for Akron," *Beacon Journal* clipping, no date, vol. 3, Tuesday Musical Club Collection, University of Akron Archives.

9. "Matter of Pride," *Akron Beacon and Republican*, April 4, 1896, 3; Kenfield, *Akron and Summit County*, 1:162–270.

10. "Matter of Pride"; "Devotees," *Akron Beacon Journal*, January 7, 1899, 9; "A Fanfare for Fine Music," *Beacon Magazine*, October 4, 1987; "Music . . . has done for Akron," *Akron Beacon Journal*, no date, vol. 3, Tuesday Musical Club Collection, University of Akron Archives.

11. "Gratifying Report," *Akron Beacon and Republican*, June 23, 1894, 1. For details about Theodore Thomas and the Chicago Symphony Orchestra, see Philo Adams Otis, *The Chicago Symphony Orchestra: Its Development and Organization, 1891–1924* (Chicago: Clayton Summy Co., 1924); "A Grand Concert," *Akron Beacon and Republican*, May 21, 1895, 2; "A Musical Treat," *Akron Beacon and Republican*, December 7, 1895, 1; "The First Concert," *Akron Beacon and Republican*, December 5, 1895, 1.

12. "The Ladies," *Summit County Beacon*, June 9, 1898, 3.

13. Helen Storer married Winfield Collins in 1901. When they were married, he was an employee of Storer and Co. Five years later, he was assistant secretary and treasurer of Akron Roofing Tile.

14. "History," *Akron Beacon Journal*, March 21, 1904, no page number, clipping, vol. 2, Tuesday Musical Club Collection, University of Akron Archives.

15. Ibid.

16. Ibid.

17. Ibid.

18. "A People's Chorus to Be Organized by the Tuesday Musical Club," poster, and "It Is Reorganized," *Akron Beacon Journal*, November 13, 1903, no page noted, clipping, both in vol. 2, Tuesday Musical Club Collection, University of Akron Archives.

19. "It Is Reorganized," *Akron Beacon Journal*, November 13, 1903, no page number, clipping; "Tuesday," *Akron Beacon Journal*, November 14, 1903, no page noted, clipping; and "Two Societies Merged," *Akron Beacon Journal*, December 16, 1903, no page number, clipping, vol. 2, Tuesday Musical Club, University of Akron Archives.

20. "Tuesday," *Akron Beacon Journal*, November 14, 1903, no page noted, vol. 2, Tuesday Musical Club Collection, University of Akron Archives.

21. "Four," *Akron Beacon Journal*, May 10, 1904, no page noted, vol. 2, Tuesday Musical Club Collection, University of Akron Archives.

22. Ibid.

23. "DON'T LET THE TUESDAY MUSICAL CLUB GIVE UP ITS CONCERTS," *Akron Beacon Journal*, December 16, 1905, 1; "Why Tuesday Club Gives Up Concert," letter to the editor, *Akron Beacon Journal*, vol. 2, Tuesday Musical Club Collection, University of Akron Archives.

24. "DON'T LET THE TUESDAY MUSICAL CLUB GIVE UP ITS CONCERTS," *Akron Beacon Journal*, December 16, 1905, 1; "Knockers Can Kill the Tuesday Musical Club," *Akron Beacon Journal*, December 19, 1905, 1. "The Tuesday Club," clipping not identified or dated, vol. 2, Tuesday Musical Club Collection, University of Akron Archives.

25. Mary Zipperlen Schumacher, second wife of Ferdinand Schumacher, the so-called cereal king of the city, left $50,000 to the organization to underwrite the cost of the concerts, "Mary Zipperlen Schumacher," Akron Women's History website, http://www3.uakron.edu/schlcomm/womenshistory/schumacher_m.htm, retrieved July 8, 2004.

26. During the 1910 evening season, subscribers could attend the entire series of concerts for $2.50, while the afternoon series of twelve concerts was even less, $1.50. "Tuesday Musical Club Prospectus, 1910–1911"; "Tuesday Club Getting Ready for Next Season," *Akron Beacon Journal* clipping, no date, no page number; "Did Splendid Work," *Akron Beacon Journal* clipping, no date, no page number; "Tuesday Musical Club Chooses Mrs. Bruot," *Akron Beacon Journal* clipping, no date, no page number; all in vol. 3, Tuesday Musical Club Collection, University of Akron Archives.

27. "Tuesday Musical Club Is Growing," *Akron Beacon Journal*, September 18, 1910, clipping, vol. 3, Tuesday Musical Club Collection, University of Akron Archives.

28. The Tuesday Musical Club stayed true to its commitment to classical music during this time period. "Tuesday Musical Club Prospectus, 1910–1911" and "Tuesday Musical Club of Akron, 1914–1915," both in vol. 3, Tuesday Musical Club Collection, University of Akron Archives.

29. Kathleen Waters Sander, *The Business of Charity: The Woman's Exchange Movement, 1832–1900* (Urbana: University of Illinois Press, 1998), 26 and 121–123.

30. "Woman's Exchange Has Worthy Object," *Akron Beacon Journal*, November 19, 1904, 6; *Akron Official City Directory* (Akron: Burch Directory Co., 1904).

31. "Akron Woman's Exchange," *Akron Beacon Journal*, April 28, 1904, 6.

32. "Akron Woman's Exchange," *Akron Beacon Journal*, April 28, 1904, 6; "What It Can Do for Women," *Akron Beacon Journal*, June 11, 1904, 10; and "Woman's Exchange Has Worthy Object," *Akron Beacon Journal*, November 19, 1904, 6.

33. *Akron Official City Directory* (Akron: Burch Directory Co., 1911); *Akron Official City Directory* (Akron: Burch Directory Co., 1912); *Akron Official City Directory* (Akron: Burch

Directory Co., 1913); *Akron Official City Directory* (Akron: Burch Directory Co., 1914); *Akron Official City Directory* (Akron: Burch Directory Co., 1915); *Akron Official City Directory* (Akron: Burch Directory Co., 1916); *Akron Official City Directory* (Akron: Burch Directory Co., 1917); *Akron Official City Directory* (Akron: Burch Directory Co., 1918); *Akron Official City Directory* (Akron: Burch Directory Co., 1919); *Akron Official City Directory* (Akron: Burch Directory Co., 1920).

34. Endres, *Rosie the Rubber Worker*, 21–38.

35. Records of the Woman's Exchange of Akron were not retained. The only material available on this organization appeared in the newspapers of the day.

36. "Woman's Exchange Has Worthy Object," *Akron Beacon Journal*, November 19, 1904, 6; "Brief Local Items," *Akron Beacon Journal*, May 3, 1905, 3.

37. Mary S. Sims, *The YWCA—An Unfolding Purpose* (New York: Women's Press, 1950), 3–4, 114; Kenfield, *Akron and Summit County*, 1:168.

38. Mrs. J. B. Wright, "Y.W.C.A. Becomes Vital Factor in Akron's Progress," *Akron Beacon Journal*, January 26, 1931, 10; Kathleen L. Endres and Cheryl Flox, "The YWCA of Summit County: A History" (Akron: YWCA of Summit County, 2001), 6–7.

39. Endres and Flox, "YWCA of Summit County," 6–7.

40. Social conventions and legal requirements that required women to assume their husbands' surnames at marriage make it difficult to trace family ties within the women's organizations of Akron or anywhere else. However, it appears that the largest number of the leaders of these women's organizations had a mother or father involved in club and/or organizational work.

41. Federal Census, U.S. Census Office, 10th Census, 1880; *Akron Official City Directory* (Akron: Burch Directory Co., 1900); Kenfield, *Akron and Summit County*, 2:448; Endres, "Calista Willard Wheeler," Akron Women's History website, http://www3.uakron.edu/schlcomm/womenshistory/wheeler_c.htm, retrieved July 6, 2004; Fox, "Margaret Chapman Barnhart, 1874–1913."

42. Federal Census, U.S. Census Office, 10th Census, 1880; *Akron Official City Directory* (Akron: Burch Directory Co., 1900); Kenfield, *Akron and Summit County*, 2:577.

43. "The Y.W.C.A.," *Summit County Beacon*, December 5, 1901.

44. The five were: 1901, Rosella Meredith; 1902, Jane Wheeler; 1902, Lella Johnson; 1904, Ruth Wheeler; and 1904, Jessie Peasley. Peasley was replaced by Adella Ogden in 1907. Mrs. J. B. Wright, "Y.W.C.A. Becomes Vital Factor in Akron's Progress," *Akron Beacon Journal*, January 26, 1931, 10; "New Secretary," *Akron Beacon Journal*, August 30, 1902, 3; "Y.W.C.A. Complimentary Concert Friday Evening," *Akron Beacon Journal*, May 18, 1907, 16.

45. Helen Geib, "A YWCA Director 50 Years," *Akron Beacon Journal*, March 27, 1951, 20; "A Lusty Infant," *Akron Beacon Journal*, January 28, 1902, 1; "Good Health," *Akron Beacon Journal*, February 27, 1902, 2; Endres and Flox, "YWCA History," 8; "The Y.W.C.A.," *Akron Beacon Journal*, January 14, 1902, 4; undated, handwritten note from

Rosella Meredith, folder: History Documents, Handwritten Originals, box 42, YWCA of Summit County Collection, University of Akron Archives.

46. Secretary's Minutes, February 13 and April 10, 1905, 35 and 39, box 44, YWCA of Summit County Collection, University of Akron Archives; "What the Y.W.C.A. of Akron Needs," *Akron Beacon Journal*, April 30, 1904, 7; "The Y.W.C.A.," *Akron Beacon Journal*, January 14, 1902, 4.

47. Minutes, June 6, 1904, 32, and November 13, 1905, 57, box 44, YWCA of Summit County Collection, University of Akron Archives.

48. With Lyon's appointment, the title shifted from extension secretary to industrial secretary. In 1904, the term was extension secretary; see "What the Y.W.C.A. of Akron Needs," *Akron Beacon Journal*, April 20, 1904, 16.

49. "The Y.W.C.A. in Factories of Akron," *Akron Beacon Journal*, June 7, 1907, 10; "Sarah Scudder Lyon," *One Hundred Year Biographical Directory of Mt. Holyoke College, 1837–1937*, bulletin series 30, no. 5, published and compiled by Alumnae Association of Mt. Holyoke College, South Hadley, Mass., as found at http://www.mtholyoke.edu/~dalbino/women20/slyon.html, retrieved June 20, 2004.

50. "Y.W.C.A. Notes," *Akron Beacon Journal*, January 25, 1908; "Great Work Done by Y.W.C.A. Depts.," unidentified clipping, June 9, 1909; and "Need More Shop Girls and More Home for Them," unidentified clipping, October 26, 1909, both in scrapbook 1, box 46, YWCA of Summit County Collection, University of Akron Archives; Minutes, Annual Meeting, June 1906, 74–76, box 44, YWCA of Summit County Collection, University of Akron Archives; "Need More Shop Girls and More Homes for Them," *Akron Beacon Journal*, October 26, 1909, 6.

51. "Goodyear Branch Y.W.C.A.," *Wingfoot Clan*, November 1, 1912, 2; "By All Means," *Wingfoot Clan*, September 27, 1913, 2; "The Domestic Arts," *Wingfoot Clan*, October 11, 1913, 2; "Second Honors," *Wingfoot Clan*, October 14, 1916, 1; "Membership Contest," *Wingfoot Clan*, September 19, 1914, 2.

52. Women paid twenty-five cents to register with the employment bureau and twenty-five cents for securing employment. Employers paid fifty cents for listing week work and twenty-five cents for listing day work. Minutes, January 11, 1909, 179–81, box 44, YWCA of Summit County Collection, University of Akron Archives. See also Minutes, March 9, 1908, 145–47, box 44, YWCA of Summit County Collection, University of Akron Archives. For nurse's registry details, see "Y.W.C.A. Notes," *Akron Beacon Journal*, October 31, 1903, 12.

53. "What the Y.W.C.A. of Akron Needs," *Akron Beacon Journal*, April 30, 1904, 16; Minutes, June 1905, 47, box 44, YWCA Collection, University of Akron Archives.

54. "Y.W.C.A. Has Bright Outlook for Future," *Akron Beacon Journal*, June 3, 1911, 4.

55. The Union Charity donated the Grace House to the YWCA. In return, the YWCA had to continue the Charity's Penny Savings program, use the Grace House name, and teach domestic training classes. "Auspicious Opening of New Y.W.C.A.

Building," *Akron Press*, no date or page number provided, scrapbook 1, box 46, YWCA Collection, University of Akron Archives; "Y.W.C.A. Has Bright Outlook for Future," *Akron Beacon Journal*, June 3, 1911, 4.

56. Minutes, January 14, 1908, 140, box 44, YWCA of Summit County Collection, University of Akron Archives.

57. "Conditions Here Good, Says Y.W.C.A. President," *Akron Press*, April 30, 1912, and "Resent Slander," *Akron Times*, April 30, 1912, both in scrapbook 1, box 46, YWCA of Summit County Collection, University of Akron Archives.

58. "Annual Meeting of Y.W.C.A. Draws Very Large Attendance," January 18, 1913, 11.

59. "Monthly Reports, February 1913," folder 3, box 31, YWCA of Summit County Collection, University of Akron Archives; "Federation Is Newest Idea in Y.W. Work for Girls," *Akron Beacon Journal*, February 7, 1916, 7.

60. "Two Institutions to Divide $100,000 From Col. Perkins," *Akron Beacon Journal*, September 13, 1910, 1.

61. "Society and Personal," *Akron Beacon Journal*, December 10, 1912, 7; "First Move for Girls' Dormitory," *Akron Beacon Journal*, July 2, 1915, 14; "Big Demand for Y.W.C.A. Rooms," *Akron Beacon Journal*, May 24, 1916, 7.

62. "One Bright Spot in Dreary Search for Room in Akron," *Akron City Times*, March 2, 1917, 7.

63. Janelle Baltputnis, "Anna Trowbride Viall Case, 1883–1965," Akron Women's History website, http://www3.uakron.edu/schlcomm/womenshistory/case_a.htm, retrieved July 1, 2004; "New Secretary of Y.W.C.A. Here," *Akron Beacon Journal*, January 13, 1917, 16; "One Hundred Year Biographical Directory of Mt. Holyoke College, 1837–1937."

64. Scrapbook 2, box 46, and "Properties of the YWCA—1950," folder 14, box 4, both in YWCA of Summit County Collection, University of Akron Archives; Endres and Flox, "YWCA of Summit County," 24; Minutes, September 9, 1918, 152, box 44, YWCA of Summit County Collection, University of Akron Archives.

65. "Young Women's Christian Association of Akron, Ohio," annual statement, 1923, 3, 10, and 17. See also Endres and Flox, "YWCA of Summit County," 24–25.

66. For a fuller discussion of the YWCA's youth activities, see Endres and Flox, "YWCA of Summit County," 11–13.

67. "Dr. Kurt, First Woman Physician in Akron, Is Dead," *Akron Beacon Journal*, September 13, 1910, 3.

68. Kenfield, *Akron and Summit County*, 1:162–270 and 2:192; Federal Census, U.S. Census Office, 10th Census, 1880; *Akron Official City Directory* (annual) (Akron: Burch Directory Co., 1911–14, 1916).

69. Kenfield, *Akron and Summit County*, 1:229; *Akron Official City Directory* (annual) (Akron: Burch Directory Co., 1911–14, 1916).

70. Mrs. Abbie Field took over as WCTU matron in 1912 but does not appear to have had a lengthy tenure with the organization. The WCTU moved from its room at

70 Main Street and began meeting at the YWCA headquarters at the Grace House. "W.C.T.U. Divided," *Akron Beacon Journal*, January 29, 1901, 1.

71. Letter from Mrs. A. Adamson, Hannah Louise Uhler, Louise T. James, and Katherine Kurt to Mrs. J. Park Alexander, February 19, 1901, box B-16, series 2, folder 8, Summit County Historical Society Collection, University of Akron Archives; "A Fine Year," *Akron Beacon Journal*, September 3, 1902, 6; "Woman's Christian Temperance Union," *Akron Beacon Journal*, October 3, 1902, 6; "The Crusaders' Work," *Akron Beacon Journal*, March 17, 1903, 3; "W.C.T.U. Will Fight Billboard Nuisance," *Akron Beacon Journal*, January 23, 1906; "For Half Holidays," *Akron Beacon Journal*, March 14, 1911, 5.

72. "New Crusade to Be Undertaken by W.C.T.U.," *Akron Beacon Journal*, January 23, 1906, 1; "Politics Rotten, Therefore Women Ought to Vote," *Akron Beacon Journal*, May 4, 1910, 2; "To Continue the Suffrage Fight," *Akron Beacon Journal*, September 14, 1912, 6; "Votes for Women," *Akron Beacon Journal*, April 9, 1914, 4.

73. The New Century Club had started in 1893, after the Columbian Exposition. In 1892, Elias Fraunfelter, superintendent of Akron Public Schools, asked his wife Laura to get Akron women to promote the Columbian Exposition in Chicago. Fraunfelter and neighbor/friend Katherine Claypole organized the Columbian Club, an organization designed to have a short life. In this group, Akron women would study historical events and produce material that would be displayed in the Woman's Building at the exposition. After the exposition, the members decided to carry on their organization under a new name for the new century. Thus, the New Century Club was organized as an educational and social group. Kenfield, *Akron and Summit County*, 1:231.

74. Lane, 472; Kenneth Nichols, "Akron's Adam Is a Man with Lots of Firsts," *Akron Beacon Journal*, February 24, 1965, clipping, in local history file, Akron Public Library.

75. "Akron and Summit County Federation of Women's Clubs, 1924–1925," folder: Akron Federation of Women's Clubs, box E1, Summit County Historical Society Collection, University of Akron Archives; Janelle Baltputnis, "Isabel Agnes Bradley, 1864–1953," Akron Women's History website, http://www3.uakron.edu/schlcomm/womenshistory/bradley_i.htm, retrieved July 23, 2004; Penny Fox, "Helen Seiberling Wolle, 1884–1974," Akron Women's History website, http://www3.uakron.edu/schlcomm/womenshistory/wolle_h.htm, retrieved July 23, 2004; "Will Ask Mayor to Give Health Job to Woman," *Akron Beacon Journal*, December 31, 1914, 1; "To Ask Health Board About Appointment," *Akron Beacon Journal*, January 7, 1915, 1; "Naming of Kuhlke Is Direct Slap at Big Clean-Up Campaign," *Akron Beacon Journal*, January 12, 1915, 1; "Women to Urge Mayor to Name Dr. Bradley," *Akron Beacon Journal*, January 6, 1915, 1.

76. The Busy Bee Hive, the first formed in Akron, pioneered insurance for women, at a time when few afforded that protection. The group offered a cooperative plan through which thousands of Akron women got insurance. In all, there were four

"hives" in Akron in the mid-1920s. The groups also offered programs and services for young women. Kenfield, *Akron and Summit County*, 1:263–64.

77. "Its Annual Meeting," *Akron Beacon Journal*, November 19, 1903, 1; "The Literary Clubs of the Women of Akron," *Akron Beacon Journal*, October 17, 1903, 9; Kenfield, *Akron and Summit County*, 1:230.

78. "Akron and Summit County Federation of Women's Clubs, 1924–1925," pamphlet, folder: Akron Federation of Women's Clubs, box E1, Summit County Historical Society, University of Akron Archives; Kenfield, *Akron and Summit County*, 1:224.

79. "Want a Juvenile Court," *Akron Beacon Journal*, November 20, 1903, 8; "Its Annual Meeting," *Akron Beacon Journal*, November 20, 1903, 8; "The Women of This City Meeting Today," *Akron Beacon Journal*, November 20, 1904, 3; "Mothers of Akron Want the Kindergarten Work Investigated," *Akron Beacon Journal*, June 11, 1904, 1; "To Beautify City of Akron," *Akron Beacon Journal*, March 29, 1905, 8; "Women's Council Stands for Good," *Akron Beacon Journal*, November 18, 1907, 8; Kenfield, *Akron and Summit County*, 1:168–70.

80. "Women's Council a Lively Factory," *Akron Beacon Journal*, November 4, 1903, 3.

81. "Women's Council Wants Juvenile Court," *Akron Beacon Journal*, May 29, 1909, 3; "Cottage Plan or One Building for Children's Home," *Akron Beacon Journal*, November 4, 1909, 1; Penny Fox, "Margaret Chapman Barnhart, 1874–1913," Akron Women's History website, http://www3.uakron.edu/schlcomm/womenshistory/barnhart_m.htm, retrieved August 8, 2004; and Kenfield, *Akron and Summit County*, 1:170.

82. "Women Enlisted in White Plague Fight," *Akron Beacon Journal*, May 6, 1909, 3; Kenfield, *Akron and Summit County*, 1:170; "Crusade Against Smoke Started," *Akron Beacon Journal*, July 29, 1909, 8.

83. "Woman's Council to Open Crusade for Flyless City," *Akron Beacon Journal*, June 4, 1914, 1, 7; "Free Ice Project and Fly Crusade Ok'd by Chamber," *Akron Beacon Journal*, June 16, 1914, 11; "Naming of Kuhlke Is Direct Slap at Big Clean-up Campaign," *Akron Beacon Journal*, January 12, 1915, 1; "Women to Urge Mayor to Name Dr. Bradley," *Akron Beacon Journal*, January 6, 1915, 1; "Week of April 12 to See Akron Get Thoroughly Clean," *Akron Beacon Journal*, March 17, 1915, 1; "Will Ask Mayor to Give Health Job to Woman," *Akron Beacon Journal*, December 31, 1914, 1; "To Ask Health Board about Appointment," *Akron Beacon Journal*, January 7, 1915, 1; "Club Women Declare War on House Fly," *Akron Beacon Journal*, May 12, 1916, 1.

84. "Asks Housewives to Observe Boycott and Cut Food Prices," *Akron Beacon Journal*, December 16, 1916, 1; "Women Join Food Boycott to Cut Prices," *Akron Beacon Journal*, December 4, 1916, 1.

85. Kenfield, *Akron and Summit County*, 1:169–72.

86. Marie Ellene Seibel Olin served as president of the Women's Council from 1910–1912. Born in Cleveland, Olin grew up in Mantua, in northern Portage County. She was the daughter of Mary Ann Johnson and Charles M. Seibel, one of the earliest music teachers in the town. Oscar Olin, her husband, was a much-loved teacher at

Daughters of Jerusalem," *Akron Beacon Journal*, March 21, 1906, 6. It is difficult to trace the activism of the Daughters of Jerusalem because the city newspapers did not consistently cover the organization—or the group did not consistently inform the newspapers of its activities.

17. "Jason Brown at the Closing Session," *Akron Beacon Journal*, September 16, 1906, 5; "Tells of Progress of Race in United States," *Akron Beacon Journal*, September 25, 1911, 7.

18. "First Session Will Be Held Tonight," *Akron Beacon Journal*, September 13, 1905, 3; "Dayton Gets the Convention Next," *Akron Beacon Journal*, September 15, 1905, 3; "Colored Society Is Meeting Here," *Akron Beacon Journal*, September 14, 1905, 5; "Daughters of Jerusalem's Social," *Akron Beacon and Republican*, December 19, 1896, 1.

19. Endres, "Mary Peavy Eagle, 1909–2003," Akron Women's History website, http://www3.uakron.edu/schlcomm/womenshistory/eagle_m.htm, retrieved July 25, 2004.

20. See, for example, the German immigrant activities at Zion Lutheran Church, "The History of Zion Evangelical Luther Church Akron, Ohio, Related by Mr. Alvin Gravesmuehl to the Meeting of the Concordia Historical Institute, Cleveland Chapter, Sunday afternoon, April 16, 1978," 6.

21. "YWCA, Akron, Annual Announcements, 1912–1913," folder 8, box 43, YWCA of Summit County Collection, University of Akron Archives; Sims, *The YWCA—An Unfolding Purpose*, 10; "Y.W.C.A. School," *Akron Beacon Journal*, November 14, 1905, 10; "History—International Institute," http://www.iiakron.org/page1.html, retrieved July 17, 2004; Endres and Flox, "YWCA of Summit County," 15–17.

22. "25th Anniversary of the International Institute, Y.W.C.A.," December 2, 1942, folder 16, box 43, YWCA of Summit County Collection, University of Akron Archives; Sims, *The YWCA—An Unfolding Purpose*, 10; Minutes, September 6, 1916, and March 12, 1917, 107–8 and 117, YWCA of Summit County Collection, University of Akron Archives; "History—International Institute," http://www.iiakron.org/page1.html, retrieved July 17, 2004; Endres and Flox, "YWCA of Summit County," 15–17; and Baltputnis, "Anna Trowbridge Viall Case."

23. "25th Anniversary of the International Institute, Y.W.C.A.," December 2, 1942, folder 16, box 43, YWCA of Summit County Collection, University of Akron Archives; Annual Report, 1923, folder 15, box 1, and Monthly Reports, February 1924, folder 1, box 1, both in International Institute Collection, University of Akron Archives.

24. "25th Anniversary of the International Institute, Y.W.C.A.," December 2, 1942, folder 16, box 43, YWCA of Summit County Collection, University of Akron Archives; Mrs. J. B. Wright, "Y.W.C.A. First Organized in Akron March 25, 1901," *Akron Times*, January 25, 1931, 2; Annual Report, 1923, folder 15, box 1, International Institute Collection, University of Akron Archives.

25. The institute had to take those classes over again in 1931 when the schools gave them up in a cost-cutting move during the Depression. Women's clubs also existed in the newly established, ethnically based churches in the city. Mrs. J. B. Wright, "Y.W.C.A. First Organized in Akron, March 25, 1901," *Akron Times*, January 25, 1931, 2; "25th An-

niversary of the International Institute, Y.W.C.A.," December 2, 1942, folder 16, box 43, YWCA of Summit County Collection, University of Akron Archives; Endres and Flox, "YWCA of Summit County," 16–17; International Institute, "History."

26. See, for example, "Twenty-fifth Anniversary of Swiss Ladies Club, 1942," folder: Progress of the Akron Institute; "International Institute of the Akron Y.W.C.A.," folder: Programs and Yearbooks of Other Institutes; and "Homelands Exhibit, Sept. 15–20, 1925," typed manuscript, folder: no name, all in box 40, YWCA of Summit County Collection, University of Akron Archives.

27. The YWCA Girl Reserve program was segregated. The native-born girls met in separate clubs. The immigrant girls and daughters of foreign-born met in Girl Reserve organizations that were affiliated with the International Institute. The YWCA also ran Girl Reserve clubs for African American girls. Women's clubs also existed in the ethnically based newly established churches in the city. "Y.W.C.A. Head Pleads for a Dormitory," November 10, 1918, clipping, scrapbook 2, box 46, and "Suggested Ways in Which Miss Isobel Lawson Can Help Akron's Negro Community," typescript manuscript, scrapbook 2, box 46, both in YWCA of Summit County Collection, University of Akron Archives; Mrs. J. B. Wright, "Y.W.C.A. First Organized in Akron, March 25, 1901," *Akron Times*, January 25, 1931, 2; "25th Anniversary of the International Institute, Y.W.C.A.," December 2, 1942, folder 16, box 43, YWCA of Summit County Collection, University of Akron Archives; Ruth Putnam, "And the English May Eat with Irish," *Akron Times Press*, March 18, 1943, no page number, folder 18, box 43, YWCA of Summit County Collection, University of Akron Archives; Annual Report, 1923, 4, folder 1, box 1, and Monthly Reports, May 1925, folder 12, box 1, both in International Institute Collection, University of Akron Archives; "The International Institute," *The Ys and the Other Ys*, January 1927, 2, folder: Ys and other Ys, series V, box 42, YWCA of Summit County Collection, University of Akron Archives; Endres and Flox, "YWCA of Summit County," 16–17; International Institute, "History."

28. "The International Institute," *The Ys and the Other Ys*, January 1927, 2, folder: Ys and other Ys, series V, box 42, YWCA of Summit County Collection, University of Akron Archives. See also Alice Edison, "Picture Brides and Victims of Sharp Land Hogs Helped by Y.W. Institute," *Sunday Times*, March 31, 1919. In that story, Eleanor Schopke of the International Institute said, "We reach the foreigners through nationality workers who were educated in their own countries so that they understand the customs, traditions and ideals and backgrounds of the people and speak their language."

29. For details of the growing tension between the central administration of the YWCA and the International Institute, see Endres and Flox, "YWCA of Summit County," 17–19.

30. "Annual Report of the Akron Young Women's Christian Association for 1929," folder: Annual Meetings, box 42, YWCA of Summit County Collection, University of Akron Archives.

1. "Woman," *American Democrat,* April 4, 1844, 4.

2. Howard Wolf, "Tuesday Musical Club Founded 40 Years Ago," *Akron Beacon Journal,* October 1, 1927, vol. 1, Tuesday Musical Club Collection, University of Akron Archives.

3. For a fuller discussion of domestic feminism, see Karen J. Blair, *The Clubwoman as Feminist: True Womanhood Redefined, 1868-1914* (New York: Holmes and Meier, 1980), 4–5.

Bibliography

MANUSCRIPT COLLECTIONS

Akron and Summit County Federation of Women's Clubs Collection, University of Akron Archives, Akron, Ohio.

Archives of Trinity Lutheran Church, Trinity Lutheran Church, Akron, Ohio.

B. F. Goodrich Corp. Collection, University of Akron Archives, Akron, Ohio.

First Congregational Church Archives, First Congregational Church, Akron, Ohio.

First Grace United Church of Christ Archives, First Grace United Church of Christ, Akron, Ohio.

Goodyear Tire and Rubber Co. Collection, University of Akron Archives, Akron, Ohio.

High Street Church of Christ Archives, High Street Church of Christ, Akron, Ohio.

Hosea Paul Collection, Western Reserve Historical Society, Cleveland, Ohio.

International Institute Collection, University of Akron Archives, Akron, Ohio.

J. Park Alexander Collection, Western Reserve Historical Society, Cleveland, Ohio.

Mary Day Nursery and Children's Hospital Collection, Children's Hospital Archives, Children's Hospital, Akron, Ohio.

Morgue Files, *Akron Beacon Journal*, Akron, Ohio.

Summit County Historical Society Collection, University of Akron Archives, Akron, Ohio.

Tuesday Musical Club Collection, University of Akron Archives, Akron, Ohio.

U.S. Sanitary Commission Collection, Western Reserve Historical Society, Cleveland, Ohio.

United Universalist Church Archives, United Universalist Church, Akron, Ohio.

Young Women's Christian Association of Summit County Collection, University of Akron Archives, Akron, Ohio.

NEWSPAPERS

Akron Beacon and Republican
Akron Beacon Journal
Akron Buzzard and Buckeye Water Nymph
Akron City Times
Akron Daily Argus

Akron Daily Beacon
Akron Daily Democrat
Akron Daily Tribune
Akron Eagle
Akron Free Democrat
Akron Free Democratic Standard
Akron Herald
Akron Press
Akron Republican
Akron Times Press
Akron Weekly Times
American Democrat
Cascade Roarer
Daily Standard
Evening Journal
Grace Church Reformed Herald
Honest Truth
The Lutheran
The People
Second Advent of Christ
Summit Democracy
Summitonian
Tee-Total Mechanic
Trinity Luther Leaguer
Wingfoot Clan

REPORTS

The History of Zion Evangelical Luther Church Akron, Ohio, Related by Mr. Alvin Gravesmuehl to the Meeting of the Concordia Historical Institute, Cleveland Chapter, Sunday afternoon, April 16, 1978. Akron: Zion Lutheran Church, 2004.

Directory of Social and Civic Agencies: A Classified and Descriptive Directory of the Social, Civic and Religious Resources of the City of Akron, 1913. Akron: Charity Organization Society, 1913.

Minutes of the Woman's Christian Temperance Union of the State of Ohio at the Seventh Annual Meeting, Xenia, September 1–3, 1880. Columbus: Nevins and Myers, 1880.

Minutes of the Woman's Christian Temperance Union of the State of Ohio at the Tenth Annual Meeting, Bellefontaine, June 20–23, 1883. Cleveland: Leader Printing, 1883.

Minutes of the Woman's Christian Temperance Union of the State of Ohio at the Twelfth Annual Meeting, Kenton, June 10, 11, 12, 1885. Xenia: Chew Printing, 1885.

Minutes of the Woman's Christian Temperance Union of the State of Ohio, Elyria, June 6–8, 1877. Cincinnati: A. H. Pugh, 1877.

Twenty-third Annual Meeting of the Woman's Christian Temperance Union of the State of Ohio, 1896, Youngstown, Ohio, October 7–9, 1896. Columbus: Hann and Adair, printers, 1896.

Van Kirk, Mrs. H. D., ed. *Ohio Woman's Christian Temperance Union 58th Annual Year, Convention Held at Dayton, October 20, 21, 22, 23 [1931].*

PAMPHLETS

Akron Woman's City Club, Directory, 2002–2003. Akron: Woman's City Club, 2002.

Akron as Seen by the Outsider [Probably 1917].

The Children's Concert Series, 1947–1997, 50th Anniversary. Akron: Children's Concert Series, 1997.

Constitution, By-Laws and Rules of the Cascade Division, Number 88, of the Sons of Temperance of the State of Ohio: Instituted September 7, 1846. Akron: Bro. H. Canfield, 1848.

Ervin, Mary B. *Ohio Woman's Christian Temperance Union: Historic Highlights.* Columbus: WCTU, 1949.

Scullen, Father. *Story of the First One Hundred Years, 1837–1937, of St. Vincent de Paul Church, Akron, Ohio.*

Seiberling, John. *Memorial of the Twenty-fifth Year.* Akron: Trinity Evangelical Lutheran Church, 1896.

Simon, Ruth J. *Heritage: A Centennial History, 1868–1968.* Akron: Evangelical Lutheran Church of the Holy Trinity, no date.

Taylor, Harold J. *135 Year History of the High Street Christian Church, 1839–1974.* Akron: High Street Christian Church, 1974.

WPA. *Play Spots: Akron and Summit County.* Akron: Community Chest, 1941.

GOVERNMENT DOCUMENTS

Federal Census, U.S. Census Office, 10th Census, 1880.

THESES AND DISSERTATIONS

Bright, Gerald D. "History of the High Street Church of Christ, Akron, Ohio, 1839–1942." PhD diss., Butler University, 1952.

Kaplan, Helga Eugenie. "Century of Adjustment: A History of the Akron Jewish Community, 1865–1975." PhD diss., Kent State University, 1978.

McClain, Shirla Robinson. "The Contributions of Blacks in Akron: 1825–1975." PhD diss., University of Akron, 1975.

Mikesell, Ralph H. "The Woman Suffrage Movement in Ohio, 1910–1920." Thesis, Ohio State University, 1934.

Povenmire, Kenneth Willet. "The Temperance Movement in Ohio 1840 to 1860." Master's thesis, Ohio State University, 1933.

Stanton, Mary Margaret. "The Woman Suffrage Movement in Ohio Prior to 1910." Master's thesis, Ohio State University, 1947.

Whitaker, Francis Myron. "A History of the Ohio Woman's Christian Temperance Union, 1874–1920." PhD diss., Ohio State University, 1971.

BOOKS AND ARTICLES

Akron City and Summit County Directory. Akron: Burch Directory Co., 1883/84.

Akron City and Summit County Directory, 1884–1885. Akron: Burch Directory Co., 1884.

Akron City and Summit County Directory. Akron: Burch Directory Co., 1885/86.

Akron City Directory, 1887–1888. Akron: Burch Directory Co., 1887.

Akron City Directory. Akron: A. R. Talcoit, 1873–1874.

Akron City Directory. Akron: Burch Directory Co., 1879/80.

Akron City Directory. Akron: Burch Directory Co., 1888/89.

Akron City Directory. Akron: Burch Directory Co., 1890/91.

Akron Official City Directory. (Annual.) Akron: Burch Directory Co., 1894–1921.

Atwater, George Parkin. *Annals of a Parish: A Chronicle of the Founding and of the Growth and Development of the Church of Our Saviour, Akron, Ohio, Together with a Personal Narrative by the Reverend George Parkin Atwater, Who Served the Parish as Pastor, Priest and Rector from November 20, 1897 to October 1, 1926.* [Akron]: Privately published, 1928.

Banks, Olive. *Faces of Feminism: A Study of Feminism as a Social Movement.* New York: St. Martin's Press, 1981.

Beard, Mary Ritter. *Woman's Work in Municipalities.* New York: D. Appleton, 1915.

Beecher, Catharine E. *A Treatise on Domestic Economy, for the Use of Young Ladies at Home, and at School.* New York: Harper and Bros., 1849.

Beecher, Catharine E. "The Peculiar Responsibilities, and Difficulties, of American Woman." As reprinted in *Roots of Bitterness: Documents of the Second History of American Women,* edited by Nancy F. Cott, Jeanne Boydston et al., 134 (Boston: Northeastern University Press, 1996).

Beecher, Catharine E., and Harriet Beecher Stowe. *The American Woman's Home, Or, Principles of Domestic Science; Being a Guide to the Formation and Maintenance of Economical Healthful, Beautiful, and Christian Homes.* New York: J. B. Ford, 1869.

Blair, Henry William. *The Temperance Movement; or, the Conflict Between Man and Alcohol.* Boston: William E. Smythe, 1888.

Blair, Karen J. *The Clubwoman as Feminist: True Womanhood Redefined, 1868–1914.* New York: Holmes and Meier, 1980.

Blocker, Jack S. Jr. *American Temperance Movements: Cycles of Reform.* Boston: Twayne, 1989.

———. *Alcohol, Reform and Society: The Liquor Issue in Social Context.* Westport, Conn.: Greenwood, 1979.

Bordin, Ruth. "'A Baptism of Power and Liberty': The Woman's Crusade of 1873–1874." *Ohio History* 87 (Autumn 1978): 393–404.

Bryce, James. *The American Commonwealth,* vol. 2. London: Macmillan, 1889.

A Centennial History of Akron, 1825–1925. Akron: Summit County Historical Society, 1925.

Cook, Sharon Ann. *"Through Sunshine and Shadow": The Woman's Christian Temperance Union, Evangelism, and Reform in Ontario, 1874–1930.* Montreal and Kingston: McGill-Queen's University Press, 1995.

Cott, Nancy F. *The Bonds of Womanhood: Woman's Sphere in New England, 1780–1835.* New Haven, Conn.: Yale University Press, 1977.

———, ed. *History of Women in the United States: Historical Articles on Women's Lives and Activities.* Vol. 16. *Women Together: Organizational Life.* Munich: K. G. Saur, 1994.

———. *History of Women in the United States: Historical Articles on Women's Lives and Activities.* Vol. 17. *Social and Moral Reform,* pt. 1. Munich: K. G. Saur, 1994.

Cowen, B. R. *Our Beacon Light or, The Youth of our Land The Hope of our Country Devoted to Employment, Education and Society.* Columbus, Ohio: F. L. Patrick and Co., 1884.

De Tocqueville, Alexis. *Democracy in America: Part the Second, The Social Influence of Democracy.* Translated by Henry Reeve, Esq. New York: J and H. G. Langley, 1840.

Doyle, Don H. "The Social Functions of Voluntary Associations in a Nineteenth-Century American Town." *Social Science History* 1 (Spring 1977): 333–55.

Edwards, Wendy J., and Carolyn D. Gifford, eds. *Gender and the Social Gospel.* Urbana: University of Illinois Press, 2003.

Endres, Kathleen L. *Rosie the Rubber Worker: Women Workers in Akron's Rubber Factories during World War II.* Kent, Ohio: Kent State University Press, 2000.

Endres, Kathleen L., and Cheryl Flox. *The YWCA of Summit County: A History.* Akron: YWCA of Summit County, 2001.

Epstein, Barbara Leslie. *The Politics of Domesticity: Women, Evangelism, and Temperance in Nineteenth-Century America.* Middletown, Conn.: Wesleyan University Press, 1981.

Flanagan, Maureen A. "The City Profitable, the City Livable: Environmental Policy, Gender and Power in Chicago in the 1910s." *Journal of Urban History* 22 (January 1996): 163–90.

———. *Seeing with Their Hearts: Chicago Women and the Vision of the Good City, 1871–1933.* Princeton, N.J.: Princeton University Press, 2002.

Fry, Linda L., and Cheryl M. Urban. *Politics & the Women of Summit County.* Akron: Women's History Project of the Akron Area, 1992.

Fulton, Rev. F. B. *Woman as God Made Her: The True Woman.* Boston: Lee and Shepard, 1869.

Galbreath, Charles B. *History of Ohio.* 2 vols. Chicago: The American Historical Society, 1925.

Giele, Janet Zollinger. *Two Paths to Women's Equality: Temperance, Suffrage, and the Origins of Modern Feminism.* New York: Twayne, 1995.

Ginzberg, Lori D. *Women and the Work of Benevolence: Morality, Politics and Class in the Nineteenth-Century United States.* New Haven and London: Yale University Press, 1990.

Gottlieb, Agnes Hooper. *Women Journalists and the Municipal Housekeeping Movement, 1868–1914.* Lewiston, N.Y.: Edwin Mellen, 2001.

Grismer, Karl H. *Akron and Summit County.* Akron: Summit County Historical Society, no date.

Hardesty, Nancy A. *Women Called to Witness: Evangelical Feminism in the Nineteenth Century.* Nashville: Abingdon Press, 1984.

Hewitt, Nancy A. *Women's Activism and Social Change: Rochester, New York, 1822–1872.* Ithaca: Cornell University Press, 1984.

Hoy, Suellen M. *Chasing Dirt: The American Pursuit of Cleanliness.* New York: Oxford University Press, 1995.

James, John Angell. *The Marriage Ring; or How to Make Home Happy.* Boston: Gould, Kendall and Lincoln, 1842.

Johnson, Lorenzo D. *Martha Washingtonianism, or History of the Ladies' Temperance Benevolent Societies.* New York: Saxton and Miles, 1843.

Jordan, Philip D. *Ohio Comes of Age, 1873–1900.* Columbus: Ohio State Archaeological and Historical Society, 1943.

Kenfield, Scott D., ed. *Akron and Summit County, 1828–1928.* Chicago and Akron: S. J. Clarke, 1928.

Knepper, George W. *Akron: City at the Summit.* Tulsa, Okla.: Continental Heritage, 1981.

––––––. *New Lamps for Old: One Hundred Years of Urban Higher Education at the University of Akron. A Centennial Publication.* Akron: University of Akron, 1970.

––––––. *Summit's Glory: Sketches of Buchtel College and the University of Akron.* Akron: University of Akron Press, 1990.

Lane, Samuel A. *Fifty Years and Over of Akron and Summit County.* Akron: Beacon Job Department, 1892.

Oana, Katherine D., and Karen B. Amodeo, eds. *Her Story in the Making: A Who's Who of Akron Area Women.* Vol. 1. Akron: Women's History Week Committee.

Olasky, Marvin. *The Tragedy of American Compassion.* Washington, D.C.: Regnery Gateway, 1992.

Olin, Oscar Eugene. *Akron and Environs—Historical: Biographical, Genealogical.* Chicago: Lewis, 1917.

Otis, Philo Adams. *The Chicago Symphony Orchestra: Its Development and Organization, 1891–1924.* Chicago: Clayton Summy, 1924.

Perrin, William Henry. *History of Summit County.* Chicago: Baskin and Battery, 1881.

A Portrait and Biographical Record of Portage and Summit Counties, Ohio, Containing Biographical Sketches of Many Prominent and Representative Citizens, Together with Portraits and Biographies of all the Presidents of the United States and Biographies of the Governors of Ohio. Logansport, Ind.: A. W. Bowen and Co., 1898.

Randall, Emilius O., and Daniel J. Ryan. *History of Ohio: The Rise and Progress of an American State.* Vols. 1–6. New York: Century History, 1912.

Ryan, Mary. "The Power of Women's Network: A Case Study of Female Moral Reform in Antebellum America." In *History of Women in the United States: Historical Articles on Women's Lives and Activities,* vol. 17, *Social and Political Reform,* pt. 2, ed. Nancy F. Cott. Munich: K. G. Saur, 1994.

Sander, Kathleen W. *The Business of Charity: The Woman's Exchange Movement, 1832–1900.* Urbana: University of Illinois Press, 1998.

Sandford, Mrs. John. *Woman, in Her Social and Domestic Character.* Boston: Otis, Broaders and Co., 1842.

Schlesinger, Arthur M. "Biography of a Nation of Joiners." *American Historical Review* 50 (October 1944): 1–25.

Sills, David L. "Voluntary Associations: Sociological Aspects." In *International Encyclopedia of the Social Sciences,* ed. David L. Sills, 16:362–79. New York: Macmillan and Free Press, 1968.

————. *The Volunteers: Means and Ends in a National Organization.* Glencoe, Ill.: Free Press, 1957.

Sims, Mary S. *The YWCA—An Unfolding Purpose.* New York: Women's Press, 1950.

Smith, Virginia Thrall. "The Kindergarten." In *The Congress of Women: Held in the Woman's Building, World's Columbian Exposition, Chicago, U. S. A., 1893,* ed. Kavanaugh Oldham Eagle, 178–80. Chicago: Monarch Book Company, 1894.

Smith-Rosenberg, Carroll. "Beauty, the Beast, and the Militant Woman: A Case Study in Sex Roles and Social Stress in Jacksonian America." *American Quarterly* 23 (Winter 1971): 562–84.

The Story of the Children's Hospital, Akron, Ohio. Akron: no date.

Sweet, Leonard I., ed. *The Evangelical Tradition in America.* Macon, Ga.: Mercer University Press, 1984.

Taylor, Harold J. *135-Year History of the High Street Christian Church, 1839–1974.* Akron: High Street Christian Church, 1974.

Turner, Elizabeth Hayes. *Women, Culture and Community: Religion and Reform in Galveston, 1880–1920.* New York: Oxford University Press, 1997.

Tyler, Helen, *Where Prayer and Purpose Meet: The WCTU Story, 1874–1949.* Evanston, Ill.: Signal, 1949.

Tyrell, Ian R. *Sobering Up: From Temperance to Prohibition in Antebellum America, 1800–1860.* Westport, Conn.: Greenwood, 1979.

Utter, William T. *The Frontier State, 1803–1925.* Columbus: Ohio State Archaeological and Historical Society, 1942.

Weisenburger, Francis P. *The Passing of the Frontier, 1825–1950.* Columbus: Ohio State Archaeological and Historical Society, 1941.

Welter, Barbara. "The Cult of True Womanhood: 1820–1860." *American Quarterly* 24 (Summer 1966): 151–74.

Williard, Frances E. *Woman and Temperance; or, The Work and Workers of the Woman's Christian Temperance Union.* 1888. New York: Arno Press, 1972.

Young, Elaine, ed. *Summit County Women as Winners.* Akron: Women's History Project of the Akron Area, 1986.

Zonsius, Patricia M. *Children's Century: Children's Hospital Medical Center of Akron, 1890–1990.* Akron, Ohio: Children's Hospital Medical Center of Akron, 1990.

Index

0359   38